The Economics
of Human Resource
Management

The Economics of Human Resource Management

Edited by

**Daniel J. B. Mitchell and
Mahmood A. Zaidi**

Basil Blackwell

First Published 1990

HF
5549
E317
1990

Basil Blackwell Ltd.
108 Cowley Road, Oxford OX4 1JF, UK.

Basil Blackwell Inc.
3 Cambridge Center, Cambridge, MA 02142, USA.

British Library Cataloguing in Publication Data
The Economics of human resource management.
  1. Personnel management. Economic aspects.
  I. Mitchell, Daniel J. B.   II. Zaidi, Mahmood A.
  658.3

  ISBN 0–631–16897–4

Library of Congress Cataloging in Publication Data
The Economics of human resource management / edited by Daniel J.B.
  Mitchell and Mahmood A. Zaidi.
      p.   cm.
  Includes bibliographical references.
  ISBN 0–631–16897–4
  1. Personnel management.   2. Industrial relations.   3. Labor
economics.   I. Mitchell, Daniel J. B.   II. Zaidi, Mahmood A.
HF5549.E317   1990
331—dc20   90–41442
                                                          CIP

Typeset by Photo·graphics, Honiton, Devon.
Printed in Great Britain by Dotesios, Trowbridge.

CONTENTS

Introduction

DANIEL J.B. MITCHELL and MAHMOOD A. ZAIDI*

ECONOMICS AND THE FIELD of industrial relations have had an uneasy relationship at best. The Industrial Relations Research Association, for example, owes its formation (in 1948) at least in part to the frustration many labor economists felt over the seeming inapplicability of then-standard economic research to industrial relations, especially in the area of collective bargaining. Those in the field of personnel management, which at the time covered the nonunion sector, never had economics as even a reluctant parent. Their academic backgrounds were more likely to be in behavioral science and psychology.

Over the years, the linkage between human resource management and industrial relations (HRM&IR) and economics grew still more tenuous. Labor economists reduced their emphasis on collective bargaining and focused more on human capital and—later—on household production. The heavy overlay of regulation in the labor market, initially concerning collective bargaining, but later encompassing such fields as Equal Employment Opportunity (EEO), occupational safety, and the tax code's implications for benefit plans, elevated the position of the legal profession in the field. Historians broadened their interests in the labor area from union histories and biographies of labor leaders to the development of internal firm practices. Sociologists brought concepts such as "trust" to bear on employment relationships.

* The authors' affiliations are, respectively, Institute of Industrial Relations, and Anderson School of Management, University of California at Los Angeles; International Program Development, Carlson School of Management, and Industrial Relations Center, University of Minnesota. The authors wish to thank the following individuals who assisted in developing the symposium to which this paper is an introduction: Kyoungsik Kang, Vivian Richman, and Kiyoshi Takahashi. They also wish to thank Francine Blau, Morris Kleiner, Solomon Polachek, and Michael Reich for acting as discussants at the December 1988 Industrial Relations Research Association meeting where the papers were originally presented.

During the seventies and eighties, economists began to turn their attention again toward HRM&IR. What is sometimes now termed the "new economics of personnel" developed. Issues that once might have been considered institutional (and thus not of great interest to mainstream economists), such as alternative compensation systems, were now examined and analyzed and attempts were made to place them within the usual economic assumptions of rationality, profit maximization, and utility maximization. At the same time, empirical research—in the form of econometrics—also advanced. Longstanding data series, such as indexes of wages and employment, were scrutinized with modern statistical techniques. Facilitated by technological advances in computers, new micro-level data sets were developed and "mined" for their insights.

At issue now is whether the models, viewpoints, and findings in the new economics literature can be of use to the noneconomists in the HRM&IR field. A clue to the answer lies in other disciplines that economics has influenced during the past two decades. For example, the "law and economics" movement has had a profound effect on legal education and public policies such as antitrust. Economic modeling has also spilled over into sociology, political science, and history. It would be surprising if the same were not to be true in the HRM&IR field.

The symposium that follows was assembled in recognition of this potential influence of economics in HRM&IR. Two provisos are in order. First, even in eight papers, it was not possible to provide full coverage of the relevant economics literature, or to pay proper attention to the diversity of views within economics. Second, the symposium contributors were encouraged to do more than simply summarize recent literature. Some papers contain critiques of, rather than praise for, the new approaches.

In the first paper, Daniel J.B. Mitchell and Mahmood A. Zaidi assert that the stylized facts that concern macroeconomists must also be of concern to HRM&IR scholars. They consider largely demand-side influences, usually associated with short-term cyclical fluctuations, and they look mainly at decisions and practices at the firm level. The macro variables considered are employment, unemployment, price inflation, and profits. At the firm level, the HRM&IR functions affected are (1) recruitment, retention, and layoffs, (2) the effective use of employees, (3) the employee-relations climate, and (4) wage setting.

In the Mitchell-Zaidi view, the labor market is usefully seen as often *not* being cleared, evidence of which can be found in cyclical fluctuations of unemployment and vacancies. Business cycle fluctuations are met with quantitative adjustment more than nominal pay adjustments. Incumbent "insider" workers tend to be protected by employers from the underbidding of job-seeking "outsiders." The future challenge for HRM&IR practitioners, as Mitchell and Zaidi see it, will be to design policies which reconcile employee needs for job stability with increasing firm needs for managerial flexibility.

International competition has been one of the factors generating employer demands for flexibility. The second paper, by Drusilla K. Brown and David M. Garman, presents models of international trade which depart from simple assumptions such as constant returns to scale. Gains from trade can come from such features as the intensification of competition and the increase in product variety. Where competition is imperfect, Brown and Garman find that seemingly inefficient devices, such as export subsidies or import tariffs, can improve national welfare. Their analysis should comfort those who have advocated activist government trade policies—notably organized labor and some employers in import-competing industries. Brown and Garman also point to circumstances under which immigration policies can improve national welfare.

Perhaps it should have been obvious long ago that if assumptions underlying simple trade models were relaxed, and imperfections were allowed, the usual free-trade conclusions would become special cases rather than general results. Of course, even when cases for optimal government interventions exist, governments with an activist stance may not always choose optimal policies. Nonetheless, the Brown-Garman review of recent economic analysis tends to return the free-trade-versus-intervention debate to its roots in *political* economy. Much depends on assumptions of how well governments will do in selecting appropriate policies. Intervention to improve labor's welfare is not ruled out. However, models of union behavior in pursuing protection do not suggest that policies which provide gains to individual unions must necessarily coincide with some larger national interest.

One aspect of the international impact on the domestic employment relationship Brown and Garman do not consider is the worldwide transition to flexible exchange rates in the early seventies. Especially in the eighties, wild swings in currency values created pressures in product markets which inevitably spilled over into labor markets. Internal HRM policies aimed at raising productivity and cutting labor costs can easily be overwhelmed by a sharp change in exchange rates. Thus, employer pressures for flexibility may have originated in part from the financial side of the international economy rather than simply from the broadening of markets through the trade side.

In the third contribution, by Myra H. Strober, the focus shifts to the firm level. HR managers can influence the productivity of their organizations by affecting the quality and characteristics of employees. One possibility is to screen new hires for desirable behavioral traits. Another is to provide—

or require—education, training, and experience. Human capital has been concerned with the degree to which education directly raises individual productivity and the degree to which it is a sorting device, screening employees for characteristics correlated with educational attainment. Strober notes that human capital theory has traditionally been based on a supply-side approach. It was formulated before internal labor markets and efficiency wage theories, and other newer forms of analysis, all of which suggest the importance of employer (demand-side) policies. For example, an association between tenure on the job and earnings could be taken as a sign that experience raised the stock of individual human capital and thus increased its return. But alternative theories now suggest an incentive for employers to create upward-sloping wage-tenure profiles as a way to limit shirking.

Human capital theorizing and empirical analysis has extended into explanations for wage differentials associated with gender or race. In particular, as a result of the controversy over "comparable worth" as a legal doctrine, a substantial literature has developed concerning the source of such differentials. A common approach has been to standardize earnings by taking account of human capital differences across groups (such as education and experience) and then examining what fraction of the wage differential remained. The usual finding is that a significant fraction is left over, adding support to the argument that the differential reflects employer policy rather than variations in individual productivity.

Although not reviewed by Strober, one of the interesting stylized facts of the eighties was a steady rise of the female-to-male wage ratio after an earlier period of stagnation. This rise in the ratio cannot be explained away by reference only to readily available human capital indicators. One possible interpretation is that the rising ratio reflects a deterioration in the kind of internal labor market which has been modeled by the new economics of personnel, i.e., one with long-term attachments, career ladders, etc. Put another way, demand levels in traditionally male labor markets fell relative to those which have been traditionally female. The missing variable may thus be a shift toward more of a "spot" labor market, ironically coming just at a time when economists were devoting their attention to long-duration relationships.

Michael L. Wachter and Randall D. Wright's paper examines employer-employee contracts within the internal labor market. They begin with the assumption that observed contractual behavior exists because it furthers the goals of both parties. Four central economic factors—match-specific investments, risk aversion, asymmetric information, and transaction costs—influence employment contracting. Wachter and Wright stress the tradeoffs that must be made in the search for an optimal labor contract. For example, they analyze match-specific investments, such as certain types of worker training programs, that lock employees into the employment relationship. They then show the complications that arise when the other factors that should be reflected in the employment contract are considered.

Contracting in internal labor markets raises the possibility that opportunistic behavior might occur, with one party "exploiting" the other. Industrial relations specialists have traditionally focused on potential employer advantages in the relationship, usually summed up as an inequality of bargaining power. An important issue is whether employment contracts are self-enforcing or whether some kind of third-party enforcement mechanism is utilized. Union contracts make use of third-party enforcement, as do external labor market contracts. But nonunion internal labor market contracts—which cover far more employees in the American work force than union contracts—tend to be self-enforcing.

One of the features of nonunion contracting is that agreements are generally unwritten. Contracts cannot be written for every contingency, but the existence of written contracts in the union sector indicates that more formalization of nonunion terms and conditions would be possible than is generally found in practice. One possibility, not explicitly considered in the Wachter-Wright paper, is that such formalization will occur in the future, spurred perhaps by wrongful discharge litigation, or paradoxically, by a possible weakening of the employer-employee attachment associated with flexible specialization and volatile markets. If employee mobility increases thanks to such forces, unwritten contracts based on mutual trust may prove to be unreliable.

The most elaborate long-term arrangement commonly found in the labor market is the defined-benefit pension plan. Edward P. Lazear focuses on pensions and deferred compensation and notes that such devices are more than simple tax-avoidance schemes. Whether by design or not, they influence worker turnover and effort levels. They can also substitute for mandatory retirement policies (which are now illegal) by inducing voluntary retirement. It appears that HRM policy regarding pension formulas is sometimes undertaken without analysis of the incentive effects created, producing perverse results which do not serve employer interests.

Similarly, the choice between pensions and other forms of deferred compensation (or arrangements such as stock options) is also more than a matter of providing an array of benefits to employees. The different programs will vary in attractiveness to employees and will also have different incentive effects. Again, HR managers need to reflect on these effects and develop benefit packages which go beyond tax code considerations.

There is a tradition in the industrial relations field of emphasizing collective employee (and sometimes employer) behavior. As Lloyd Ulman points out in his paper, such collective—or concerted—action need not always involve unionization. The issue arises especially with regard to the preference in the labor market for quantity rather than price adjustment. Ulman notes that implicit contract theory and efficiency wage theory may offer some explanation of why wages do not easily fall in the face of labor surpluses. Human capital approaches, with the firm making an investment in its work force, might provide an explanation of labor hoarding, essentially a reluctance to see rapid depreciation of a past investment. Thus, unions need not necessarily be the sole explanation of wage rigidity. Indeed, given the very low unionization rate remaining in American private employment, reliance on such union effects would be unrealistic. However, firms might have adopted internal labor markets with unionesque features in the past for reasons of union-avoidance and then perpetuated these institutions.

On the other hand, the actual presence of a union may intensify certain kinds of behaviors. Voice mechanisms (such as grievance machinery) will receive special attention in unionized situations. To some extent, positive productivity effects of employee voice might offset the impact of union wage differentials on employment, although, as Ulman notes, the last word on the productivity effect (or even its sign) has yet to be written.

Management's complaints of workrule inflexibilities are not always accepted at face value in the economics literature; indeed, some efficient contract theories find rationale for such restrictions. Efficient bargaining would have the union negotiate both the wage and the employment level (with the latter being a restriction on management's perceived right to establish the rate of labor utilization). In effect, the union should extract lump-sum transfers as the least distortive means of payment. As Ulman points out, such approaches assume extensive knowledge of the firm's economic circumstances on the union's part, a view that finds its ultimate expression in the belief that unions in the seventies deliberately followed a "take-the-money-and-run" (or end-game) strategy in industries that they could "see" would decline in the eighties.

There is a tendency in the economics literature to seize on a current phenomenon in the labor market, view it with hindsight, and then portray the outcome as the inevitable result of behaviors of rational players. Some European countries, Ulman reminds us, experienced high unemployment in the eighties along with an inability to lower the real wage during expansions. In the European case, the result was the development of the theory of insiders (incumbent workers) who make their wage desires felt (even absent a union) at the expense of outsiders. This approach was based on the evident union tendency to cater to senior workers within the work force, i.e., to put a lower weight on the preferences of juniors vs. seniors; it extended this propensity to suggest a zero weight on the preferences of yet-to-be juniors.

Ulman finds the current literature on collective action as lacking synthesis. If one wants to explain such developments as two-tier wage plans—which clearly favor insiders over outsiders—the insider/outsider approach is adequate. But he finds the practice of examining and explaining one behavior at a time potentially misleading.

While Ulman's review considers concerted activity generally (including nonunion examples), Robert J. Flanagan's contribution concentrates on the economic approach to traditional collective bargaining and related institutions. As Flanagan notes, analysis of union wage effects has a long history in labor economics. And new studies seem to reinforce the earlier conclusion that unions do push up wages relative to comparable nonunion situations.

An important issue from both the union and management perspective is whether unions have a productivity effect which reduces costs (thus possibly offsetting the wage effect) or raises costs (thus possibly reinforcing it). Even if the net union effect were not to raise costs, Flanagan notes that principal-agent problems could make management officials (agents of the stockholders) actively oppose unionization. Such behavior could arise if management officials perceived union-related limits to their discretion or status.

Flanagan notes deficiencies in economic modeling of both union and managerial choice. Unions are confronted by three influences: product markets, changing technology, and worker preferences. Managers face choices, particularly as markets expand, of enlarging pre-existing union facilities, opening new nonunion facilities, or retaining unionization but changing the micro-level industrial relations system through QWL-type techniques.

A third party—government—has long been considered active in industrial relations at the national level. In the U.S., the chief regulatory agency has been the National Labor Relations Board. Economic literature has begun to focus on the NLRB's policies, and the laws which underlie them. Both unions and management are seen as performing a cost-benefit analysis concerning such basic decisions as whether to comply with the letter of the law. From the managerial perspective, the net costs of compliance rise with the union wage premium.

Given the existence of a union-management relationship, the issue of conflict resolution arises. Conflicts of interest between labor and management are not lacking in nonunion situations, but these conflicts rarely surface as strikes. Strikes pose theoretical puzzles for economists, as Flanagan notes, because they do not appear to be caused by random mistakes in judgment— as some bargaining theories suggest. Some newer models modify the mistake approach and provide better insights, however.

Long-term contracts do not seem to avoid or reduce strikes, but rather to schedule them in a more orderly fashion from the management viewpoint. However, the parties could agree to interest arbitration as a means of dispute resolution. Flanagan points out that analysis of interest arbitration has challenged the view that arbitrators simply split the difference between the offers of the two parties. It may be that the arbitrator has an independent view of the appropriate settlement and that the parties group themselves around it. Although not referenced by Flanagan, recent economic literature on political posturing and behavior with the electorate as the constituent (rather than an arbitrator) might contribute to an understanding of interest arbitration (Nordhaus, 1989).

The focus of economic research on unions and bargaining is shifting from empirical measurement to explanation of behavior. In part, this reflects economists' efforts to fill a void in their research agenda; another factor may be the reduction in available data on the American union sector. The decline in unionization in the U.S. suggests that further data reductions could easily occur, as budgets for official data collection are squeezed.

Of the eight commentators on the economic analysis of HRM&IR, Sanford M. Jacoby is the most critical, although he recognizes analytical contributions of the new literature. The new approach shares a "mixed parentage" from both the older institutional labor economists and more modern economic theorizing. Jacoby finds that the theoretical parent provides the dominant traits. The result is a timeless rationalization of existing practice which ignores historical development and the details surrounding the broad stylized facts which are examined. His suggestion—not surprisingly—is that economists should equally honor their institutional parent.

The case in point for Jacoby is the analysis of the internal labor market within large firms. If the institutional features of such markets were simply the product of rational contracting between employer and employee, they should have sprung into existence once the "technology" became known. The actual linkage of these features with periods of war and union threat suggests that more than static optimality was involved. Similarly, Jacoby argues, jockeying over exactly what is in the employment contract now seems to occur in courts and legislatures as frequently as in the workplace (e.g., evolving doctrines of wrongful discharge).

If market failures (such as shirking) are taken as the roots of the more complex phenomena that interest economists, why should it be assumed that only markets produce the responses to these failures? Moreover, even problems such as shirking are more complex than is often appreciated, since such forces as social acculturation may influence outcomes. In some countries, bribery of public officials is the norm. In others it is considered scandalous. Why should not similar differences be found in the degree of trust in the workplace?

Jacoby traces the tension between economic theorists and institutionalists from the nineteenth century through the fifties. In many respects, the issues that existed in the past remain today. Institutionalists tended to view both social forces and economic forces as endogenous. They were unsure that unique optimal solutions emerged from the forces they observed, so they accumulated facts as such, and when they did produce theory, they often ended with difficult-to-test models. Depending on one's viewpoint, these outcomes may be depicted as the products of powerful minds capable of rising above oversimplification or the result of inadequate analytical skills.

The criticisms which have been leveled at the new economic approach to HRM&IR by Jacoby and others are important. There is indeed a timeless quality to the theoretical studies; a tendency to assume that what exists is optimal at the moment it is observed; and a tendency to assume unique solutions to problems which potentially may have multiple outcomes. Yet in certain respects, developments during the eighties have pushed the labor market to behave more as the classical model would suggest. Wages may become more flexible via contingent pay arrangements such as profit sharing. Employer-employee attachments appear to have weakened, as indicated by the growth of a contingent work force (temporaries and similar workers) and a decline in the length of on-the-job tenure. The large bureaucratic firms which may be considered models of implicit contracting have declined in their share of the work force (Mitchell, 1989). Such events suggest, ironically, that just when economists began rationalizing the lethargic institutions of the labor market, the lethargy decreased.

However, the labor market did not become a classical auction market in the eighties, and it will not become one in the nineties. Rather, there has been a move along a spectrum toward more "flexible" labor market arrangements than once prevailed. While economists may not have forecast these changes, neither did institutionalists. Given the pace of change, rejecting the insights available from economics would be a mistake for students of HRM&IR. As always, the field must be open to alternative views and models.

Macroeconomic Conditions and HRM-IR Practice

DANIEL J.B. MITCHELL and MAHMOOD A. ZAIDI*

Although macroeconomic developments may seem removed from the world of micro-level HRM-IR practices, such practices are heavily influenced by the macro economy. Wage and price inflation, for example, are closely related, and the general state of the economy influences decisions on hiring, layoffs, and hours. The labor market's tendency toward periods of extended labor surplus or shortage condition the nature of the employer-employee relationship. Economic circumstances affect the labor relations climate and that climate has a bearing on national productivity trends. Government policy in the future may seek to encourage certain kinds of compensation systems, such as profit sharing, for macro reasons. HRM-IR practitioners, too, may benefit by reconsidering policies which make wages relatively inflexible.

DESPITE THE SEEMING DICHOTOMY between macroeconomic developments and the micro level of human resource management and industrial relations (HRM-IR) practitioners, the same stylized macro facts that are of concern to macroeconomists ought to be of concern to HRM-IR practitioners as well. Perhaps the true dichotomy is between empirical macro—the type of work which characterizes economic forecasting—and theoretical macro. Here, we focus on stylized macro facts and their significance for practitioners.

Empirical macro analysis has tended to be pragmatic and often atheoretical. Theoretical macro analysis is divided between those who see the macro world as characterized by potential market failures—especially the underutiliz-

* The authors' affiliations are, respectively, Institute of Industrial Relations, and Anderson School of Management, University of California at Los Angeles; and International Program Development, Carlson School of Management, and Industrial Relations Center, University of Minnesota. The authors wish to thank Michael Keane, Erica L. Groshen, and Michael Reich for comments on an earlier draft.

ation of labor—and those who see macro outcomes as basically efficient, particularly if "appropriate" economic policies are followed.[1] In the fifties and sixties, for example, this divide took the form of Keynesians versus monetarists. The former tended to see a need for fiscal activism to balance the economy carefully between unemployment and inflation; the latter tended to believe that the economy would stabilize itself, given a predictable and consistent monetary policy.

By the seventies, the division was between a kind of modified Keynesianism that had absorbed monetarist criticism and the rational expectations view. Rational expectationists provide little scope for activism in macro policy because in their view such policy would come to be anticipated by the micro players (wage and price setters, consumers, etc.). In the eighties, the debate has been between "new Keynesians," who have absorbed aspects of rational expectations, and advocates of real business cycle theory. The latter see macro fluctuations as largely the result of supply-side disturbances, again suggesting little scope for demand management. The new Keynesians draw heavily on such micro-level theories as efficiency wage models and implicit contracting models.[2]

Ultimately, all of these approaches must measure up to the empirical facts. Empirical macro facts, while suggestive of some theoretical explanations, do not necessarily neatly fit the views of any one camp. Almost all contemporary macro theorists attempt to link their models to an assumption of optimal micro behavior; in the labor market this means that firms maximize profits in hiring, firing, and wage setting while workers maximize utility in searching for work, accepting jobs, and quitting jobs. Yet the empirical facts may also be consistent with the view that HRM-IR practices are the product of institutional history and "accident."

Seen in that way, it is possible that macro observations and failures point to opportunities for improvement in the conduct of micro-level firm policies. Such an agnostic approach is of greater potential use to HRM-IR practitioners than one which says that we live in the best of all possible worlds and that therefore improvements in existing technique are—by definition—not available. Below, we examine the behavior of macro variables, put forward some interpretations of what is observed, and indicate where changes in HRM-IR policy might be considered.

---

[1] We cannot do justice to these various schools in a few paragraphs. For a better presentation, see Gordon (1989).

[2] The Wachter-Wright paper in this issue discusses these approaches.

Categorization of Macro Variables

The distinction between a macro and a micro variable is often imprecise. Observations made at the firm or industry level are typically considered to be micro. Those made at the economy-wide level are macro. But it is not unusual for macroeconomists to have some disaggregate interests, as evidenced in the common practice of breaking down the Consumer Price Index (CPI) into its volatile and its underlying components. Rather than trying to draw an exact macro/micro dividing line, we instead select several variables widely held to be important to macroeconomics. The main dichotomy we use is the distinction between demand-side influences, usually associated with short-term cyclical fluctuations, and supply-side influences associated with long-term trends in factor utilization and technology. Since we focus on decisions and practices at the firm level, we give little attention to issues of labor supply.[3]

In the short-term, macroeconomics is identified with the study of the business cycle. The business cycle is usually taken to be a demand-side phenomenon in the short term, although there have been exceptions, ranging from sunspot theories earlier this century to more recent attempts to link cyclical behavior to the supply side, e.g., shocks to input prices, changes in technology, exogenous shifts in labor supply, etc.[4] For our purposes, the *source* of fluctuations is less important than the *reaction* to them of key variables of relevance to HRM-IR.

Employment. In the long run, the level of employment is mainly a function of the size of the working-age population and the propensity of that population to participate in the labor force. The industrial and occupational composition of the work force reflects technical, production function requirements. These influences are regularly projected by the U.S. Bureau of Labor Statistics (BLS) and are available to practitioners for employment planning.

Real private GNP rises faster than employment in the long run, reflecting rising productivity. In the short term, however, changes in employment

---

[3] The Brown-Garman paper in this issue examines variables associated with the international sector.

[4] The real business cycle theory has been associated with Edward Prescott (1986) and others. Shapiro and Watson (1988) find important roles in output and other macro variable fluctuations for demand and supply influences (including labor supply). It should be noted, however, that fluctuations involve more than simply recession and recovery. If the primary interest is in the cause of recessions (rather than all period-to-period fluctuations), demand considerations—combined with OPEC shocks in the seventies—are likely to be seen as major factors.

levels mirror changes in real GNP, although often with some lag.[5] Firms show some reluctance to hire immediately as product demand fluctuates. This tendency suggests that firms perceive costs in hiring and layoffs.

Unemployment. Unemployment is defined for statistical purposes as a situation in which an individual is actively seeking work, or is on layoff awaiting recall, and is without a job in the survey period.[6] Individuals can become unemployed by losing or quitting their jobs, re-entering the labor force, or entering the labor force for the first time. To the extent that unemployment has frictional and structural components, the number of unemployed can be expected to grow in the long term with the labor force and employment. But unemployment is highly cyclical in the short run.[7]

The phenomenon of cyclical unemployment variation is important because it represents a failure of the labor market to "clear" in the auction-market sense of that word. During recessions, there is an increase in the number of unemployed workers who are willing to work at the going wage but who nevertheless are unable to find jobs. There are macro theorists who attempt to "explain" cyclical unemployment (particularly that attributable to job loss) largely in terms of worker preferences and leisure substitutions. From a human resource perspective, such approaches tend to blur the implications for the employer-employee relationship that flow from the possibility of joblessness.[8]

---

[5] Simple regressions of the per cent change in private, full-time equivalent employment (CF) against the per cent change in real, private gross national product (CGNP) are improved by adding a lagged change in real GNP term. For 1949–1987, the regression is $CF = -1.59 + .77CGNP + .23CGNP_{-1}$ ($R^2 = .78$), with all coefficients "significant" at the 1 per cent level. The equation suggests that three-fourths of the employment adjustment to a change in output is made in the first year and the remaining fourth in the second year.

[6] Unemployed persons are those in the noninstitutional population, 16 years of age and older, who did not work in the survey week but were available for work except for temporary illness and looked for jobs during the preceding four weeks. Persons who did not look for work because they were on layoff or waiting to start new jobs within the next 30 days are also counted as unemployed.

[7] A regression of the civilian unemployment rate (U) against the ratio of real private gross national product (in 1982 dollars) to its long-term trend (GNP) over 1948–1987 produces the following results: $U = 41.34 - 35.78GNP$ ($R^2 = .91$; $ar(1) = .77$; D-W = 1.97), with all coefficients significant at the 1 per cent level. (The trend in real gross national product is benchmarked to its actual levels at the cyclical peaks of 1948 and 1979.) In other words, over the observation period, when real gross national product has been at its trend level, the unemployment rate has been about 5.6 per cent. Each 1 per cent increment in real gross national product above its trend is associated with a .3 −.4 percentage point reduction in unemployment. However, there is serial correlation in movements in the unemployment rate, a kind of lagged sluggishness.

[8] It is not true, as some commentators seem to believe, that the Current Population Survey (CPS) counts people as unemployed who have decided to substitute leisure for work, so as

In principle, persons counted as unemployed could convert themselves to an officially employed status by becoming self employed. They could offer to cut their neighbor's grass, for example.[9] Generally, however, the unemployed cannot simply employ themselves in their previous occupation due to economies of scale and other barriers which prevent workers from hiring capital (Weitzman, 1982). There may be an incentive for the creation of more worker-owned firms during business cycle downturns.[10] But, in the general case, capital hires labor and rations job availability. Apart from the labor market significance of these observations, the forces involved are fundamental to an economic understanding of why firms are formed and why there are employers in the first place.

When unemployed workers hunt for jobs in "loose" labor markets, they may be told there are no vacancies. At other times, in "tight" labor market periods, firms may experience long durations of vacant jobs. Except for a brief period ending in the early seventies, the U.S. has not collected vacancy data. But a proxy, help-wanted advertising, is available.

Help-wanted advertising, unfortunately, is not an ideal indicator of vacancy trends. It is affected by changes in EEO requirements regarding job advertising, shifts in the industrial organization of the newspaper industry, and other factors. Attempts have been made to adjust for these influences (Abraham, 1987), but especially in the late eighties, help-wanted advertising moved in unexpected ways. Still, it is clear that in the short run, help-wanted advertising is highly pro-cyclical.[11] Thus, vacancies and unemployment move inversely, as do unemployment and voluntary quits. When unemployment is low, workers can be selective about the jobs they take and may readily leave jobs they dislike. Employers must cater to employee preferences when labor markets are tight. The reverse occurs when

---

to give a false cyclical picture of nonmarket clearing behavior. For example, Knieser and Goldsmith (1987, p. 1249) state that some workers might "interpret the Current Population Survey as asking 'Would you take a job at your *normal* wage, w(0)?' instead of asking, 'Would you take a job at the *current* wage, w(1)?" In fact, as the text notes, the CPS does not ask about wages at all, only about search behavior and layoff status.

[9] The self-employment option generally would involve a substantial cut in earnings. As Greenwald and Stiglitz (1987) point out, the existence of a sector in which displaced workers can be employed at earnings substantially below the going rate in the sector from which they came is inconsistent with classical labor market clearing behavior.

[10] Avner Ben-Ner reports to us that his research indicates an increase in the creation of worker-owned firms during recessions.

[11] A regression on the ratio of help-wanted advertising to its long-term trend (HELP) on the ratio of real private gross national product (in 1982 dollars) to its long-term trend (GNP) produces the following results: HELP = −3.78 + 4.55GNP (R^2 = .77; ar(1) = .77; D-W = 1.04), with all coefficients significant at the 1 per cent level. The difficulty in correcting for autocorrelation illustrates how hard it is to capture the shifting longer-term influences on job advertising.

labor markets are loose; during such periods, employer preferences tend to dominate in the employment relationship.

Price inflation. Unlike the variables discussed above, inflation of prices is a product market, not a labor market, phenomenon. Price inflation is usually assumed to be an important guide to wage determination, although—as we discuss below—some macroeconomists dispute that view. What is clear is that price inflation, as measured by an index such as the CPI, and wage inflation are highly correlated.[12] However, the empirical history of wage movements also indicates that (1) the real wage (the ratio of wages to prices) does not always advance, and that (2) in particular, real wage declines have been prone to occur during periods of external price shocks, such as those of the mid- and late seventies.

Inflation is also widely viewed as an important influence on nominal interest rates. The newspaper explanation of this connection is often that lenders will not "accept" a reduction in their real return due to inflation. In fact, lenders must accept what the financial markets provide, and there were periods of negative *ex post* interest rates in the seventies.

The impact of inflation on interest rates is especially important to HRM-IR practitioners where deferred benefits must be funded, e.g., in defined-benefit pensions. If inflation pushes up wages, without producing corresponding increases in nominal interest rates, the current funding costs of such benefits are increased. Similarly, a fall in interest rates and an increase in asset values (as occurred during the low inflation period of the mid-eighties) can lead to pension plan changes. Employers may retrieve "excess" assets from the fund or even terminate the plan and liquidate the assets. Changes in the costs and status of pension plans have obvious employee relations implications.

Profits. At the micro level, private firms must ultimately be profitable to survive. Profitability, therefore, is important for job security and job opportunities. In principle, profits could play an important role in wage determination. Increased profitability could be viewed as an increased "ability to pay" by employers. Where there are formal profit-sharing plans, bonuses paid to workers do reflect profitability. However, an important question is whether the wage system itself functions as a *de facto* profit-sharing plan, even where no formal profit sharing exists.

Recently, there have been proposals—based on macroeconomic

---

[12] The gross correlation between the per cent change in the Consumer Price Index (CPI-W) and the per cent change in private compensation per full-time equivalent employee is quite high, but not perfect. During 1948–1987, the R^2 between these two measures was .72.

considerations—to increase the proportion of the work force covered by profit sharing. The need for such coverage is lessened to the extent that the wage system has an implicit profit-sharing component. Defining an appropriate measure of profits for testing for such a relationship poses a variety of problems. During the postwar period, there has been virtually no ongoing correlation between wage change and the ratio of after-tax domestic corporate profits to labor compensation. Other profitability measures, in particular data sets and time periods, will sometimes show a wage-profits linkage. The key point is that such a connection does not appear to be close.

Long-term economic performance variables. Macroeconomics is often limited to the study of short-term economic fluctuations. Nevertheless, the evaluation of aggregate economic performance has an important long-term component. An economy that avoided any cyclical fluctuations, but produced a steady decline in real per capita income, could not be considered a success.

Unemployment, discussed above from a cyclical perspective, is also of long-term significance. Although the unemployment rate shows little trend, the lowest rates achieved at successive business cycle peaks did show a marked upward trend through the late seventies. Particularly in Europe, where joblessness was historically high in the eighties, there has been recent discussion about whether increased labor market "flexibility" could improve the unemployment situation. The word "flexibility" has various connotations in this discussion, but generally it is linked to HRM-IR practices, particularly with regard to layoffs and wage setting.

Although productivity exhibits a pro-cyclical influence, its long-run trend has been considered more important as an index of economic performance. Until the early seventies, an upward trend in output per labor hour of 3 per cent per annum was considered "natural" by U.S. economists. Empirically, real wages over long periods have risen at approximately the trend rate in productivity growth. This observation was built into wage guidelines used in wage-price control programs in the sixties and seventies, and into the "3% plus COLA" collective bargaining formula in certain industries, especially autos.

Lower productivity growth after the early seventies, not only in the U.S., but in most other countries, led to a resurgence in productivity research. Over the long haul, the productivity trend may influence work force composition and the social climate within which public policies toward the labor market are enacted. Sluggish real wage growth may disappoint workers who were expecting tangible gains in remuneration. Participation rates may be affected; the growth of the female work force in the seventies is sometimes attributed to families' need to make up for the lagging real wages of the household head.

The Impact of Macro Variables: Recruitment, Retention, and Layoffs

There are many aspects of the HRM-IR function which might be influenced by macroeconomic conditions. We divide these functions into the following four categories: (1) recruitment, retention, and layoffs; (2) the effective use of employees; (3) the employee relations climate; and (4) wage setting. We then discuss how the previously identified variables influence these functions.

Decisions on *recruitment, retention, and layoffs* are reflections of the firm's demand for labor. The strongly cyclical nature of employment fluctuations suggests that a good macro forecast would be of use to HRM-IR practitioners for short-term planning. It would seem unwise for firms to make costly employment commitments if the economy were soon to turn down. On the other hand, there might also be some benefit in hiring ahead of forecast upturns to avoid the skill shortages that might accompany decreased cyclical unemployment. Yet, as noted earlier, employment adjustments show some lag in responding to output.

Trends in structural unemployment are usually attributed to long-term influences such as demographics. But there could be a cyclical element, too, so that short-term internal firm policies could translate into a long-run social problem. If so, public policy issues arise. In this section, we take up issues relating to employment, cyclical unemployment, and secular unemployment.

Employment considerations: hours vs. jobs. Firms have various options in meeting fluctuations in their labor demand. One possibility is to change the intensity of labor utilization by varying weekly hours rather than employment. Indeed, during periods of high unemployment, e.g., the Great Depression and the early eighties, spreading work around via hours reduction is inevitably advocated as an offsetting macroeconomic measure.

Despite such advocacy, postwar empirical evidence suggests that weekly hours variation, while correlated with employment variation, is of a much smaller magnitude. Yearly hours variation has been affected on a long-term basis by a gradual trend toward part-time employment. Similarly, yearly employment variation has been affected by the gradual shift toward reduced average weekly hours per employee. When corrected for these trend influences, the two measures are positively, but not tightly, correlated. The lack of tight correlation is to be expected since hours variation in part deflects the need for employment variation. Nonetheless, employment shows substantially more variability than weekly hours. During the postwar period, yearly hours variation has generally stayed within a ±2 per cent range, whereas employment fluctuations have occurred within a ±6 per cent range.[13]

Various explanations could be offered for this tendency. Micro theorists might point to employee tastes for weekly income stability and the existence of legally mandated overtime premiums as barriers to hours variation. We do know that workers not covered by overtime pay requirements tend to work longer hours, suggesting that the mandated wage premium after 40 hours per week does act as a constraint on employers. Another possibility is that rigidity stems from seniority-related arrangements whereby juniors are most prone to layoff. Under such systems, the inframarginal worker might be unwilling to trade off hours (and income) variation for more employment stability, since the added stability benefits the marginal worker. (Similar considerations regarding wage flexibility are discussed below). In fact, workers are more likely to indicate they would like to work more hours, not less, other things equal (Shank, 1986).

Public policy—in the form of unemployment insurance (UI)—may contribute to the preference for layoffs, as opposed to hours reductions, during downturns. The typical state UI system does not pay benefits to workers whose incomes decline due to reduced weekly hours. In the eighties, several states modified their laws to allow some benefits in cases of work sharing, however. These changes appear to have resulted in some employment stabilization for employers who took advantage of the option; only a negligible fraction of employers have participated, however. One factor in this employer disinterest may be that fringe benefit costs are not proportional to hours and so rise on a per hour basis when hours are reduced.

The lower variability of hours relative to employment may indicate a potential for achieving greater job security. HRM-IR practitioners might carefully examine the employment/hours tradeoffs they are making. In the eighties, after a severe slump in the early part of the decade, and with employee nervousness due to mergers, acquisitions, exchange rate movements, etc., the taste for job security may have increased. Workers might accept more hours variability packaged with assurances of increased employment security.

---

[13] During 1948–1987, the standard deviation of annual changes in adjusted weekly hours per production and nonsupervisory employee in the private, nonagricultural sector was .7 percentage points compared with 2.7 percentage points for adjusted employment change. The positive correlation between the two measures, as indicated by the R^2, was .30.

Employment stabilizing strategies. Apart from hours variation (or pay variation as discussed below), firms have options for increasing job security. To protect the employment stability of a group of core employees, the incidence of variable labor demand can be shifted to a "contingent" group. There appeared to be an increase in the use of such contingent worker groups as temporaries, part-timers, and subcontractors in the eighties.

Those working in the contingent labor force do not necessarily prefer such arrangements. Use of employees from temporary help services accelerated in the early eighties, just as the economy was beginning to recover from a very severe recession. This timing suggests that employers were reluctant to make permanent commitments to regular workers, due to the uncertain economic outlook, and met rising employment demand through temporaries. Nonetheless, for workers in the protected core, and for HRM-IR managers seeking to have both flexibility to meet peaks of demand and a loyal core work force, the contingent option is an important alternative.

Cyclical unemployment. Business cycle fluctuations are met using quantitative adjustments more than by using nominal pay adjustments. During booms, employers react by expanding hours and employment, rather than just raising pay (Okun, 1981). During downturns, hiring is frozen, layoffs occur, and merit and promotion opportunities are reduced.

The cause of this preference for quantity rather than pay adjustment has long been debated. In the thirties, wage rigidity was blamed for unemployment by pre-Keynesian economists. Keynesian theory tended to shift the blame away from wage determination, but it nevertheless accepted wage rigidity as an empirical fact. In the seventies, wage determination was again seen as an important element in quantitative adjustments and new theories were developed to explain it. These new approaches include the implicit contract approaches discussed by Wachter and Wright (in this issue). The new models, because of their starting assumption of rationality, do better at explaining real rather than nominal wage rigidity.

All of these approaches, however, suggest that "insiders" (incumbent workers) are protected by their employers from underbidding and/or displacement by queues of "outsiders" (job seekers) (Lindbeck and Snower, 1986). When insiders are laid off, they may remain attached to the employer through recall systems. From the employer's perspective, there are costs to providing insider protections. The employer is foregoing the possibility of using outsiders who may be superior to incumbents.

Insider protection must contribute to unemployment, since it creates hurdles for outside job searchers. The resulting unemployment contributes to insiders' fears of displacement. Displaced workers in the eighties often experienced long periods of joblessness. In a world of unemployment, it is rational to fear it. HRM-IR practices that contribute to unemployment give rise to demands for other practices to cushion workers from it.

Recent literature on efficiency wages argues that unemployment is a disciplinary device. Under efficiency wage theory, employers need to have a penalty for misconduct. They pay higher than a market clearing wage so that employees will pay a penalty if they are dismissed. The labor market always has a worker surplus as a result. Thus, unemployment benefits individual employers through maintenance of employee discipline.

Since job insecurity can trigger public interventions which limit employer flexibility, employers *as a group* still may be better off in a tight labor market (i.e., with low unemployment). The enactment in 1988 of federal requirements for advance notice of mass layoffs and plant closings is an example of such an intervention which was strongly opposed by business groups. During the past two decades, employee protections also have grown through court decisions—eroding the at-will doctrine. Workers' compensation and EEO programs have been used increasingly to address worker grievances, including those arising out of discharges.

Thus, employers who individually may be rationally following strategies which cause unemployment may be imposing eventual hardships on other employers and themselves. Because of the highly decentralized U.S. economic system, such externalities are difficult for employers to confront. Business groups can lobby against public interventions in the workplace, but they have no authority to modify employer policies which lead to such interventions.

Despite the efficiency wage argument, high unemployment does not necessarily contribute to good macro productivity performance. Productivity growth, for example, was much higher during the incredibly tight labor markets of World War II than during the very loose labor market of the Great Depression.[14] Employers with stubbornly high rates of unfilled vacancies are forced to find ways to economize on labor.

Labor shortages. General labor shortages have occurred less frequently than surpluses. They have been associated with wartime labor markets and historically have influenced subsequent HRM-IR practices. During World War I, for example, the attributes of the workplace aspects of welfare capitalism were developed. Internal labor market practices were further

---

[14] Official productivity indexes do not go back to these periods. However, real GNP per full-time equivalent employee rose by only 0.5 per cent per annum during 1929–1941 and by 4.9 per cent per annum during 1941–1945.

enhanced during the labor shortages of World War II (Jacoby, 1985).

Defining the precise boundaries of the labor market has always been a problem. Even in 1982, a recession trough, more people who entered employment did so from being outside the labor force than from being unemployed. An average of over 4.5 million workers entered the labor force each month while a similar number departed. The overall labor force participation rate fluctuates pro-cyclically, so that more people enter the labor force in good times than in bad.

The evidence suggests that as the labor market tightens, not only are people sucked into the labor force, but job mobility also increases. Quits rise as workers face improved external opportunities. And there is an upgrading of the labor force into better jobs as hiring and promotion standards are relaxed. Employers fill vacancies from all sources, not only from the unemployed. There is a spectrum of labor market attachment ranging from the presently employed, to the unemployed, to individuals not officially in the labor force who express some interest in working, to those who currently have no such interests but who might be enticed under some circumstances. During labor shortages, HRM-IR managers need strategies to tap these pools of labor.

Structural unemployment issues. Initially, the issue of structural unemployment was viewed skeptically by Keynesian economists. Such arguments were seen as diverting attention from the appropriate macroeconomic remedies. Macroeconomists became concerned about structural unemployment when it appeared that traditional monetary and fiscal policy might be unable to drive down the rate of unemployment without causing accelerating inflation. Milton Friedman (1968) suggested the concept of a "natural" rate of unemployment, below which inflation acceleration was inevitable. However, the natural rate tended to be seen as determined by labor force composition and therefore susceptible to lowering by public training programs. These programs would match the skills of available workers with those required by employers, thus removing the structural barrier to lower unemployment without rising inflation.

Although the popular press has tended to present training programs as boondoggles, some of them, at least, did improve the lot of their clients. It would be difficult to argue, however, that the natural rate has been substantially lowered by government training programs. Indeed, it may be that the problem with persistent structural unemployment involves the wage-setting process and is not purely a matter of demographics and skills. Generally, economists who are willing to consider a role for wage setting prefer to substitute the nonaccelerating inflation rate of unemployment

(NAIRU) for the natural rate concept. The implication of the wage-setting view is to shift public resources and attention away from training programs and toward modifying the wage system.

Much of the discussion of the interaction between wage setting and the natural rate has occurred abroad. In Europe and elsewhere, countries which had remarkably low unemployment rates in the sixties found themselves with high unemployment in the seventies and eighties, sometimes substantially exceeding American levels. Several studies suggested that real wages in Europe had become too high, and that therefore what was being observed was "classical" rather than "Keynesian" unemployment (Sachs, 1983).

One explanation was that nominal wages were indexed, formally or through bargaining, to prices, and that external oil price increases in the seventies had pushed wages up relative to domestic (internal) prices. The resulting profit squeeze would trim the demand for labor. Another view was that there was simply a worldwide increase in labor militancy—reflected in strikes and industrial unrest—which pushed wages up (Nordhaus, 1972). Whatever the cause, it may be that once real wages rose, still-employed insiders kept the wage high at the expense of unemployed outsiders, creating "hysteresis" (continuation) in unemployment (Blanchard and Summers, 1986).[15]

The interaction of wage (W) setting and price (P) setting could produce a rise in the NAIRU. Assume that over some period, the labor market attempts to set a real wage W/P and the product market tries to establish a price markup over costs. At any one firm, costs are often largely purchases from other firms. But at the macro level, interfirm transactions net out and the main cost is wages; ultimately, the product market can be seen as trying to set P/W.[16] Obviously, desired W/P must equal the inverse of desired P/W or there will be disequilibrium in the form of accelerating inflation or deflation. Heightened economic activity, as proxied by a fall in the unemployment rate (U), can be expected to raise desired W/P, either as a result of employer bidding for labor or through changing union bargaining strength. It will also influence the ability of firms to obtain markups, as their demand curves shift. That is, we would expect a decrease in U to raise

---

[15] An alternative explanation for hysteresis might be that the job skills of the unemployed deteriorate with disuse, reducing these individuals' employability.

[16] It should be noted that we are dealing with adjustment over an extended period of time. If one argues, as Gordon (1988) recently did, that wage costs empirically have little to do with price trends and *vice versa*, then the model in the text breaks down and a natural rate of unemployment or NAIRU would have to depend on other explanations. Many would be reluctant, however, to accept a lack of any linkage between wages and prices, particularly in view of the evidence discussed below.

both desired W/P and P/W.[17]

At any point in time, there is one level of the unemployment rate (U*) which reconciles labor and product market wage and price setting. Lower rates will accelerate inflation. Higher rates will decelerate inflation and ultimately lead to deflation. The reconciling U* is the NAIRU in this model. Rather than being a fixed number geared to demographics and skills, it is a variable which can be raised by such events as spontaneous increases in labor militancy or OPEC price increases. If the monetary authorities wish to prevent inflation acceleration, they will keep the economy at or below the NAIRU.

Although doubts have been raised about the real wage model in the European context, there is casual evidence that changes in wage and price setting had an impact on the NAIRU in the U.S. in the seventies. During those years, it became difficult for the U.S. to lower the unemployment rate without inflation acceleration. The seventies were characterized by OPEC oil price shocks, which pushed up desired wage targets and markups. Escalation of union contracts rose, thus incorporating oil price movements into wages. The inflation-biased treatment of housing in the CPI also tended to boost union wages. Union wages rose relative to nonunion, suggesting wage pressures in that sector, despite deteriorating productivity performance (Mitchell, 1980). Finally, long-term contracts happened to be timed so that union wages "missed" the impact of restrictive policy and recession in 1974–1975 (Mitchell, 1982).

In contrast, in the eighties, oil prices fell, unions were significantly weakened, escalation declined (see below), and wage norms seemed to shift downward. Employers reported less of a propensity to look outward at wages, and more of a tendency to look toward their own internal economic circumstances (Freedman, 1985). Unemployment declined without returning the economy to the inflation rates of the late seventies. There seemed, in short, to be a two-way interaction between macroeconomic events and firm-level labor relations policy. Macroeconomic shocks caused changes in firm wage-setting practices. The perceived change in these practices allowed the monetary authorities to push the unemployment rate down further. For HRM-IR practitioners, the evidence suggests that shifts in the macro climate occur from time to time, changing the power balance in the labor-management relationship. This point is discussed further below.

---

[17] We do not attempt to specify a dynamic path for actual W/P. Empirically, markups tend to rise procyclically, as does productivity growth. So profits capture a disproportionate share of the procyclical productivity effect.

The Impact of Macro Variables: The Effective Use of Employees

Because the causes of the U.S. productivity slump in the seventies are not well understood, attention has focused not only on traditional economic variables (such as capital/labor ratios) but on the possibility that HRM-IR policies and tensions in the workplace added to the problem (Weisskopf, Bowles, and Gordon, 1983). More generally, there has been interest in the impact of such policies on firm performance. This section examines macro influences on the effective utilization of the work force.

Turnover control. Macro fluctuations clearly affect employee turnover. As noted above, quits are pro-cyclical, rising as external job opportunities increase. Layoffs are anti-cyclical, rising as the economy turns down. In both cases of employee departure, the firm faces an erosion of its investment in its employees. Firms can use wage policy to reduce quits, although, as discussed earlier, they seem reluctant to do so (Salop, 1979). Deferred benefits, with less-than-complete vesting, also dampen voluntary outward mobility.

Firms can limit their use of layoffs, through devices already discussed, such as hours variation and use of contingent workers. Most firms do not follow a full employment policy—IBM is probably the only *major* U.S. firm which claims to do so. But other firms with "enlightened" employment policies do use elements of layoff avoidance. They do not guarantee full employment, but they do try to enhance job security.

Adapting to secular change. One view of even such enlightened policies is that they arise from market pressures, which inevitably drive firms to install the most efficient labor practices. If firms do not vary wages in accordance with quits, or if they choose to follow full-employment policies, they are seen as pursuing optimal approaches, given their circumstances. Yet, norms of what is good practice seem to change over time, often in response to historical shifts and accidents. At the very least, there may be a lag in adapting to changing economic circumstances. Those who develop appropriate HRM-IR practices early on have a competitive advantage in the marketplace.

For example, there have been predictions that the economy is evolving toward smaller firms which will produce customized products for changing markets (Piore and Sabel, 1984). And there is evidence of a decline in average firm size in the U.S. Smaller firms in more erratic markets would have to evolve policies which enabled them to obtain needed skills quickly, but they would be less able to maintain a cadre of overhead workers for this purpose. Unions might function in such industries as referral services, as they do in fragmented industries today, such as construction and film production. Given the potential weakening of employer-employee attachments, unions might focus on providing services to members other than traditional bargaining representation.

Adjusting to such long-term macro changes will require redesign of existing HRM-IR practices. Simply following fads—such as team production—will not necessarily improve performance. The challenge is to design systems reconciling employee needs for stability and firm needs for flexibility. Alternatively, the old macro policy goal of full employment must be given new prominence so that stability in employer-employee attachments is less important. If displaced workers can readily find alternative employment, the cost of displacement is substantially reduced. Ultimately, macro goals and micro HRM-IR practices need reconciliation. Ease of labor mobility may be impeded by certain benefit plans, wages linked to seniority, and other practices which were designed on the assumption of long job tenures.

Productivity measurement. Since the early sixties, macro perspectives on the sources of productivity growth have been enhanced by the use of "growth accounting," a term associated with Edward F. Denison (1985). Such accounting breaks down the sources of output increase by considering both capital and labor inputs and then adjusts these inputs for detailed quality changes where possible. What remains is a residual involving changes in technology and managerial technique, a factor that "explained" over two-thirds of the growth of output per employed person in the nonresidential business sector during 1929–1982. It also accounted for over half of the decline in this measure between the periods 1948–1973 and 1973–1982.

Denison explicitly accounted for formal education, demographic shifts in the work force, and time lost to strikes. Remaining within his residual are the general climate of the employment relationship and the stock of human capital accumulated on the job or outside the formal educational system. By definition, we cannot say how much of the residual effect is due specifically to changes in the employment relationship. But micro-level evidence increasingly suggests that the climate at the workplace "matters."

There are no comprehensive surveys concerning the extent to which firms measure productivity. But there are reasons to suspect that productivity measurement is often not systematically undertaken, particularly outside the large firm setting. HRM-IR managers and consultants would do well to borrow some of the techniques developed by economists in the macro productivity field and adapt them for use at the micro level.

The labor relations climate. As noted above, there is evidence that the labor relations climate affects firm performance within the union sector. Workplace frictions, as measured by grievances, strikes, etc., influence the effective use of employees by the firm. Although less work has been done on analogous conditions in the nonunion sector, the same conclusions are likely.

The business cycle influences the climate of labor relations in complex ways. Strikes seem to be pro-cyclical and are influenced by the degree wages keep up with, or fall behind, general inflationary trends in the economy. During periods of union weakness, as measured by low wage settlements, strike frequency also seems to decline.[18] Unfair labor practice charges filed with the NLRB also are affected by the level of, and direction of change in, business conditions (Mitchell, 1980).

Apart from its impact on general wage trends (discussed below), unexpected price inflation can complicate labor-management relations by creating pressures for "catch up," especially if wages are not subject to an escalator clause. Because such clauses tend to award cost-of-living adjustments as flat cents-per-hour payments, they can narrow the relative (percentage) wage structure and give rise to pay inequities and reduced promotional incentives (Mitchell, 1980). Inflation variation, by increasing uncertainty over likely future inflation rates, can increase the probability of a strike when union contracts expire, especially if the parties do not use escalator clauses (Gramm, Hendricks, and Kahn, 1988; Gray, 1978).

An increase in price inflation can induce strife over union demands for installation of new escalator clauses. And it can lead to management proposals to eliminate or cap escalation in periods when the inflation is external (e.g., due to OPEC or exchange rates) since full indexation is not optimal under such conditions. All of these problems cropped up in the seventies and gave rise to limitations on both the escalator formula and the number of workers covered by it during the concession years of the eighties.

Indeed, escalation in the seventies may have been part of the mechanism which triggered union wage concessions in the eighties. Union wages rose relative to nonunion during the seventies, and escalated union wages rose faster than nonescalated. The widening union-nonunion wage differential is believed to have increased management incentives to resist unionization (Freeman and Medoff, 1984). And the wage concessions that followed have been seen as "corrections" of the earlier widening. The dampening effect of import prices in the eighties also may have reduced wage inflation (Vroman and Abowd, 1988).

Although, as noted earlier, less is known about the effects of macro

---

[18] The early sixties and the eighties were such periods.

variables on the employee relations climate in nonunion settings, it is likely that inflation has a distorting effect there, too. Nonunion firms are more likely than union to rely on individual "merit" adjustments in wages. In fact, managements at nonunion firms may state that they make no general adjustments and award pay increases only on merit.

Such merit-only policies pose obvious problems during periods of high inflation, since some way must be found to keep average wages increasing. There is weak evidence that claimed exclusive reliance on merit falls in such periods (Jacoby and Mitchell, 1983). But firms which persist in merit-only policies find themselves having to find almost all workers to be meritorious in order to keep up with external wage trends. Such practices tend to undermine the supposed incentive effect of merit awards.[19]

The deterioration of long-term productivity growth in the seventies was initially felt more in the nonunion than in the union sector (Mitchell, 1980). Real wage trends in the nonunion sector reflected the productivity trend more than in the union sector. Perhaps the previously noted "3% plus COLA" principle continued to influence unions, even after the 3 per cent productivity factor had disappeared from the economy. Thus, the productivity decline may have contributed to the widening union-nonunion wage gap in the seventies, and, therefore, to the subsequent union concessions and membership losses. Some argue that unions made a deliberate choice in the seventies to obtain short-term gains despite long-run consequences (Lawrence and Lawrence, 1985). However, the tradeoffs may not have been clear. With the benefit of hindsight, unions may want to take a longer-run perspective on issues such as escalation and annual improvement factors in the future.

Fair dealing. Recent economic literature, with its emphasis on implicit, long-term contracts in the labor market, suggests that firms make an investment in "trust" between employer and employee. Where physical capital is concerned, it is sometimes said that managers can act to maximize short-term (accounting) profits—at the expense of long-run owner interests—by cutting back on maintenance. The temptation to do so may be particularly great when economic circumstances are adverse. And much the same may be true about the firm's investment in the trust and goodwill of its employees.

The onset of the Great Depression ultimately produced a substantial burst of unionization, despite the fact that historically union membership had been pro-cyclical. As firms fell on hard times, they apparently dropped some

---

[19] A merit plan which has been distorted by inflation may still provide some differentiation between good and bad performers. Inflation, however, tends to reduce the signal-to-noise ratio of the plan.

of the more humane features of welfare capitalism, triggering a backlash from their workers, both directly and through legislation (Jacoby, 1985). It may be that the soft labor markets of the early eighties, which for certain industries remained soft for several years, created a similar change in climate. Under a banner of a need for "competitiveness," firms may have spent previous accumulations of worker goodwill.

Other macro variables may have interacted with the general economic climate to produce situations in which trust was allowed to depreciate in the eighties. For example, falling nominal interest rates and a rise in stock price values led to the "overfunding" of some defined benefit pension plans. There were instances in which managements terminated such funds, and reclaimed the assets, giving vested workers annuities only for what they were legally owed. However, legally required funding rules do not correspond to the liabilities of such plans when viewed as part of implicit contracts. Workers may suffer losses when plans are terminated, even if paid what they are technically owed.[20]

The Impact of Macro Variables: Wage Setting

There is a long-term, close correspondence between real wage trends and productivity trends. In the short run, though, considerable divergence occurs. There is a substantial literature involving the estimation of short-run (quarterly or annual) econometric equations explaining wage change.[21] Although this literature is far too voluminous to summarize, it has some basic features. The wholesale estimation of wage equations goes back to the Phillips curve study which found that nominal wage inflation slowed during periods of high unemployment in Britain (Phillips, 1958). Subsequent studies added other variables and modified the original specification in many ways.

The modified Phillips curve approach was subject to both theoretical and empirical criticisms. On the theory side, although the inclusion of unemployment seems to give the relation a demand-supply flavor, that flavor is not consistent with an auction market. The Phillips curve does not predict wages to fall when there is excess supply; rather, they are forecast to rise more slowly. Moreover, the modified equations are not necessarily consistent with constant natural rates of unemployment or NAIRUs.

---

[20] Defined-benefit pension plans typically have "lumpy" benefit schedules, e.g., vesting after five years of service, early retirement at age 55, normal retirement at age 65, etc. Thus, workers who fall short of the discrete points in the benefit formula are shortchanged in pension terminations.

[21] In principle, wage change refers to movements in total compensation (wages plus benefits). Often, however, actual studies rely on wage-only indexes, mainly for reasons of data availability.

These criticisms are not necessarily devastating. They may simply reflect the deviation of the real world labor market from the theoretical model. In the post-World War II period, nominal wage cuts—while not unknown (especially in the concession-prone eighties)—seem to be unusual. Lags operate to prevent wage changes from immediately reacting, or reacting fully, to unemployment increases. And the NAIRU may be a variable, not a constant, for reasons explored earlier.

More of a problem for the econometric wage equations is the fact that they seem to be empirically unstable. Their coefficients vary considerably, depending on the time period chosen for estimation. Thus, it seems unwise to draw conclusions from nuances in any one specification or estimate. Some very general conclusions, however, can be reported.

Inflation effects. The evidence suggests that two kinds of variables influence short-run wage change: inflation variables and activity variables. There are three basic candidates for inflation variables: (1) the official CPI, (2) some other price index in which volatile external price elements may play a smaller role than in the CPI, and (3) past wage trends. In addition, some researchers have been interested in separate specification of external (versus domestic) prices (Vroman and Abowd, 1988). The official CPI is an obvious candidate for a price inflation measure, since we know that escalators are virtually all based on it. But nonunion workers—who constituted six out of seven private employees in the mid-eighties—rarely have formal escalation. And the majority of union workers are also not covered by escalators. Thus, the existence of CPI escalation for a small minority is not evidence that the vast majority of workers have their pay set based on the CPI. Indeed, the existence of only a small union sector and an even smaller escalated subsector within it may account for lesser real wage rigidity in the U.S. than abroad.

Movements in the CPI may reflect factors external to most employers, such as jumps in energy prices or farm prices; therefore, they do not necessarily indicate employer "ability to pay." For that reason, a price index which is less sensitive to external forces might be preferable. Generally, price indexes taken from the national income (GNP) accounts are less volatile than the CPI and are more domestically oriented.

It is possible, however, that the inflation effect on wages is not through prices directly, but through wages themselves. Some studies have argued that the relevant explanatory inflation variable for current wage change is lagged wage inflation (Gordon, 1988). That view implies that wage determination is largely unhinged from general economic forces in the short run. As will be seen below, real activity measures and other variables do not strongly influence short-term wage change. So if prices do not influence wages, wages would be left to determine themselves.

Activity effects. Since the original Phillips study, it has been traditional to use the unemployment rate as a measure of the state of the labor market. Sometimes, unemployment rates for specific groups are used instead, or the overall unemployment rate is corrected for demographic shifts in the labor force. Studies using unemployment implicitly assume that the state of the job market—proxied by excess labor supply—is of concern to wage setters.

Alternative views are possible. For example, given the nonclearing nature of the labor market, a variable geared to excess demand, i.e., unfilled job vacancies, could plausibly be suggested as the appropriate activity index. The insider-outsider view suggests that the queue at the factory gate would matter less in wage setting than an absence of needed job applicants. Finally, it might be that labor market variables such as unemployment are simply a reflection of the overall stage of the business cycle. In that case, what matters is the business cycle itself—which influences employer "ability to pay"— rather than the state of the labor market *per se*.

Other possible effects. It could be that variables other than those relating to inflation or the level of economic activity influence wage determination. Obvious candidates are profits and productivity, both of which seem linked directly to ability to pay. Of course, these variables are themselves heavily influenced by the business cycle.

Wage estimations. Annual wage equations estimated over the period 1954–1987 are presented below for illustrative purposes. Our goal is to show general tendencies only and to give a sense of what wage researchers are likely to find. In all cases, the dependent wage-change variable is the annual per cent change in compensation per full-time equivalent employee from the national income accounts.

To measure price inflation, we use the annual change in CPI-W and the less volatile annual change in the private GNP deflator, both lagged one period.[22] The alternative notion that lagged wage inflation determines current wage inflation simply involves using lagged wage change as an explanatory variable rather than price inflation.

Various alternatives were used to construct activity measures: the inverse of the official civilian unemployment rate, the ratio of help-wanted advertising to trend, the ratio of average weekly hours of production and nonsupervisory

---

[22] Experiments with alternative lag schemes suggested that the one period lag "worked" best. Studies with more elaborate lag schemes tend to be those using quarterly rather than annual data.

workers (standardized to 40 hours) to trend, and the ratio of real private GNP to trend.[23] Also included in some regressions in Table 1 are equations utilizing the ratio of after-tax corporate profits to corporate labor compensation, lagged one period, and a productivity variable—the per cent change in business output per hour.

The first lesson from Table 1 is that all specifications perform reasonably well, with fit (measured by the adjusted R^2) ranging from just under .6 to just over .8. Some estimations are better than others. Given the known sensitivity of such equations to the period of estimation and to precise variable definition, it is best not to draw strong conclusions from minor differences.

Second, it appears that profits and productivity do not work well in aggregate wage-change equations, as can be seen from equations (2) and (3). Thus, arguments that U.S. wage setting functions as a *de facto* share economy are not supported. It is quite possible that there are firms which reflect profitability and productivity in wage decisions. Profits have been found to influence wages in disaggregated union situations, for example (Mitchell, 1980). But they are not important enough in the aggregate to move the overall wage index for the U.S. used for the regressions in Table 1.[24]

Third, the use of lagged wage change, rather than lagged price change, in the equations does not improve the results. To the contrary, the lagged wage equation (1) exhibits the poorest fit. Employers may look at wage changes around them as a guide to their own wage decisions, but price movements—if they are of domestic origin—reflect the demand for labor. Thus, they provide "information" on demand as well as the cost-of-living effect. A boot-strap model of wage setting, in which wages set wages, does not appear realistic.

Fourth, the coefficients on lagged prices (all equations except [1]) are less than 1. This result is common in wage equation estimates. It could be that the price effect is being incorrectly measured by the specifications chosen, biasing the coefficient downward. The equations, though, seem to be saying that wages react less than fully to inflation in the short run. Wage setters may look to price inflation as a guide, but they see it as an external indicator which need not be followed mechanically. Thus, periods of unexpected

---

[23] Some of the variables used in this section have been cited and defined in previous footnotes. In all cases, the trend was based on 1948 to 1979, with both years being cyclical peaks. The ratio variables—other than weekly hours—were thus equal to 1 in 1948 and 1979. The weekly hours ratio is equal to 40 in both years. (In 1948, average weekly hours were just 40.)

[24] Early studies by Kuh (1967) and by Siebert and Zaidi (1971) found significant effects of productivity in U.S. wage equations.

TABLE 1

ANNUAL WAGE-CHANGE REGRESSIONS[a]
(STANDARD ERRORS ARE IN PARENTHESES)

Equation number	(1)	(2)	(3)	(4)	(5)	(6)	(7)	(8)	(9)	(10)
Constant	.54	−.07	.29	−.90	−73.87*	−16.76**	.07	−.40	−58.81**	−14.50**
	(1.40)	(1.38)	(1.17)	(.93)	(33.85)	(3.66)	(1.04)	(.94)	(26.73)	(3.22)
Lagged change in CPI	—	.54**	.54**	.49**	.52**	.60**	—	—	—	—
		(.09)	(.08)	(.05)	(.11)	(.05)				
Lagged change in private GNP deflator	—	—	—	—	—	—	.71**	.60**	.74**	.73**
							(.08)	(.06)	(.11)	(.05)
Lagged change in wages	.85**	—	—	—	—	—	—	—	—	—
	(.12)									
Inverse of the unemployment rate	7.69	20.80**	19.53**	—	—	—	15.06**	—	—	—
	(5.13)	(5.71)	(4.99)				(4.47)			
Help wanted advertising ratio	—	—	—	6.09**	—	—	—	4.85**	—	—
				(1.11)				(1.16)		
Weekly hours ratio	—	—	—	—	1.92*	—	—	—	1.53*	—
					(.84)				(.66)	
Private GNP ratio	—	—	—	—	—	20.17**	—	—	—	17.36**
						(3.58)				(3.13)
Lagged after tax profits ratio	—	−.01	—	—	—	—	—	—	—	—
		(.10)								
Change in business productivity	—	—	−.12	—	—	—	—	—	—	—
			(.12)							
ar(1)	—	.43**	.36	.27	.52*	−.02	.05	.07	.15	−.20
		(.18)	(.18)	(.18)	(.21)	(.19)	(.20)	(.19)	(.19)	(.18)
$\bar{R}^2$	.59	.77	.78	.83	.72	.81	.74	.78	.70	.80
Standard error	1.32	.97	.96	.84	1.09	.89	1.04	.96	1.11	.91
Durbin–Watson	—	2.17	2.15	2.11	2.15	1.90	2.00	1.95	1.96	1.95
n	34	34	34	34	34	34	34	34	34	34

[a] The dependent variable is current per cent change in wages for all equations. The period of observation is 1954–1987. Lags refer to one-year periods. (See text for details.)
* Significant at .05 level; ** significant at .01 level.

inflation acceleration or deceleration may lead to real wage losses or gains.

As for the choice of price index, some of the equations involving the CPI require autoregressive corrections; those using the GNP deflator do not.[25] This difference suggests that the CPI for an extended period deviated from what wage setters considered relevant to their decisions. Problems with the CPI in the seventies, particularly regarding housing costs, seem to be the main cause. In the aggregate, wage setters, especially those without mechanical escalators, will apparently discount the CPI when it departs from reality as they see it.

Lagged prices in wage-change equations may be interpreted in two ways. There may be a backward-looking process, in which today's wages are adjusted to make up for yesterday's inflation. Or there may be an expectations process in which yesterday's inflation is used to forecast tomorrow's inflation. It is difficult to distinguish between these effects empirically. We did not include direct measures of inflation expectations in the regressions. But studies using direct measures indicate that such expectations move sluggishly with past inflation, suggesting that the two processes—backward looking and forward looking—are virtually the same. Even when people explicitly try to forecast inflation, they have looked back at recent inflation in an adaptive process.[26] This tendency seems to be a stylized fact of U.S. wage setting.

For the union sector, the escalator option can be used to deal with future inflation, if it is considered to be a problem. And in the nonunion sector, wage decisions are basically annual and can be "re-opened" by management at any time. That may explain why the effect of inflation on wages is essentially a backward-looking process.

Fifth, it is difficult to distinguish the activity variables in terms of which one is "best." The GNP variable works about as well as the labor market variables. Help-wanted advertising seems to work better than the other labor market variables, but this feature is a function of the estimation period chosen. All we can say is that in good times, nominal wages rise faster than in hard times, other things equal.

Sixth, the effect of good times and hard times is attenuated. For example,

---

[25] All equations, except the one with the lagged dependent variable, include an autoregressive correction. The autoregressive parameter, however, is not significant in the equations not involving the CPI.

[26] Thus, Vroman and Abowd (1988) find little difference when they use an expected inflation measure based on lagged CPI changes, or one based on the Livingston expected inflation survey, in wage equations covering over 2,700 union contracts in U.S. manufacturing. We experimented with inclusion of actual future inflation and with bond yields (which presumably include an inflation expectations element) in our wage equations, but the results were less satisfactory than the equations shown in Table 1.

the unemployment coefficient in equation (2) indicates that a one percentage point increase in unemployment from 6 per cent to 7 per cent would slow wage inflation by only 0.5 percentage points. It is this type of observation which gave rise to the implicit contract research described earlier. Firms react to hard times with layoffs much more than with changes in wage policy.

Economists have suggested possible rationalizations for such behavior; if those rationalizations do not ring true to HRM-IR specialists, perhaps they need to articulate and examine the causes of this deviation from the market model. Perhaps the insensitivity of wage decisions to real economic conditions—which long puzzled economists—would also puzzle HRM-IR practitioners, *if* they explicitly considered it. Indeed, perhaps such consideration would lead to more flexible pay policies.

Implications

The key lesson from this survey is that macroeconomic variables have an important influence on micro-level labor-management policies and the general climate of employer-employee and employer-union relationships. Thus, HRM-IR practitioners need to be concerned with the macro economy. Indeed, the HRM-IR function can be influenced by macro conditions via political mechanisms as well as economic.

In the postwar period, dissatisfaction with macro conditions has led to various public policies which especially affected employment practices at the firm level. These included anti-inflation wage-price controls and guidelines and the creation of anti-unemployment job training subsidies for employers and hiring incentives for disadvantaged workers. Concern over unemployment also resulted in federal requirements of advance notice for mass layoffs and plant closings in the late eighties. With an aging (and thus security-conscious) work force in the nineties, other restrictions on employer ability to lay off workers may be considered.

Proposals were made in the eighties for special tax subsidies to companies implementing profit sharing, on the grounds that such plans tend to stabilize and expand employment (Weitzman, 1984). Britain adopted such incentives in 1987 and the idea could spread to the U.S. in the nineties, depending on macro trends. The interest in improving U.S. productivity performance could also stimulate public policies aimed at fostering alternative pay systems. Both students and practitioners of HRM-IR ought to play an active role in such macro-related policy debates.

Human Resource Management and International Trade

DRUSILLA K. BROWN and DAVID M. GARMAN*

This article reviews recent developments in international trade theory that relate to issues of human resource management and industrial relations. Some trade models with imperfectly competitive goods markets and their links to strategic trade and industrial policy are described. These models' results are shown to be sensitive to the incorporation of labor market imperfections. Applications of trade theory to international labor migration and human capital acquisition are also included.

INTERNATIONAL TRADE THEORY has had limited overlap with the analytical orientation of practitioners in the field of human resource management and industrial relations. This is unfortunate since both areas are concerned with industrial growth, employment, and income distribution—issues that are closely related to international comparative advantage and commercial policy. Recently, trade economists have begun to explore the implications of international trade for issues that have previously been considered the domain of labor economists, such as the individual's decision to acquire an education, the likelihood of labor action in an industry, and the size of the union wage premium over a competitive sector. This review is intended to stimulate economists interested in human resource management and industrial relations to consider general equilibrium influences on the behavior of labor and to invite suggestions concerning the treatment of labor issues in international trade models.

The traditional analysis of international trade under perfect competition, as developed by Heckscher, Ohlin, Samuelson, Rybczynski, and others, produced a powerful demonstration of the role of factor abundance in

* The authors' affiliation is Department of Economics, Tufts University. The authors benefited from the comments of Solomon Polachek, Jeffrey Pliskin, and an anonymous referee on an earlier draft of this paper.

determining the pattern of trade, the gains from free trade, and the impact of protection on factor income and employment. A typical Heckscher-Ohlin-Samuelson model assumes a two-good, two-factor world with perfect competition and constant returns to scale technology. Both trading partners are assumed to share identical homothetic preferences and production technology.

This model has been used to illustrate three remarkable propositions concerning the effect of trade and commercial policy on the distribution of income. First, the Heckscher-Ohlin Theorem demonstrates that the country relatively abundantly endowed with labor will produce relatively more of the labor intensive good and therefore will export that good. Second, the Factor-Price Equalization Theorem shows that free trade will equalize the price of goods across countries, which will also equalize the wage-rent ratio across both countries. Third, the Stolper-Samuelson Theorem identifies the effect of import protection on the returns to capital and labor. Protection will tend to raise the domestic price of the imported good. The real income of the factor used relatively intensively in the production of the import will rise and the return to the other factor of production will fall.[1]

The analysis of international trade and commercial policy changed course in the eighties as a result of influential work by economists such as Paul Krugman, James Brander, and Barbara Spencer.[2] This new literature was spurred by developments in the field of industrial organization[3] and by a growing discontent with the ability of traditional trade theory to explain such puzzles as the existence of significant intra-industry trade in homogeneous products and protectionist behavior by governments. The central element of both the new international trade theory and the new industrial organization is the relinquishing of the convenient assumption of perfect competition. This leads to the unsettled world of imperfect competition, rents, and strategic interaction.

The results from the new models of imperfect competition pose a challenge for the advocates of minimal government intervention in domestic or international trade. Imperfect competition can generate "excess" profits or rents that accrue to the factors employed in particular firms or particular

---

[1] For discussions of these theorems' assumptions and qualifications, see standard textbooks such as Chacholiades' (1978).

[2] Since it is not possible to mention all the contributors to this area of research, we present a representative selection of the most visible and provocative contributors. Kierzkowski (1984), Helpman (1984), Dixit (1987), and Helpman and Krugman (1985, 1989) provide excellent overviews of imperfect competition, strategic interaction, and international trade theory and policy.

[3] In particular, see Dixit and Stiglitz (1977) and Spence (1976). For a review of strategic industrial organization, see Tirole (1989).

industries. In certain cases, it may be possible to strategically manipulate trade or domestic policy in order to capture larger market shares in these industries. Imperfect competition also may increase the likelihood of beneficial spillovers from R&D expenditures or experience, and could provide another justification for promotion of an industry by direct subsidy, import protection, or export promotion.

In the first part of this paper, we examine the modifications to the Heckscher-Ohlin-Samuelson view of international trade required by the incorporation of scale economies and imperfect competition and note some implications for commercial policy. Several applications that focus on the returns to labor are used to illustrate the basic results. The second part of the paper summarizes work done by trade economists in areas other than strategic trade and industrial policy which nevertheless includes labor-related topics. A common component of these studies is the recognition by trade economists that their models can be improved by eliminating the assumption that labor is a homogeneous input that is traded in a perfectly competitive market.

Our discussion of these models is subdivided as follows: First, we examine the models that incorporate imperfectly competitive labor markets. The inclusion of labor rents dramatically increases the potential gain from strategic trade and industrial policy. Then we review some international labor migration issues, such as the impact of migration on economies with unemployment. Lastly, we outline some recent work on the influence of international trade on human capital acquisition. These models incorporate feedback effects of trade on the incentives to acquire human capital. We close with a summary and concluding comments.

Gains from Trade in the Presence of Internal Economies of Scale

Recent work in international trade has focused on models of increasing returns to scale (IRS) technology and imperfect competition. The presence of imperfectly competitive firms can reverse the conclusion that all countries will gain from free trade. Yet, paradoxically, the loss of guaranteed gains has been accompanied by the presumption that there is potentially more to be gained from international trade under imperfect competition than under perfect competition. The gains from international trade in an IRS model of identically endowed countries stem primarily from two sources. First, trade can intensify the degree of competition, reduce a firm's profit maximizing mark-up of price over marginal cost, and thereby increase output. Second, trade can increase the product variety enjoyed by consumers.

Homogeneous products. The benefit from improving the competitive environment is illustrated simply by Brander (1981). He posits an identical pair of two-sector economies in which the first sector is characterized by perfect competition and constant returns to scale (CRS), and the second sector has a monopoly producer with IRS technology. In the absence of trade, the monopolist in each country will set a profit-maximizing mark-up of price over marginal cost.

In the presence of trade, each former monopolist will want to take advantage of the profit opportunities available by selling its product in the foreign market. The duopolists created by the advent of trade in the imperfectly competitive sector will take into account the potential response of the other to any intrusion into the foreign market. Several patterns of strategic response have been explored, but a popular assumption is that the two firms will behave as Cournot duopolists.

Since two Cournot duopolists will sell more to a single market than will a single monopolist, output must rise and price must fall in the imperfectly competitive sector, and the allocation of resources between perfectly and imperfectly competitive sectors will be improved. This source of gain is sometimes referred to as the "pro-competitive" effect of trade in imperfectly competitive markets and is shared by both trade partners. A second source of gain, the realization of scale economies, will also emerge in this example. Both of the IRS firms will increase output, moving down the average total cost curve, so that the average productivity of at least one factor will rise.

Although Brander's model assumed that the second sector was monopolized in autarky, there are similar gains under other imperfectly competitive market structures. Markusen (1981) analyzed the case in which the imperfectly competitive sector is characterized by relatively free entry so that profits are driven to zero. The IRS industry (sector 2) is assumed to consist of n Cournot firms that each choose a profit-maximizing price and output while taking the output of other firms as fixed. The equilibrium number of firms in this model is determined by the zero-profits condition.

Now consider the possibility of trading with an identical country. The market for good 2 will become an international market with total market demand doubled and the number of firms doubled to 2n. The autarky price-quantity combination will no longer be an equilibrium position. The representative firm still takes the output of the other 2n-1 firms as fixed, but it now perceives its demand curve to have become more elastic. With the market twice as large as in autarky, a small reduction in price by a representative firm will yield a much larger expected increase in quantity demanded.

This increase in the firm's perceived elasticity of demand will result in a lower profit-maximizing price and higher output. As in the Brander model, higher firm output generates movement down the average total cost curve and an increase in factor productivity. Productivity increases reflect the pro-competitive effect of trade that will occur even when extra-normal profits are dissipated through entry.

Differentiated products. The development of the IRS model has not been restricted to homogeneous products and Cournot behavior. The approach pioneered by Krugman (1979, 1980), Helpman (1981), and Lancaster (1979, 1980) assumes that consumers prefer variety and that each firm sells a slightly differentiated product. This class of models introduces an additional source of gain from international trade—increases in the variety of available products.

Krugman's (1979) model of differentiated products assumes that there is only one industry, but that each firm produces a differentiated product using IRS technology and labor as the only factor of production. Consumers have a utility function of the form

$$(1) \quad U = \sum_{i=1}^{n} v(c_i), v' > 0, v'' < 0$$

where c_i is consumption of the variety produced by the ith firm, and n is the number of firms. Demand functions derived from (1) have the property that an increase in quantity consumed is accompanied by a fall in the elasticity of demand. Firms set a profit-maximizing price and quantity, taking the price of other varieties as fixed, and free entry is assumed to yield zero profits.

Due to the resource constraint, attempts to raise output must lead to some exit, but the total number of firms in the world will not fall below n. Thus, consumers' utility is higher because they can consume a greater variety of goods, and firms reap economies of scale because of increased output. The usual gains from greater factor productivity are supplemented by the gains from greater product variety.

There are two implications for labor in Krugman's model. First, the increase in the scale of production will increase the productivity of labor. Second, two-way trade occurs in identical or very similar products in the IRS models. That is, each country imports and exports the same good, a phenomenon well documented in the trade statistics. As a result, increased trade does not necessarily require that labor must be reallocated between sectors. The existence of intra-industry trade leads each country to produce a larger quantity of a smaller number of varieties so that factor employment in the industry could remain close to the autarky level.

The U.S.-Canada free trade area. The theoretical developments in international trade with imperfectly competitive markets have practical benefits, some of which are illustrated by the recently ratified free-trade agreement between the United States and Canada. Canadian economists and policymakers have been concerned for some time with the sizable difference between labor productivity in Canada and the United States. Low Canadian productivity has persisted despite broad similarities between the two countries in tastes, factor endowments, technology, and labor force quality. Recent Canadian interest in an agreement stems from studies (e.g., see Eastman and Stykolt, 1967; Economic Council of Canada, 1975; and Wonnacott and Wonnacott, 1967) that have found that steep tariff protection in Canada has resulted in sub-optimal plant size and an excess of locally produced varieties, which could explain the gap between labor productivity in the United States and Canada.

Thus, Canadian policy analysts have emphasized the gains of a reciprocal trade agreement. Tariff reductions by Canada would have a strong pro-competitive effect on Canadian firms, which would be expected to lower price-cost margins, stimulate firm output, increase the scale of production, and raise labor productivity. In addition, reciprocal tariff reductions by the United States would give Canadian firms tariff-free access to a large market, further raising the scale of production and factor productivity.

Empirical evidence supports the claimed benefits. Wonnacott (1975), using a partial equilibrium model, estimated that removal of pre-Tokyo Round tariffs on U.S.-Canada bilateral trade would raise Canadian GNP by 8.2 per cent. Harris (1984) used a computable general equilibrium model to generate the estimate that multilateral tariff removal would raise Canadian GNP by 8.6 per cent.[4] Across the 29 sectors of the model, labor productivity rises by an average of 32.5 per cent. More recent work by Harris and others place the gain to Canada from a free trade agreement at a smaller but still sizable 1.5 to 2.5 per cent of GDP.

The existence of scale economies for Canadian firms has also been documented by Baldwin and Gorecki (1986). They treat scale as consisting of the interrelated effects of plant size, number of products per plant, and length of production runs. Using a 4-digit SIC level of disaggregation, they calculate relative labor productivity levels of matched Canadian and U.S. manufacturing industries for 1970 and 1979. Their results show productivity in Canadian plants to be as much as 20 per cent below U.S. productivity,

---

[4] The effects of multilateral free trade on Canada provide a reasonable approximation to the effects of U.S.-Canada bilateral tariff removal because the United States, Canada's largest trade partner, accounts for 80 per cent of Canada's trade.

and they are able to explain about a third of this gap by scale differences between the two countries. Scale disadvantage for Canadian manufacturing plants could be explained in part by high Canadian tariffs and seller concentration in import-competing industries and by smaller plant sizes in areas where Canadian firms have a comparative advantage but find their exports restricted.

Strategic Trade Policy

The traditional Heckscher-Ohlin-Samuelson trade model generally leads to the prescription of free trade as an optimal policy. In particular, small countries enjoy their largest welfare gains when there are no trade restrictions and they have no economic incentive to interfere with free trade.[5] These results change with the introduction of imperfectly competitive goods markets and IRS technology. Market imperfections that are commonly thought to be welfare reducing in autarky can provide new opportunities for using interventionist trade policy to a country's national advantage.

Below, we outline some simple models in which strategic trade policy can be welfare improving. Early versions of these models did not focus on the returns to labor or on labor's participation in the policy game, but later versions have made labor a key component. This shift in attention is illustrated by an evaluation of the strategic potential of the automobile industry, a case in which the benefits to labor may predominate.

The transfer of economic rent. Strategic trade policy's primary role is in transferring economic rent from a foreign producer to a domestic producer, consumer, or government. For example, Brander and Spencer (1985) demonstrate that an export subsidy can raise national welfare when a pair of domestic and foreign firms that act as Cournot duopolists are competing for market share in a third country.

An export subsidy paid to the domestic firm effectively reduces marginal cost, thereby increasing the profit-maximizing level of output and lowering price. The subsidy will also disturb the Cournot equilibrium. In a Cournot equilibrium, the lower cost firm has a larger market share; thus, the fall in net marginal cost of the domestic firm raises the domestic firm's market share at the expense of the foreign firm.

The subsidy will not generate a domestic welfare gain, however, unless

---

[5] Advocates of protectionism sometimes cite the presence of market imperfections such as wage rigidity or interindustry factor immobility as a justification for their position. The best policy for correcting market imperfections which cause losses from international trade usually involves a direct intervention in the affected market rather than at the border.

the increase in profits of the domestic firm exceeds the amount of the subsidy. Perhaps surprisingly, this will always be the case. Domestic welfare must increase because the export subsidy can be thought of as correcting a "market failure" in the sense that the domestic firm is not truly maximizing its profits when it treats the output of its competitor as fixed. The domestic firm would do better if it took into consideration the reaction of its competition and behaved as a Stackelberg leader.[6] The export subsidy simply increases output to the level that would be chosen by a Stackelberg leader.

This model also illustrates some of the difficulties with strategic trade policies. First, it is presumed that the government recognizes the gain from Stackelberg leadership even though the firm does not. This assumption is troubling since it is difficult, if not impossible, to determine the strategic content of a firm's observed behavior. However, the model's conclusion can be generalized. Even though firms have an incentive to increase profits through entry-deterring activities, governments will possess entry-deterring tools not available to firms and may be able to act with greater credibility. Second, the model ignores the potential for retaliation, which is likely because the export subsidy lowers the market share of the foreign competitor.

This type of analysis can also be used to evaluate the optimal policy of the importing country. The government in the importing country may realize that the foreign firm is extracting monopoly rents from domestic consumers. Brander and Spencer (1984) have examined some cases in which an import tariff can be used to transfer economic rent from the foreign producer to domestic firms or the government. They begin with a model in which domestic consumers are supplied by a monopolistic foreign firm which sets a profit maximizing price and quantity. The pre-tariff position has an equilibrium price, P_o, and an import quantity, q_o, as shown in Figure 1. If a specific tariff, t, is imposed on imports, it would raise the consumer price to P_1 and imports would fall to q_1.

The tariff will be beneficial if it can be shown that the tariff revenue is greater than the lost consumer surplus. Lost consumer surplus is shown by area A + B in Figure 1, and tariff revenue is shown by area C. The case of linear demand provides a simple illustration. Marginal revenue, MR, is twice as steep as the demand curve, so area C is twice as large as area A. As long as imports fall by less than 66 per cent, B is no larger than A, and the tariff revenue will exceed the lost consumer surplus. The tariff is a rent-shifting policy since it has captured monopoly profits from the foreign firm for the benefit of the domestic treasury.

---

[6] A Stackelberg leader calculates its profit-maximizing level of output incorporating the information that its competitor will behave in a Cournot manner.

FIGURE 1

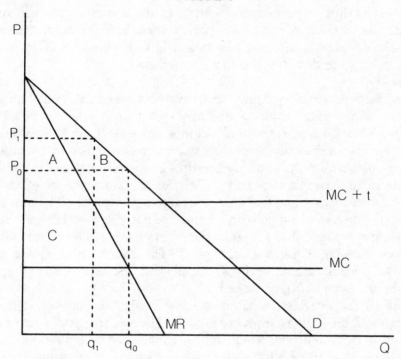

This model also provides an opportunity to illustrate the sensitivity of the results to the specification of the underlying model. The example of Figure 1 can be easily modified such that an import subsidy is the optimal policy. Recall that the possibility that tariff revenue would exceed lost consumer surplus turned on the assumption that the MR curve is steeper than the demand curve. However, for a wide class of demand functions, such as the constant elasticity of demand case, the MR curve may be flatter than the demand curve.

Thus far, it has been shown that an import tariff can extract economic profits from a foreign firm that sells to the domestic market. Remarkably, an import tariff can also help a domestic firm extract rent from foreign consumers, as illustrated by the apparent success of the newly industrializing countries of Asia in expanding their export base through import protection.

Krugman (1984) formalized these observations in a model in which one local and one foreign firm play a Cournot game in each other's markets, and marginal cost is assumed to be declining in output. An import tariff effectively raises the cost to the foreign firm of doing business in the domestic market. This increase in cost will alter the equilibrium in the domestic market by lowering the foreign firm's market share and raising output of the domestic firm. The increased output of the domestic firm will reduce its marginal cost, thus raising its market share in the foreign market, as well. Hence, exports rise and the domestic firm obtains a larger market share in both the domestic and foreign markets.

Other motives. Welfare-improving intervention policies also exist in models without extra-normal profits and barriers to entry. Venables (1985) has analyzed a market segmentation model in which a tariff can be used to force both domestic and foreign firms to cover their fixed costs with charges to foreign customers only, thus transferring consumer surplus from foreign consumers to domestic consumers. This model assumes a set of Cournot firms in each country and free entry guarantees zero profits. The model also makes the strong assumptions that firms are not able to arbitrage between national markets and that a representative firm has a greater relative market share on domestic sales than on exports. The absence of arbitrage allows firms to price discriminate between the two markets, with a separate equilibrium price emerging in each.

Consider the Venables model in the case in which country A imposes an import tariff on imports from country B. The net receipts for country B firms would fall and they would face negative profits. Equilibrium prices must adjust so as to raise profits for country B firms while maintaining zero profits for country A firms. This is accomplished by an increase in the price paid by country B consumers, where country B firms have a relatively large market share, and a fall in the price paid by country A consumers. The tariff-imposing government will earn extra revenue and consumer prices in country A will fall, raising consumer surplus. The tariff effectively transfers consumer surplus from country B consumers to country A consumers, thus raising country A welfare even in the absence of rents.

The role of organized labor. Recent strategic trade policy modeling has recognized that labor differs from other factors of production because of its ability to legally organize and behave in concert. These formulations have included labor as an actual or potential actor in policy games. However, it is important to note that the treatment of labor in international trade models remains incomplete; the work reviewed in this section relies on primitive unionization models which do not make use of an efficient bargaining environment.[7]

---

[7] This point was noted by an anonymous referee.

Brander and Spencer (1988) examined the strategic response of organized labor when an optimal trade policy is pursued for a unionized oligopoly.[8] They focused on the ability of the union to capture part of the benefits of a rent-shifting subsidy or tariff and the impact of this behavior on the optimal level of intervention. The essence of their model can be seen in the standard example of an international Cournot duopoly. The previous model is modified by assuming that the supply of labor to the local firm is controlled by a union which maximizes some function of real wages and total union employment.

Equilibrium will be determined by a two-stage game. In the first stage, the union and the firm bargain over the wage. In the second stage, the level of employment is the outcome of the Cournot rivalry between the domestic and foreign firms. The game is said to be sub-game perfect since the firm and the union understand the implications of the wage set in the first stage for output, price, and employment of the second stage. As would be expected, if the union increases the domestic wage, it will directly lower the firm's profits. More importantly, there will be a profit loss due to the weakened competitive position of the domestic firm relative to the foreign firm.

Government can be added to this game as a third player. The government will be assumed to know how the other players will respond to each potential policy and to pick the policy that will maximize national welfare. A production subsidy would lower the domestic firm's perceived marginal cost, which improves its competitive position relative to the foreign firm. The domestic firm's market share increases, so that the subsidy has a rent-shifting effect.

Increased profitability of the firm is likely to raise union wage demands, which in turn can reduce the effectiveness of the government policy by raising the firm's marginal cost. The higher marginal cost for the firm weakens its competitive position and results in a smaller market share. A greater subsidy would be required to accomplish the same degree of rent-shifting from the foreign firm, which implies that the optimal production subsidy will tend to be higher in the presence of the union.

This model, however, is subject to the criticism that the union is not following a sophisticated strategy that maximizes the return to the domestic industry and divides the resulting quasi-rents via the collective bargaining agreement. The major implication of this model arises from an inefficient linking of the negotiated wage rate to the product price, instead of using

---

[8] Matsuyama (1987) obtained similar results.

the wage rate in a purely allocative fashion to divide the *ex-post* quasi-rents.[9]

The interests of labor. The practical applicability of the theoretical gains from a strategic trade policy is problematic. A recent survey of the issues and evidence by Katz and Summers (1989) seems to rule out rents to capital as a basis for a strategic trade policy. They conclude that labor market rents are likely to be a more important motivation for adopting an industrial policy (see also Dickens and Lang, 1988).

Katz and Summers examine a variety of data sources to determine whether significant compensation differences across two-digit categories of U.S. industries exist that cannot be explained by the characteristics of the workers, the characteristics of the industries, or the degree of unionization. They find substantial unexplained wage differences in the measures they construct from 1984 Current Population Survey data; and they find that these differences hold up over finer occupational disaggregation, over time, and over countries.[10] The possibility that these differences are due to compensating differentials or unobserved ability instead of rents is rejected based on the persistence of the differences, evidence on quit rates, and data on wages of individuals who move between industries.

Katz and Summers use a stylized model of an economy with one primary and one secondary sector to illustrate the point that policy measures to expand employment in the "premium wage" sector will be welfare improving. They find the standard deviation of the unexplained nonunion wage differences to be about 18 per cent, which suggests that a primary sector wage subsidy could generate a substantial welfare gain. The authors also develop further evidence on the likely benefits of export promotion versus import protection by comparing the skill adjusted wage differentials for imports and exports of manufactured goods. Export industries resemble primary sector firms and have wages that are 11 per cent above the manufacturing average. Import industries, with the exceptions of autos and steel, resemble secondary sector firms and have wages that are 15 per cent below average. Between 1960 and 1980, the number of jobs lost due to imports was roughly equal to the number of jobs gained from exports. This should have generated a substantial welfare gain for the United States and further gains might accrue from policies that promote the continuation of this trend.

Dixit (1988) approached the question of the potential benefits from a

---

[9] For examples of models which incorporate an efficient bargaining environment, see Brown and Ashenfelter (1986) or Card (1986).

[10] Schultze (1989) and Topel (1989) doubt that the analysis is able to capture important unobserved differences.

strategic trade policy very differently. He focused on the U.S. automobile industry as possibly benefiting from such policies because of the potential for strategic rivalry between the United States and Japan, oligopoly in production, and monopoly rents to labor. He investigated the benefits of an "optimal" tariff or subsidy policy using a simple static model of the United States and Japan.

His model treats demand as linear, marginal cost as constant, and differentiates the various car models only by national origin of production. Oligopolistic behavior is modeled as a Nash equilibrium with conjectural variations. Although the conjectural coefficients are not structural values, they provide a convenient way to represent differing degrees of competition and can be determined by calibration using data for the years of interest. The model is used to examine optimal policies for 1979 and 1980; it is calibrated by reproducing the initial equilibrium with only the MFN tariff applied to Japanese imports.

Dixit ran simulations over alternative policies and parameter values and found that the degree of monopoly rents in U.S. labor costs plays a major role in determining the optimal trade policy. Under the assumptions of central parameter values and no labor rents, the optimal tariff is 17 per cent. If the optimal tariff were imposed, U.S. real income would have increased by $80 million in 1979. Under the assumption that half of U.S. labor cost is monopoly rent, however, the optimal tariff for 1979 is 24 per cent, which would increase national income by $185 million. Nevertheless, a production subsidy rather than an import tariff proved to be a superior policy. If no monopoly rent is assumed to exist, the optimal production subsidy yields a gain of $251 million and the monopoly rent case yields a gain of $1.94 billion in 1979.

Dixit emphasized that his results are preliminary and give only an upper bound for the benefits of a strategic trade policy. The gains could be greatly reduced by dropping the assumptions that only the United States engages in policy, that there is no retaliation to U.S. policy, and that subsidies do not stimulate increased monopoly in the output or labor markets. Still, the results effectively illustrate the points that gains from strategic trade policies are likely to be small unless there are large labor rents to be captured and that the optimal policy may be promotion rather than protection.

Labor Market Imperfections and International Trade

Incorporating labor market imperfections has affected discussions of strategic trade policy and modern theoretical explanations of the pattern and gains from trade. This section outlines several areas in which abandoning the assumption of competitive labor markets has led to qualifications of the standard results of theoretical trade models.

We begin by reviewing the effect of unionized labor on the basic results of trade theory. What is labor's interest in protectionism and under what circumstances will a consensus for protectionism develop within an industry? We use this framework to consider how the presence of a labor union affects the ability of an economy to adjust to changing comparative advantage. These models provide an explanation for the surprising observation that the union wage premium sometimes rises in declining industries.

Labor's interest in protectionism. Recent experience with appeals for protection suggests that protectionism will be supported by all factors of production within a sector. This unanimity runs counter to the Stolper-Samuelson Theorem's conclusion that protection benefits factors of production rather than industries. According to this theorem, protection of a capital-intensive industry lowers the wage and increases the return to capital. Thus, the owners of labor and capital should not agree on which industry to protect. The observed unanimity has been explained by short-run models in which factors are sector specific, but the existence of imperfect labor markets provides an alternative view.

Hill (1984) finds that import protection may be sought by unionized labor in a capital-intensive industry if the import protection allows the union to increase its wage premium over the nonunion wage. Hill considers a standard two-good, two-factor model in which one sector has a unionized labor force. The mark-up of the optimal union wage over the nonunion wage follows the monopoly pricing rule and is inversely related to the elasticity of the demand for labor in the unionized sector. That elasticity varies positively with labor's cost share and, therefore, with the wage-rent ratio (as long as the elasticity of substitution between capital and labor is less than unity).

Consider now the effect of a tariff-induced increase in the domestic market price of the unionized good. According to the Stolper-Samuelson Theorem, an increase in the output price of the unionized sector will raise the return to the factor used intensively in that sector. If the unionized sector is capital intensive, then the wage-rent ratio will fall in both sectors. Labor, then, is worse off in terms of both goods. However, the decline in the wage-rent ratio will also raise the mark-up of the union wage over the nonunion wage. For sufficiently small values of the elasticity of substitution between capital and labor, the gap between the union and nonunion wage may rise enough that the real income of union members actually rises, making support for protection unambiguously in the union's interest. Thus, we may find both factors of production in the unionized sector supporting protection.

The Hill model is, of course, vulnerable to the same criticism applied to the Brander and Spencer (1988) model of union behavior. If Hill had used an efficient contract framework, then the union would benefit as long as the rents to the protected industry rose by enough to offset the lower competitive wage rate resulting from protection.

Unions and changing comparative advantage. Trade economists have also used unionization to help explain why an economy might adjust slowly to declining competitiveness and increased imports. Grossman (1984) considers the contribution of a seniority system for hires and layoffs to slow union wage adjustment in the face of declining demand. His model is similar to Hill's, but Grossman assumes an extreme production technology in order to focus on the effect of union behavior on wage demands.

The union is modeled as setting wages by majority vote, so that the expected utility of the median voter is maximized. Union members are employed in order of seniority, with the most senior hired first or laid off last. The seniority of the median voter is assumed to depend on the size of the union. The smaller the union the higher the seniority ranking of the median voter, and the greater the probability of getting hired for each wage demand. Thus, the smaller the union, the higher the union wage demanded.

Grossman uses this framework to analyze the impact of an increase in international competition that reduces the world price of the union good. The decline in price reduces the probability that the median voter will be employed at the current wage and will tend to reduce the union's wage demand. However, the deterioration in the industry's competitive position will also worsen the most junior union member's employment prospects. As a result, the union will shrink and the seniority rank of the median member will rise. It is theoretically possible for the seniority rank of the median member to rise sufficiently that the wage demand actually increases.

Staiger (1988) has shown that the union wage may rise in the face of intensified international competition if import penetration leads domestic production to become more capital intensive. Increased capital intensity lowers labor's cost share, which causes the elasticity of demand for labor to fall and raises the optimal mark-up of the union wage over the nonunion wage.

Empirical evidence supports this conclusion. Lawrence and Lawrence (1985) point out that U.S. auto and steel workers receive a wage premium over the manufacturing average that is significantly higher than that received by their Japanese counterparts. They also report that during the seventies, the compensation of steel and auto workers increased 30 and 15 per cent more, respectively, than the average of the 57 3-digit SIC industries that they studied. These seemingly large wage differentials are often used to explain the loss of U.S. competitiveness, but models from international trade suggest that the causality runs in the opposite direction. Loss of international competitiveness raises the union wage. It must be stressed, however, that these models rely on union behavior which does not maximize the present value of the union's share of the industry's quasi-rents.

International Factor Mobility and Labor Migration

The proposition that international trade will equalize the returns to factors across countries is one of the major results of the traditional Heckscher-Ohlin-Samuelson trade theory. When factor-prices are not equalized, the owners of a country's relatively abundant factor will face a strong incentive to move to a country where it yields a higher return. Although this incentive exists for the owners of all factors of production, labor movements provide its most dramatic and wrenching expression.

Much of the recent U.S. interest in international factor mobility has been generated by the case of the United States and Mexico, with a labor flow from Mexico to the United States and a capital flow out of the United States. The difficult question faced by economic policy analysts becomes, "Is it better for the United States to allow labor inflows and prevent capital outflows, or should the United States prohibit labor inflows and promote capital outflows?"[11]

The Factor-Price Equalization Theorem is fairly fragile; it can fail to hold simply if there are more inputs in an economy than outputs. As a result, a modified Heckscher-Ohlin-Samuelson model with two factors of production, but only one good, has become a common framework for analyzing international factor mobility. Failure of factor-price equalization in the Heckscher-Ohlin-Samuelson model implies that producers in the two countries face different relative factor prices and thus adopt different techniques of production. The use of two different production techniques will not be as efficient as a single technique since isoquants are assumed to be strictly convex. This inefficiency will leave the world inside its production possibility frontier.

In the context of the perfectly competitive, full-employment Heckscher-Ohlin-Samuelson model, international factor mobility will equalize factor returns across national borders, moving the world economy toward the production possibility frontier. Free factor trade will be mutually beneficial

---

[11] Problems associated with illegal immigration are discussed by Ethier (1986) and Bond and Chen (1987).

for both countries, and since capital and labor are treated symmetrically, it will not matter which factor migrates.[12] Certain types of market failure that qualify these conclusions are discussed below.

Market power in factors. A large country with international market power can usually do better than free trade as long as its trading partner does not retaliate. This is the case in factors markets as well as goods markets. Hence, the United States might actually gain by limiting the export of capital to the rent-maximizing monopsony level by imposing a capital export tax.

U.S. residents could also extract foreign rents by controlling the immigration of labor. Note, however, that the restriction would have to take the form of a tax on immigrants, not the form of an immigration quota. An immigration quota would simply transfer the rents associated with the exercise of U.S. market power to the immigrant, so that the welfare of current U.S. residents would not increase.[13]

Introducing the exercise of market power destroys the symmetry of the model, so that labor imports and capital exports will generate different results. An intriguing argument first made by Ramaswami (1968), and later formalized by Calvo and Wellisz (1983), demonstrates that importing labor is superior to exporting capital! The argument in favor of labor imports is most easily made by considering each policy in turn. First, consider the capital export case. Let U.S. capital move to Mexico, subject to an optimal capital export tax. This policy leaves the return to capital in Mexico above the U.S. rate, and the return to labor in Mexico below the U.S. rate.

Now consider the creation of an enclave in the United States. This enclave would contain U.S. capital repatriated from Mexico and all Mexican workers employed by this capital. The actual national location of this capital and labor would not affect the welfare of the two countries, given the existence of the enclave. Thus, the enclave policy has the same welfare implications for both countries as the capital export policy.

The creation of an enclave would not be welfare maximizing for the United States, however. Since the capital-labor ratio in the enclave would be lower than in the rest of the country, two different techniques of production would be in use to produce the same good. Output in the United States would be increased if the barriers creating the enclave were removed and a single technique of production were adopted. The United States could guarantee that previous residents receive all of the output increase by taxing

[12] For a demonstration of the mutual gains from international factor mobility, see Ruffin (1984). (This point was first made by MacDougall [1960].)

[13] This case is analogous to the difference between an import quota and a voluntary export restraint in the market for goods.

away the increased wages of enclave laborers.[14]

The point of this exercise is to show how the restricted capital export policy can be viewed as employing U.S. capital with different techniques of production at home and abroad. There will be gains to be made by transferring capital and labor to the United States so that the techniques of production can be unified.

Jones, Coelho, and Easton (1986) have pointed out that there is no reason to limit the import of capital (and the labor it employs) to American-owned capital. The movement of a bundle of Mexican capital and labor into the U.S. enclave will produce the same result as before. Once again, total U.S. production can be increased by unifying the production process in the enclave with the production process in the rest of the United States.

The efficiency gains from the shift of Mexican capital and labor to the United States could again be captured by taxation. A tax on immigrant labor would leave Mexican workers with the same after-tax wage as they would receive in Mexico. Mexican capital would have to be subsidized in order to receive the same return as it would receive in Mexico. The tax on immigrant labor and the subsidy to Mexican capital would hold the factor payments to Mexican capital and labor constant, leaving any increased production accruing to U.S.-owned factors of production and to the U.S. government.

The labor import policy requires a discriminatory tax on immigrant labor which generally would be considered morally undesirable and politically unacceptable. Calvo and Wellisz (1983) show that the same results can be effected through a government-formed capital export cartel. This capital export cartel would follow two operating principles. First, the cartel would exercise its market power by hiring labor in Mexico at the rent-maximizing monopsony rate. Second, the cartel would export capital only up to the point where the return to capital in the two countries is equalized. Equalizing the return would guarantee that all U.S. capital uses the same technique of production, whether in the United States or Mexico.

Labor market imperfections. Many of the political objections to labor migration stem from problems generated by factor market imperfections. Imperfections in the labor market could significantly change the results of the preceding models and alter the optimal ranking of policies. For example, Brecher and Choudhri (1987) conclude that when there is a real minimum income guarantee, any labor immigration will lower national welfare.

Brecher and Choudhri's model contains a minimum income guarantee

---

[14] The wage paid in the enclave is the same as the wage received in Mexico, so enclave labor would not have an incentive to return to Mexico under this scheme.

that is provided through a package of unemployment compensation and welfare payments. The minimum real wage pegs the marginal product of labor and determines labor employment and output for each level of the capital stock. Given labor employment and the capital stock, the level of GNP is also fixed. Since total employment and output are fixed, each immigrant displaces one native worker but has no effect on total output. Any positive factor payment to immigrant labor will accordingly lower the output available for native consumption.

The Brecher and Choudhri framework contains an incentive for capital exports only if the average product of capital at home is lower than the marginal product of capital abroad. Exporting a unit of capital leaves some domestic labor unemployed and causes domestic production to fall by the average product of capital. By comparison, the capital export earns the marginal product of capital in the foreign country. As long as the domestic average product of capital is less than the foreign marginal product of capital, the capital export generates a net national gain.

On the other hand, Ramaswami's argument can be applied equally well to the Brecher and Choudhri result that labor immigration is never welfare improving for a minimum wage economy. Repatriating capital and the foreign labor that it employed to a domestic enclave would certainly have no effect on domestic welfare. Moreover, further gains would be possible if a single production process were adopted economy wide, though this would require that the minimum income guarantee scheme be replaced by a wage subsidy paid exclusively to nationals.

The Brecher and Choudhri result is further qualified if the assumption that migrant and native workers are perfect substitutes in production is relaxed. An industry which is losing its comparative advantage might increase the employment of unskilled immigrant labor to hold down production costs. This could increase home welfare by saving the jobs of skilled native labor.

Ethier (1985) has derived some interesting results on the relationship between factor substitutability and optimal migration. Consider, for example, a decline in demand for the export good which is accompanied by a decline in the real wage for migrant labor. This type of secular decline in the commodities market and the migrant labor market could occur if the host country's export market is the same as the market from which it hires migrant labor.

The introduction of this correlation will cause a decline in export demand to have both positive and negative influences on the employment of native labor. On the one hand, the fall in the cost of migrant labor will induce firms to substitute migrant workers for native workers. The higher the elasticity of substitution (σ) between migrant and native labor, the larger the employment decline.

On the other hand, the fall in the cost of migrant labor will tend to lower the cost of production, raise output, and increase the employment of native workers. The extent of this output increase will depend on the elasticity of demand for the firm's product. High values of the elasticity of demand (η) will increase the level of output and the demand for native labor. In fact, if $\eta > \sigma$, the welfare of native workers will be increased by the reduced probability of layoff under adverse conditions. However, if demand is insufficiently elastic, or migrant and native labor are very substitutable, then $\eta < \sigma$. The substitution effect will dominate and native workers will be worse off.

Strategic trade policy and international capital flows. The foregoing analysis has emphasized the interests of the capital-abundant country in its decision to import the scarce factor, labor. These results do not apply to the decision faced by a labor-abundant country with unemployment. Das (1981) has analyzed the case in which the labor-abundant country has unemployment and sets a real minimum wage. Recall that in the absence of unemployment, a labor-abundant country has an incentive to exercise its market power by taxing capital inflows. However, in the presence of unemployment, it is possible that the optimal policy is a subsidy to capital inflows that will increase employment.

There are many cases when a government could attack an unemployment problem by a policy of attracting foreign capital. Brander and Spencer (1987) compare an optimal tariff and an optimal production tax given the existence of unemployment. They analyze the optimal policy response when a foreign firm is considering whether to supply the home country market from a plant located in the foreign country or from a plant located in the home country. Typically, foreign investment in the home country will be deterred by high production taxes in the home country but promoted by a high import tariff.

The presence of high tariffs may not stimulate foreign direct investment, however, if the firm believes that once the capital is in place, the government will then replace the import tariff with a production tax. In order to induce foreign direct investment, the government must credibly precommit to a policy which will make foreign direct investment the profit-maximizing choice for the foreign firm.

The firm will prefer foreign direct investment only if it believes that its profits under an optimal production tax will always be greater than under an optimal import tariff. Remarkably, this proves to be the case. The government's motivation for taxing the foreign firm is to extract economic rents earned by the firm. If the firm undertakes foreign direct investment, taxing the firm will lead to lower firm output and higher unemployment. In contrast, if the foreign firm supplies the market through exports, raising an import tariff leads to no unemployment penalty since production is taking place in the foreign country. Consequently, the optimal production tax is lower than the optimal import tariff and the foreign firm will prefer foreign direct investment. The host government is able to credibly precommit to the production tax because of the unemployment associated with a tax-induced reduction in output.

International Trade and the Acquisition of Human Capital

The factor proportions theory of the determinants of international trade predicts that a country will export the good that intensively uses its relatively abundant factor. For example, the United States is relatively abundantly endowed with human capital, so its export bundle will require more human capital to produce than its import bundle.

To the extent that education contributes to the development of human capital, the forces of international trade can affect the decision to acquire an education. Interestingly, interaction between the trade and education sectors may actually widen the educational disparity between two trading nations. Trade could cause a decline in the human capital stock of the human capital-scarce country and an increase in the human capital-abundant country. If there are social benefits attendant to a high level of education in the population, international trade may be detrimental to the human capital-scarce country. Below, some trade models that incorporate human capital acquisition are used to illustrate the possibilities.

The acquisition of human capital. Findlay and Kierzkowski (1983) and Borsook (1987) have investigated the interaction of human capital acquisition[15] and the factor-proportions theory of international trade. Both papers assume that individuals are faced with the choice of earning the wage paid to unskilled labor or investing in an education that leads to the higher wage paid to skilled labor. Education is assumed to be produced using physical capital specific to the educational sector of the economy.[16] The output of the educational sector is increasing in the number of people seeking education, but the educational production function is subject to diminishing marginal returns. Individuals will seek education if it produces a discounted

---

[15] These papers incorporated views on human capital acquisition similar to those of Mincer (1958), Schultz (1961), and Becker (1962).

[16] Educational capital used to produce educational services should not be confused with the human capital embodied in an educated worker.

net present value of earnings that is greater than or equal to the discounted present value of unskilled worker earnings.

This familiar human capital model is imbedded in a standard Heckscher-Ohlin-Samuelson trade model in which skilled and unskilled labor are used to produce two goods. At each set of relative wages, good 1 is produced with relatively more skilled labor per unit of unskilled labor than good 2. Goods prices are given by the terms of trade on the world market, and wages are determined by the zero-profits condition.

The Heckscher-Ohlin Theorem for such a world becomes, "the country which is abundantly endowed with educational capital will export the skill-intensive good." An increase in a country's stock of educational capital will reduce its marginal product and lower the cost of an education. As additional unskilled workers find it profitable to obtain an education, the number of unskilled workers declines. Both output and exports of the skill-intensive good will rise, output of the other good will fall, and imports of the other good will rise.

One important conclusion from this model is that workers in the skill-abundant country do not gain from trade, since all gains accrue to the owners of educational capital. Prior to the opening of trade, the skill-intensive good is relatively cheap in the educational capital-abundant country, and the other good is relatively expensive. The opening of trade will relieve the relative scarcity of the good with the lower skill content, and its price will fall.

Application of the Stolper-Samuelson Theorem shows that the wage of unskilled labor must fall and the wage of skilled workers must rise, since the opening to trade causes a price increase for the skill-intensive good in the educational capital-abundant country. The wage gap will increase the demand for education, which will raise the cost of education, thereby lowering the life-time earnings of skilled workers to the new lower level of unskilled workers. Thus, both skilled and unskilled labor are worse off. However, the increase in the number of people seeking an education will increase the marginal productivity of educational capital so that the return to educational capital owners will increase. The opposite occurs in the country in which educational capital is scarce.

A second and more important conclusion from this model is that trade increases the stock of skilled labor in the educational capital-abundant country, and it lowers the stock of skilled labor in the other country. In other words, international trade depresses the incentive to obtain an education in the skill-scarce country. This change in the skilled labor stock accentuates the differences in endowment that existed prior to the opening of trade.

Heterogeneous ability. Findlay and Kierzkowski (1983) used the simplifying assumption that all individuals are identical. The introduction of hetero-geneous abilities complicates the model but provides a more realistic representation of the process of human capital acquisition. Borsook (1987) introduces heterogeneity by allowing for a continuum of abilities throughout the population. The amount of skill acquired from a given amount of education is assumed to depend on the innate ability of the individual.

The worker at the educational margin will be indifferent between acquiring an education and remaining unskilled. The conditions which determine the educational margin in this model are basically the same as those for the previous case. The difference is that the net earnings of the infra-marginal skilled worker exceed those of the skilled worker at the margin. This follows from the assumption that a dollar's worth of expenditure on education will purchase more skill units for the worker with greater innate ability.

An important implication of this extension is that international trade will not be sufficient to generate the Pareto Optimal level of education for the world as a whole. This can be illustrated by considering two identical countries that face the same prices on the world market. Holding world prices fixed, allow the stock of educational capital to increase in one country. The increase in the capital stock must cause the marginal product of educational capital to fall, so that the cost of educational capital will fall. As a result, some less innately able workers will now find it worthwhile to obtain an education, and the equilibrium return to capital will be lower in this country.

A lower return to educational capital in the capital-abundant country implies that the marginal worker receiving an education in the educational capital-abundant country is less innately able than the marginal skilled worker in the capital-scarce country. Policy intervention in the educational market, therefore, could be Pareto improving from a world point of view. Alternatively, students from the capital-scarce country will find it worth their while to attain an education in the educational capital-abundant country.

A last point to note is that trade leaves the mean skill level of the distribution of skilled workers in the educational capital-abundant country higher than in the labor-abundant country. While trade equalizes the cost of a skill unit between the two countries, the cost of educational capital in the educational capital-abundant country is lower than in the educational capital-scarce country. Therefore, net earnings of skilled workers are higher in the educational capital-abundant country.

Conclusions

The study of market imperfections has been a central focus of international economics over the last decade. This area had previously received little attention because the earliest trade theorems made a strong case that border controls were rarely the first best response to market failure. Although it was recognized that import controls could be used to exercise international market power associated with a country's size, international economists generally rejected this as a serious policy option. The optimal tariff was considered to be a "beggar thy neighbor" policy that would move the world economy below its production possibility frontier.

The focus on general equilibrium analysis, Pareto optimality, and national interest has led trade economists to analyze economic issues somewhat differently than labor economists. Trade economists have been willing to sacrifice many details of individual behavior and market function for the "greater" goal of obtaining general equilibrium results. A notable example is the way union behavior is represented in the few trade models that include it. The attention given national advantage can seem abstract and removed from the human side of real world issues. For example, the trade economists' preoccupation with the exercise of monopsony power when analyzing immigration issues must strike the labor economist as bizarre.

When the "new" international economics is placed in proper perspective, it becomes apparent that many of the conclusions of the "old" international analysis continue to hold. Deardorff and Stern (1987) argue that the motivation of many of the strategic trade polices is simply the traditional exercise of market power. An obvious example is the taxation of imports from a foreign monopolist. The essential objective of the policy is to lower the price received by the foreign monopolist for its exports.

Another idea recycled by the strategic trade proponents is the notion that market efficiency can be improved by subsidizing the producers in an imperfectly competitive market. The same optimal policy prescription that has never been attractive enough for domestic application becomes more palatable when the competing firm is in a foreign country.

Nevertheless, the new international analysis has clarified the issues involved in various trade policies. It has resulted in a rethinking of our policy of protection for the domestic automobile industry. Previously, auto protection was thought to reduce national welfare, and it was justified as temporary support to ease the movement of workers to other industries. Katz and Summers' and Dixit's analyses make a serious case for preserving auto industry jobs in order to retain rents inherent in the industry. Auto protection may actually be welfare improving. A similar reclassification applies to some export subsidies.

A practical scheme to identify the "strategic" industries that would benefit from intervention remains elusive. The *ex-post* identification of successes must be balanced by a host of failures. Moreover, policy games between governments are complex, and analytical solutions for even simple games are difficult to obtain. Computer simulations offer opportunities for utilizing more complicated models, but thus far the models have not proven to be robust. Small changes in model parameters will often shift the optimal policy from a tax to a subsidy. In spite of the lessons of the "new" international economics, the belief in the optimality of free trade remains strong among trade economists.

Human Capital Theory: Implications for HR Managers

MYRA H. STROBER*

This paper reviews some of the contributions of and challenges to human capital theory. It focuses on the alleged link between earnings and education and experience and on competing explanations for observed earnings differentials by race and by gender. The review concludes that while human capital theory provides some central insights about the supply side of the labor market, the challenges to this theory suggest that the demand side of the market, i.e., the actions of human resource managers, also play a key role in determining earnings and employment. Moreover, these challenges suggest that government policies can be instrumental in effecting a more efficient and equitable use of human resources.

"IF YOU WANT A GOOD JOB, get a good education." That advice, embodying the essence of human capital theory, is offered daily to school children, adolescents, displaced homemakers, and unemployed workers by parents, teachers, members of the clergy, outplacement counselors, and seekers of public office. Many of these advice-givers, of course, have never heard of human capital theory. Nonetheless, they believe in it deeply. Getting ahead by getting an education has become "the American way," the embodiment of democracy and meritocracy.

Human capital theory says more than simply that educational level is positively correlated with income. It specifies a particular mechanism through which this correlation results: education increases skills, and these in turn increase productivity; higher productivity is then rewarded through higher earnings (Becker, 1964; Mincer, 1974). Human capital theory also proposes a specific rationale for the positive correlation between age and earnings: people who are older earn more because they have more on-the-job experience

* School of Education, Stanford University. This paper was originally prepared for presentation at a symposium on The Economic Approach to Human Resource Management and Industrial Relations at the Annual Meetings of the Industrial Relations Research Association (IRRA), New York City, December 27–30, 1988.

(on-the-job training). As with education, on-the-job experience or "training" is said to make workers more productive and, once again, because they are more productive they are paid more. On-the-job training can provide general human capital (skills and knowledge transferable to other work settings) or specific human capital (skills and knowledge of use only in the particular company) (Becker, 1964).

Becker's contributions generated a fertile outpouring of theoretical supplements and empirical verifications. An annotated bibliography on human capital theory and empirical tests published by Blaug in 1976 contains almost 2,000 entries. Since the publication of Mincer's (1974) human capital regressions, his specification of the earnings function has become the standard for empirical work.

Human capital theory was never hegemonic among economists, however, and theoretical and empirical objections were raised early on (see Thurow, 1972, 1975). The theoretical criticisms have continued and have moved into new territory with respect to earnings differentials by race and gender; the empirical critiques have become more sophisticated. But what is perhaps most fascinating, some recent theoretical insights in other areas of labor economics have made it more and more unlikely that human capital theory can be tested definitively.

This paper reviews two challenges to human capital theory. Stated as questions, these are: (1) Do education and experience raise earnings by raising productivity or are education and experience correlated with earnings as a result of other behavioral relationships?; and (2) To what extent does human capital theory explain earnings differentials by race and by gender? The paper is a summary rather than a full elaboration of the issues raised by these two questions.[1] Moreover, except in a few instances, I omit the relationship of these challenges to other challenges, particularly those concerning the relationship of education to the distribution of income and to the rate of economic growth, the effects of retraining on workers' subsequent incomes, and the effects of preschool education. Nor do I discuss challenges to the new home economics (the theory of the allocation of time between home and labor market, and the theory of marriage and divorce) or to the economics of fertility, both of which are closely related to human capital theory.

I conclude that human capital theory provides us with some central insights about the relationship between education and earnings and the nature of earnings differentials, but that it tends to lose credence when it

---

[1] For more complete reviews, see Cain (1976, 1986); Blaug (1976b, 1985); and Willis (1986).

insists on being the only game in town. Human capital theory is basically a supply-side theory[2] and, as might be expected, demand-side forces are also operative in labor markets and need to be taken into account. Moreover, perhaps more frequently than the theoretician would like, there are feedback effects in the real world and supply and demand factors are not as independent of each other as we would like to pretend.

With respect to human resource and industrial relations managers, a more catholic view of the process of wage determination recognizes managers' propensity to be influenced by institutions and ideology, and their power and agency to act in the employment and pay-setting arena. With respect to public policy, moving away from exclusive reliance on human capital theory provides more scope for considering the extent to which policies such as equal employment opportunity legislation, affirmative action programs, and pay equity arrangements can move us toward a more efficient and equitable use of human resources.

The Productivity Connection Between Education/Experience and Earnings

The productivity connection between education/experience and earnings has been challenged on several fronts. We review here the criticism of the screening hypothesis, efficiency wage theories, internal labor market theories, and radical theories.

The screening hypothesis. The screening hypothesis has several variants; some are based on insights from the theory of statistical discrimination (Phelps, 1972), some on signaling theory (Arrow, 1973; Spence, 1973, 1974), and some on credentialist theory (Thurow, 1972, 1975). In each case, the argument is that education is positively correlated with earnings not because additional education yields higher productivity, but because employers use additional education as a screen, or filter, or signal to hire better-educated workers into jobs that pay more.

The theory of *statistical discrimination* was first put forth by Phelps (1972) with respect to race and sex. It argues that if employers believe that minorities and women are in the long-run less productive than white men, and if employers operate in a world of uncertainty where it is costly to obtain information about the individual productivity of prospective employees, then employers will assume that individual minorities and women have the

---

[2] In a personal communication, Polachek (1989) indicates that he regards human capital theory not as a supply-side theory but as a reduced form of supply and demand.

presumed lower productivity characteristics of the "average" minority or woman worker. Employers will then either pay women and minorities less or exclude them entirely from employment in a particular occupation. Skin color and gender are used by employers as bases for statistical discrimination both because numerous employers hold preconceived beliefs about the lower average productivity of minorities and women and because information about skin color and gender can be obtained by employers at zero cost.

Extending the theory of statistical discrimination to include education is straightforward. Like beliefs about the relationship between average productivity and skin color or gender, beliefs about the relationship between average productivity and educational level are widespread. Moreover, although obtaining information about educational level is not costless, it is quite inexpensive.[3]

The *signaling models* of Spence (1973, 1974) and Arrow (1973) begin with the proposition that employers may pay higher wages to more educated employees even if education has no effect on productivity. The second assumption is that ability level is correlated with productivity. Thirdly, it is assumed that potential workers with relatively high ability levels can invest more cheaply in education than can employees with lesser ability. For example, if we have in mind cognitive ability, then those with high ability can presumably go through school with less effort and less "pain" than their lower ability classmates. Depending on the cost differential to the two ability groups and the wage premium that the employer offers to higher ability workers, it may be worthwhile for higher ability workers to invest in more education and then "signal" their higher ability (and higher productivity) to employers. If firms find that indeed those with more education are more productive, they will continue to use education as a signal of higher productivity even though education itself has nothing to do with productivity enhancement.

The screening hypothesis may be given either a strong or a weak interpretation. The strong version, that schooling does nothing to enhance productivity, and that schools do nothing more than play a filtering role, seems unreasonable (see Blaug, 1985). But the weaker version, that the role of education is, in part, to act as a screen or signal in labor markets where

---

[3] One question about statistical discrimination that has concerned theorists is its efficiency. One point of view is that in situations of uncertainty it is always efficient for the employer to use information that is costless (or virtually costless, in the case of education). A recent article by Schwab (1986) questions this argument and describes two situations in which employers' use of information based on group data may "exacerbate the labor supply distortions of limited information" (p. 233). Schwab concludes that "an a priori efficiency claim cannot be used to justify statistical discrimination" (*ibid.*).

information about potential productivity is imperfect, seems credible. Why employers should continue to pay more to educated workers once they have had an opportunity to observe employees' actual productivity is best understood in the framework of internal labor market theory (discussed below).

The theories of Phelps, Spence, and Arrow are basically neoclassical in approach. Thurow's (1972) observations about the connections between education and productivity stem from a quite different conception of labor markets. He champions the *credentialist view*, namely that employers believe that higher productivity is a function not of the skills that workers have learned in school, but rather of the amount of capital that employees have to work with, the amount and type of on-the-job training that they receive and, most importantly for the credentialist hypothesis, the ability of the worker to absorb training. Education, according to Thurow, is used by employers as a signal of trainability.

In contrast to human capital theory, which views the employee's education and skills as the major source of his or her productivity, Thurow argues that the major source of an employee's productivity lies with the employer and the type of job that the employer fashions. Several important consequences flow from this way of looking at the sources of productivity. If productivity is based on the way in which employers structure jobs—their level of responsibility, their capital intensity, their promotion possibilities, etc.—and the amount and kind of on-the-job training provided by the employer, then the distribution of earnings among workers depends not upon the educational differential among workers, as human capital theory suggests, but upon the differentials in the kinds of jobs that employers provide. Thurow strongly disagrees with the human capital view that reducing the variance in the educational attainment of the work force will reduce earnings disparity. He argues that to reduce the disparity in the earnings distribution, we need to reduce the number of jobs that have a low level of productivity associated with them. In other words, with respect to income distribution, the ball is in the employers' court.

Thurow postulates that potential employees form a queue in which those with more education are at the front. Over time, as the overall educational level has increased, workers have increased their education merely to hold their place in the queue. But despite a reduction in the variance in educational level, there has not been a corresponding reduction in the variance in earnings.

Efficiency wage models. One of the contributions of human capital theory is to explicitly recognize that the labor market, unlike many other markets, deals with a long-term relationship. This emphasis is especially clear in the discussion of investment in specific human capital. For the theory discerns that, if shared cost-wise by both the employee and the employer, investment in specific human capital reinforces the mutual interest of the two parties in maintaining a long-term employment relationship.

Efficiency wage models challenge human capital theory not with respect to the connection between education and productivity but with respect to the connections between experience and productivity and between productivity and earnings. Efficiency wage models derive from the observation that when employers face high turnover costs or high costs of monitoring worker productivity, they seek to develop wage payment schemes that provide incentives for employees to remain with the firm and to continue to remain maximally productive. One way to do this is to create earnings differentials over time that do not correspond to productivity profiles. That is, employers may pay workers less than their value added during the early years of employment, but pay them more than their value added in later years. During the initial years of employment, the prospect of earning more in later years keeps employees from quitting or risking dismissal by shirking. During the later years, the actuality of earning more than their value added, combined with the knowledge that if they went to a different firm they would have to start at a job that paid only equal to (or perhaps less than) their value added, keeps employees tied to their firm and producing at a high level.

Interestingly, because employers realize a savings in turnover costs and monitoring costs by divorcing the earnings profile from the productivity profile, they are able to increase the lifetime earnings package such that in the early years of employment workers may not be paid less than their value added. The term efficiency wages is derived from the fact that such payment schemes are beneficial not only to employers, but also to workers.

The notion that employee earnings increase with seniority because of employers' need to provide employee incentives challenges the human capital view that earnings rise with experience (seniority) because they mirror workers' productivity increases that result from their on-the-job training. Moreover, the efficiency wage notion adds to the difficulty of testing human capital theory's proposed connections among on-the-job training, productivity, and earnings because it suggests that even if on-the-job training (seniority) does increase productivity, employer incentive wage schemes may obscure the connection. If empirical tests fail to find a positive correlation between experience (or seniority) and earnings, this does not prove that human capital theory is "wrong." The connection posited by human capital theory may be correct over the entire earnings profile, but it may be eclipsed by incentive pay considerations at any particular point in time. Moreover, at any point in time, the incentive schemes themselves may increase worker productivity above whatever increases may stem from on-the-job training.

Internal labor market theories. Internal labor market theory, as outlined by Doeringer and Piore (1971), stresses the demand rather than the supply side of the market, and particularly employers' structuring of jobs and job clusters. In that sense, it is similar to Thurow's credentialist theory. Internal labor market theory has its origins in Dunlop's (1957) and Livernash's (1957) concepts of wage contours and job clusters and in Kerr's (1954) discussion of the balkanization of labor markets. The basic point that Doeringer and Piore make is that while external labor markets set wages based on supply and demand, internal labor markets set wages based on administrative rules and procedures. These two labor markets are connected through certain jobs which provide ports of entry to the internal labor market. Other jobs in the internal market may be thought of as being on job ladders that rise from the jobs at the ports of entry.

Thus, jobs that are not entry level are not filled from the external market but through promotion and transfer of those who are already employed by the firm (i.e., those in the internal labor market). The wage rates for jobs in the internal labor market are not, therefore, directly affected by competition in the external labor market, although they are certainly indirectly affected. As Doeringer and Piore point out, the degree to which the construct of an internal labor market challenges neoclassical theory (including human capital theory) depends upon the rigidity of the rules of the internal labor market.

The argument of efficiency wage theorists, that one way in which management increases company loyalty and reduces turnover is by holding out an earnings carrot for long-service workers, is familiar to internal labor market theorists. For one way in which such a carrot is provided is by promoting long-service workers into high-on-the-ladder, high-paying jobs.

Internal labor markets give human resource/industrial relations managers great power, for they decide not only how much on-the-job training to provide and how to share the costs with workers (the relatively narrow range of decision-making power accorded to managers in human capital theory), but also which jobs are assigned to which job ladders, how wide or narrow the earnings differentials are between job ladder "rungs," how much, if any, cross-over there is among job ladders, and which jobs to redesign and which to contract out (see Osterman, 1984).

Although human capital theorists, if pushed, might agree that human resource/industrial relations managers are important players in labor markets, the theory itself generally ignores power issues. Since markets are competitive, it is "the market" rather than human agents who have power (see Brown, 1988), for it is in "the market" that employers must compete for workers. If there are powerful agents in the human capital framework, these are the workers, who choose how much and what type of education and on-the-job training they wish to undertake. Interestingly, efficiency wage theorists, although they are usually neoclassical economists, assign more power to managers and place more emphasis on managerial decision-making than do human capital theorists.

Internal labor market theory also helps reconcile some inconsistencies raised by other labor market hypotheses. For example, as noted earlier, one question often asked about the long-term effects of the screening hypothesis is: If employees have been on the job for some time and employers are no longer uncertain about their performance, and if educational attainment is unrelated to productivity, why do employers continue to favor better-educated workers by paying them higher wages? In an internal labor market, the screening done at the time of hiring affects not only the initial job and wage level of the employee, but also his or her entire career at the firm. The initial employment decision determines the job ladder on which the employee enters. Thus, unless the firm provides for cross-over among ladders, if only better-educated workers are placed on ladders that contain the high-paying jobs, only better-educated workers will be found in high-paying jobs. Indeed, given the operation of internal labor markets, despite the longevity of job tenure of less-well-educated workers, employers will have little opportunity to learn of these workers' potential ability to perform in high-paying jobs. Of course, to the extent that initial hiring decisions are made not only on the basis of educational level but also on the basis of race and gender, employers also will not learn of the potential of minorities and women for higher paying jobs. Thus, screening or statistical discrimination, when practiced in the context of an internal labor market, reverberates throughout employees' work lives. Those with relatively low levels of education will be in jobs which have been structured to have low productivity.

Radical theory. Bowles and Gintis (1975, 1976) propose a completely different interpretation of the link between productivity and education. Unlike the adherents of the screening hypothesis, they believe that education does increase productivity. Bowles and Gintis argue, however, that the link between education and productivity is not skill acquisition, as the human capitalists maintain, but the reproduction of the class structure of society. That is, schools teach students from the working class those skills and behaviors that are useful in working-class occupations, but they teach middle-

and upper-class students skills and behaviors needed to assume leadership roles in society.

Like Thurow, Bowles and Gintis are dissatisfied with the human capital notion that the distribution of income is determined only by differences in the characteristics of the labor supply. They emphasize that the demand side of the labor market, particularly "macroeconomic considerations, market structure, technical change, and economic dualism" (1975, p. 81) are important in determining the distribution of income. Moreover, they maintain that mechanistic laws of supply and demand are not sufficient bases for predicting the effect of more widespread education on the distribution of earnings or income; what is being taught in schools must be examined as well. They believe it is foolish to expect that more widespread education will lower income disparity when the lessons that schools teach are precisely the opposite; in their view, schools teach that economic inequality is legitimate, indeed desirable.

More recent work on education in the radical tradition argues that education may not reproduce class norms as faithfully as Bowles and Gintis suggest (see Carnoy [1981] for a review). It may be that not only does the base (the workplace structure) affect what goes on in the superstructure (the schools), but that schools may operate as agents for changing the workplace. For example, the ideology of political democracy and equality presented to students in school may lead employees to demand more "voice" at the workplace (see Hirschman [1970] on the concept of voice). Unless these demands are met, employers may find that worker productivity declines. Indeed, Freeman and Medoff (1984) maintain that the opportunity that unions provide for worker "voice" is one reason why union workers have higher productivity than nonunion workers. If more education makes worker productivity contingent upon the opportunity for employees to exercise "voice" at the workplace, then once again the relationship between education and productivity is made more complex and more dependent upon management behavior.

Empirical Tests

Attempts to test the tenets of human capital theories or those of its critics with respect to the productivity link between education and earnings and between experience and earnings have not been numerous—mainly because of the difficulty in obtaining measures of productivity. The work reviewed below provides a sense of the kinds of tests done recently, the general "ferment" in the field, and the continuing absence of resolution or consensus.

Productivity, experience, seniority, and earnings. Medoff and Abraham's tests of the link between productivity and earnings are the best known. Their first study (Medoff and Abraham, 1980) used performance ratings by immediate supervisors as the measure of productivity and looked at data on education, experience, productivity, and earnings for about 7,600 white, male, full-time managers and professional employees in two U.S. manufacturing companies. Their findings were at variance with the human capital (on-the-job training) model. They found that although experience and earnings were positively correlated, the relationships between experience and productivity were either zero or negative. Medoff and Abraham's (1981) second study yielded similar findings. Using longitudinal data from a large U.S. manufacturing company for about 8,000 full-time, white, male managers and professionals, they found that for those who remained in a particular grade level, relative earnings increased, but relative productivity (performance rating) fell over time.

Medoff and Abraham speculated that skill obsolescence and boredom might be responsible for the decrease in productivity over time.[4] They also pointed out that the absence of a relationship between productivity and earnings may nonetheless be consistent with firms' long-run profit maximization. For example, as noted in the above discussion of efficiency wages, both employers and employees may benefit by divorcing the short-term link between productivity and earnings.[5] Moreover, it is important to remember that to the extent that productivity increases are brought about by specific on-the-job training that is financed solely by the employer, one would not expect, according to human capital theory, to find the productivity increases reflected in earnings.

Another study of the experience-productivity relationship, although based on a special population and hence less generalizable than the work of Medoff and Abraham, is by Maranto and Rodgers (1984). These authors looked at 191 claims processed by 20 field investigators in the wage and hour division of a midwestern state department of labor and related the investigators' level

---

[4] In addition, they raised the possibility that opportunity for promotion may complicate the experience-productivity relationship (Medoff and Abraham, 1984). If the most productive workers are promoted to higher job levels, then we would expect to find a negative correlation between number of years in a particular grade and productivity. That is, the estimated effect of experience on performance will be biased downward. However, as Medoff and Abraham point out, under such circumstances the estimated effect of experience on earnings will also be biased downward.

[5] Medoff and Abraham also suspect that worker beliefs about "just" compensation (e.g., that older workers should be paid more) may play a role in producing a positive relationship between experience and earnings that is not based on a positive relationship between experience and productivity.

of experience to a measure of their productivity—the fraction of the wages that an employer allegedly owes an employee which the investigator is able to collect. They found that at least during the first six years on their jobs, investigators' productivity was positively related to the length of their experience.

In addition to the difference in their measures of productivity, one possible reason for the disparity between Medoff and Abraham's results and those of Maranto and Rodgers is the difference in the mean levels of experience in their samples—15 to almost 20 years versus five years.

Abraham and Farber (1987) have recently looked at the relationship between seniority and earnings. Using a sample of male household heads who participated in the Panel Study of Income Dynamics (PSID), they selected workers in nonunion, blue-collar occupations and in nonunion, professional, technical, and management occupations. They used a hazard function to estimate job duration and concluded that there is only a small average return to seniority in excess of the average return to overall labor market experience. They found that workers in jobs of long duration earn more throughout their jobs than workers in short-term jobs and speculate that the correlation between seniority and earnings may result, in part, from the fact that workers with high seniority are better workers, are in better jobs, and/or are in jobs in which their own skills are particularly well-matched to the demands of the job.

Efficiency wages. Empirical work by Lazear and Moore (1984) expands upon the efficiency wage complication of the productivity/earnings link posited by human capital theory. The authors compared the age-earnings profiles of wage and salary workers with those of the self-employed. Since self-employed workers do not need to provide anti-shirking incentives to themselves, they provide a control group. Lazear and Moore found that the age-earnings profile is considerably steeper for wage and salary workers than it is for the self-employed, indicating that the desire to provide incentives is an important factor in the steepness of age-earnings profiles for wage and salary workers. The relative importance of on-the-job training and incentives in determining the steepness of the profile for wage and salary workers depends upon the assumptions made about the similarity and differences between wage and salary workers and the self-employed.

Screening. Comparisons of the self-employed and wage and salary workers have also been used to test the relative merits of human capital theory and the screening hypothesis. (See Wolpin [1977] and Riley [1975, 1979] for earlier efforts.) Tucker (1985), using data from the 1981 Wave XIV of the

PSID, compared about 2,800 private sector employees with about 300 self-employed workers. In separate earnings regressions for the two groups, the coefficients on the education variable (number of years of formal schooling completed) were statistically significant for both groups, and "slightly higher" (.077 versus .068) for the self-employed. This finding supports human capital theory rather than the screening hypothesis. Tucker also found that, contrary to the predictions of the screening hypothesis, the percentage endowment contribution of education is greater for the self-employed than for employees. Finally, again contrary to the screening hypothesis, the self-employed received a greater percentage contribution from the difference in the education coefficients.

One problem with both Tucker's study and Lazear and Moore's is endemic to any study using earnings data for the self-employed: the percentage of total income from unincorporated business that is to be considered labor income and the percentage to be considered a return to capital is an arbitrary decision. The fact that the R^2 in Tucker's earnings regression for the self-employed was so much lower than the R^2 in the regression for the employed (.277 versus .488) may indicate that some of the so-called earnings of the self-employed was really profit or rent.

A second difficulty is possible sample selection bias. Some self-employed workers may be self-employed because they invested too little in education relative to their ability and wish to be in a situation where screening by prospective employers (but not, of course, by potential customers) is unimportant. If this is the case, the distribution of the education-ability relationships is different across the two populations, and the self-employed no longer represent an adequate control group for testing the effects of education and experience on earnings.

Although Tucker does not discuss his findings with respect to experience, they are interesting in light of Lazear and Moore's work. In Tucker's earnings regressions, the coefficient on experience is higher for employees than for the self-employed (.0058 versus .0035). (The coefficient is significant for employees but not for the self-employed.) This suggests that some of the return to experience for the employed may be due to employer incentive schemes.[6]

---

[6] The earnings regressions from which these experience coefficients are derived also include a dummy variable equal to 1 if the employee or self-employed individual received nonacademic training prior to 1980. This dummy variable was significant for employees, but not for the self-employed.

Internal labor markets. Efforts to test the relative power of human capital theory and internal labor market theory generally consist of comparing earnings regressions that include only human capital variables with earnings regressions that include only "structural" variables and seeing which set explains a larger percentage of the variance in earnings. Recently, however, three more ecumenical papers (Maxwell, 1987; Hartog, 1987; Rao and Datta, 1985) have suggested three different methods of combining supply and demand-side variables.

Maxwell uses data on 5,000 "older" men from the National Longitudinal Surveys and Rosenberg's (1979) classification scheme for primary sector and secondary sector jobs. She finds that in jobs with high wages, job security, and mobility on promotional ladders (i.e., primary sector jobs), human capital variables, particularly level of educational attainment, have the greatest influence on earnings. In secondary jobs, on the other hand, education is one of the weakest significant variables in the regression. Variables with stronger effects are SMSA residence and structural characteristics of the job, particularly whether or not current and initial jobs were in heavily unionized industries. Being black had a significant negative effect on earnings for those in the primary sector, but it had no significant effect in the secondary sector. Also, having had one's longest job working for the government had a significant negative effect on earnings for those currently working in the primary sector; it had a significant positive effect on earnings for those currently working in the secondary sector.

Hartog's (1987) use of human capital and job variables is more integrative than Maxwell's. He develops a model of an allocation process where individuals with particular levels of education are matched with jobs with particular levels of difficulty, and he emphasizes that earnings are determined by both the supply and the demand side of the market. Hartog uses data for 14,000 workers sampled from the Dutch Wage Structure Survey of 1979. The data come from firms, not from individuals, and the firms were asked to rank the job level of each individual in the survey across nine categories based on "activities performed, taking into account the necessary education or knowledge, the difficulty and the degree of responsibility."

For the sample as a whole, and for each educational level, an F test rejects the hypothesis that job level does not add to the explanatory power of a human capital regression including seven educational level dummies, age, age squared, length of experience with present employer, and gender. That is, job level matters for determining earnings even after human capital and gender are taken into account. Similarly, for the sample as a whole and for each job level, an F test rejects the hypothesis that educational level does not add to the explanatory power of the regression. In all but two job levels, earnings vary positively with education.

Hartog's findings do not support the human capital view that job level doesn't affect earnings. He does not find that for individuals with given levels of education and experience, the labor market equates earnings across jobs. Nor do his findings provide support for Thurow's notion that earnings adhere to particular jobs regardless of the incumbent's educational attainment or length of experience. Hartog's results affirm that earnings are prices and that prices are set by both the supply and demand sides of the market.

Rao and Datta (1985) use data drawn from the 1980–1981 annual report of one of the largest manufacturing companies in India. According to Rao and Datta, all private Indian companies are legally required to include an appendix in their annual report which provides information on all full-time employees who earn $3,750 or more per year. Information must be provided on the following: "name, age, educational qualifications, gross income, total experience (in years) and hierarchic status" (p. 68). The company studied had 32 hierarchical levels.

Rao and Datta model the interactions of human capital and hierarchical levels as a recursive system. In the first equation, hierarchy is a function of schooling and experience. In the second equation, earnings are a function of schooling, experience, and estimated hierarchy. Thus, hierarchy is seen as an intermediate variable "to channel the transmission effect of schooling and experience onto earnings" (p. 75). The earnings regression that includes estimated hierarchy explains about three-fourths of the variance in earnings. The earnings regression that does not include a variable measuring hierarchical level explains about half of the variance in earnings. This finding indicates the usefulness of combining supply and demand side variables when looking at the determinants of earnings.

The radical theory. The Marxist contention that education affects earnings primarily by reproducing class divisions is difficult to test. Researchers have examined the effects of family background variables on earnings after human capital and job variables have been accounted for, but this provides only a partial test since part of the theory's contention is that education socializes working-class students to accumulate less human capital. Nonetheless, this partial test does seem to confirm aspects of the radical theory. For example, Kiker and Heath (1985), using data on individuals whose families have been part of the PSID longitudinal data base, found that family background variables exert significant indirect effects on the earnings of both black and white men. The meritocracy has not yet arrived.

Summary. Human capital theory, and the criticisms leveled against it, contribute to our understanding of the positive relationship between education and earnings. Part of the reason why those who are better educated earn more than those who are not stems from the skills training and consequent productivity increase derived from their education. But those who are better educated earn more also because of their relatively higher class background and because their education gives them entre to job ladders containing the more desirable and higher paying jobs.

Similarly, some of the positive relationship between job experience and earnings results from increases in productivity as a result of on-the-job training; but some comes from employer-designed pay schemes aimed at reducing employee turnover and shirking. And some derives from the fact that workers with high seniority may be "better" workers to begin with, may be in better jobs, or may be in jobs where the job requirements and their own characteristics are particularly well-matched.

Human Capital Theory and Earnings Differentials by Race and Gender

There are substantial earnings differentials by race and gender in the American work force. Table 1 presents these differentials for 1981 for year-round, full-time workers. The causes of these race and gender differentials (and the causes of changes in them) continue to be subjects of considerable, and often acrimonious, controversy.

Human capital theory argues that race and gender differentials are explained by differences in the supply side of the market, namely differences in worker productivity, and particularly by differences in education and experience. The challenges to human capital theory argue that the differentials are due to the demand side of the market—particularly discrimination, to interactions among ideology, demand and supply, and to political movements. Lastly, proponents of alternative theories see employers as having power to set wages and to determine the gender and racial designations of occupations.

These differences are more than academic. The way in which one views the causes of the earnings differentials and the power that one attributes to employers versus potential employees directly affects one's views of appropriate public policies to remediate the differentials. All economists agree that earnings differentials *ought* to reflect productivity differentials; human capital theorists think they already do. Critics of the human capital theory think they do not. Thus, critics support such public policy initiatives as equal employment legislation, affirmative action, and pay equity (comparable worth).

TABLE 1
EARNINGS RATIOS OF YEAR-ROUND, FULL-TIME, U.S. WORKERS, 1981

Black/White and Hispanic/White Earnings Ratios by Gender

	Blacks/Whites	Hispanics/Whites
Men	.69	.72
Women	.90	.87

Female/Male Earnings Ratios by Race and Ethnicity

Whites	Blacks	Hispanics
.58	.76	.70

Female/Male Earnings Ratios by Gender and by Race and Ethnicity

White women/White men	Black women/White men	Hispanic women/White women
.58	.53	.50

Source: U.S. Bureau of the Census, Current Population Reports, Series P–60, No. 137, *Money Income of Households, Families and Persons in the United States: 1981*, Washington, D.C.: U.S. Government Printing Office, 1983, Table 55.

The human capital view. Human capital theory contends that the earnings differential between minority men and white men results from the corresponding differentials between the two groups in both the quantity and quality of their educations. The decline in the earnings differential, especially the black/white male differential, is said to be the result of the narrowing of educational attainment between white and black men and an improvement in the quality of black men's education relative to that of white men. As firm believers in the meritocracy, human capital theorists expect that when blacks (or other minorities) increase the quantity or quality of their education, the initial return that they obtain on that education will be the same as the one received by whites. And minorities' opportunity to obtain on-the-job training will be the same as for whites. Thus, the policy conclusion for human capital theorists is very straightforward: to further reduce the earnings differential, continue to improve black educational attainment and quality relative to that of whites.

With respect to the gender earnings differential, the human capital story is somewhat different, because on average men and women already have the same quantity of education.[7] Human capital theory interprets the gender earnings differential as stemming from women's own choices: (1) the choice

---

[7] It is sometimes difficult to assess whether they have the same quality, especially at the tertiary level, because so often men and women have been educated in different fields.

to obtain less education of the type that has a high payoff (e.g., scientific or technical education) (Polachek, 1978); (2) holding type of education constant, the choice to obtain jobs that have low levels of on-the-job training but high initial starting salaries; and (3) the choice to withdraw from the labor force periodically in order to raise children (Mincer and Polachek, 1974). Polachek, in a series of articles (see Polachek [1987] for a summary), has argued that in determining their desired level and type of education and on-the-job training, women choose education for occupations that will minimize the penalty for intermittent labor force participation.

The treatment of minority women in such theorizing is curious. Comparing the earnings of black women or Hispanic women to *white* men shows that these earnings differentials are the lowest (see the bottom row of Table 1). Yet human capital theory does not deal specifically with the double disadvantage of minority women as compared to white men. The theoretical work on minority women asks either why they earn less than *minority* men, in which case the explanation has to do with women's "choices"; or it asks why they earn less than white women, in which case the explanation has to do with quantity and quality of education (see Malveaux and Wallace [1987] for further discussion of this issue).

Human capital theorists think that women are paid less than men in part because women (allegedly) have different utility functions than men. This causes women not only to seek different types of education than do men, but also to seek different kinds of jobs, even if they have the same education that men have. Filer (1986) has suggested that men seek to maximize income over their lifetime (constrained only by their own talents and ambition), but that women may also be interested in other objectives, such as the social aspects of their work, or the physical surroundings of their job. And, according to Becker (1985), women may be more interested than men in finding jobs that allow them to "conserve" some of their energy for housework.

Another aspect of women's lower earnings is their higher quit rates. Goldin (1986) has suggested that one of the reasons why women's age-earnings profiles are rather flat is that because of women's higher quit rates employers find it hard to structure efficiency wage contracts for them. Without such contracts, it is costly for employers to monitor their potential shirking. Consequently, employers concentrate women in occupations where such contracts are not important.

The absence of much slope in women's age-earnings profiles is also discussed by Mincer and Polachek (1974). In their view, the profiles' flatness stems from women's *expected* discontinuous labor force participation, which leads them not to invest in much on-the-job training because they don't expect to be in the labor market long enough for such training to pay off, and from women's *actual* discontinuous labor force participation, which causes their labor force skills to depreciate.

With respect to policy, human capital theory is quite clear—"if it ain't broke, don't fix it." Some human capital theorists are in favor of public policies designed to increase the availability of child care and to change the tax disincentives to married women's labor force participation (Polachek, 1989). However, despite the existence of a large female/male earnings differential, human capital theorists' belief that the gender differential springs from women's own choices leads these theorists to support the status quo. To try to increase the female/male earnings ratio through public policy would, in their view, interfere with the efficient allocation of resources now being performed by labor markets.

Discrimination. The most important alternative explanation for the race and gender earnings differentials is that there is discrimination in the labor market; i.e., employers provide lower earnings to minorities and women even when they have the same productivity characteristics as white men. The discrimination may be of the "statistical" type discussed earlier, which attributes no ill motives to employers, but stems from employers' "rational" behavior in the face of uncertainty; or it may be "taste" discrimination, resulting from prejudice on the part of employers, employees, or customers (Becker, 1957).[8] Taste discrimination may operate directly on the earnings differential or it may be channeled into occupational segregation, where minorities or women are excluded from higher paying jobs and crowded into those that pay less.

Internal labor market theory is compatible with the concept of discrimination. Indeed, in their original elaboration of the theory, Doeringer and Piore (1971, p. 133) state: "Internal labor markets...are designed intentionally to 'discriminate'.... Sometimes the discrimination is an incidental by-product of distinctions made for other purposes.... In other cases, race is a significant consideration in decisions affecting entry, internal allocation, and wages."

Those who subscribe to the segmented labor market hypothesis also view race and gender discrimination as "expected." Unlike the internal labor market, which divides jobs into those that compete in the external market (ports of entry jobs) and those that do not, the segmented labor market divides jobs into those in the primary sector that have high wages, good

---

[8] It is ironic, and a tribute to his own powers of analysis, that the framework for the two leading competing explanations for the earnings differentials both come from Becker.

promotion prospects, good working conditions, stability of employment, and due process with respect to work rules, and those in the secondary sector which do not have these characteristics (Doeringer and Piore, 1971). In fact, however, the two schema come from the same authors and there is considerable overlap between jobs in the internal labor market and those in the primary sector.

An interactive explanation. Hartmann (1976), Strober (1984), and Strober and Arnold (1987) have argued that occupational segregation is neither a supply-side phenomenon nor simply a result of employer discrimination, but stems from the interaction of patriarchal ideology and the operation of the job market. In particular, Strober suggests that because of a widespread societal belief that men should provide financial support for their families, employers give men first choice of occupations. To do otherwise would be to court costly disapproval from colleagues, family, and community as well as from customers and male employees.

Because the job market is segregated by race and educational level, not all men get first choice of occupations. Rather, within race and educational categories, men are permitted to choose before women do. Men choose those occupations that are relatively more attractive, where attractiveness is based on income, working conditions, and opportunities for advancement. Women choose occupations, too—but only after men have made their choices. Because men choose first and prefer those occupations that are higher paying, the female/male earnings differential emerges directly from the process of occupational segregation.

The gender designations of occupations rarely change because men actively keep women out of "their" occupations and men rarely have any interest in moving into lower paid, and lower-status, female occupations. When occupations do change their gender designation, as, for example, in teaching and banktelling, it is because the occupation has become less attractive to men and men either leave the occupation or fail to increase their numbers.

The radical view.[9] Radicals think that earnings differentials are mainly a reflection of power differentials between blacks and whites and between men and women in the society at large and that the differentials change in

---

[9] See Amsden (1980) for a discussion of the differences in world view among neoclassical, institutional, and radical economists. Reich (1988) argues that the categorization of labor market theories into neoclassical, institutional, and radical is deficient, and he suggests that the three categories should instead be conservative neoclassical, liberal neoclassical, and radical-institutional. Or, better still, he thinks the last category should be political-economic. I am sympathetic to his concerns. Such a delineation would better recognize that institutional

response to political movements (see Reich, 1981). In the radical view, one important reason why employers have pay differentials by gender and race and segregate the work force by gender and race is to prevent solidarity among employees.

Empirical Findings

The black/white male earnings differential. There is widespread agreement that the black/white male earnings differential has narrowed over time; the disagreement arises over the timing and causes of that narrowing. After laboriously constructing and analyzing earnings data for blacks and whites over the period from the Civil War to 1940, and also examining microdata for the 1940–1980 Censuses, Smith (1984) and Smith and Welch (1988) conclude that the human capital argument best explains the convergence of the black/white male earnings differential.

Keifer and Philips (1988) formulate a regression model of Smith's estimates of black/white men's earnings differentials for the 1890–1930 period and compare it to two other regressions, one containing institutional variables and no human capital variables and one containing both institutional and human capital variables. The institutional variables, which were used to measure changes both in labor market institutions and in societal institutions, include the percentage of black men in the rural South and the intensity of racial repression, measured by the number of black lynchings per year. Keifer and Philips also added two dummy variables for 1970 and 1980 to proxy the existence of equal opportunity legislation and affirmative action programs during that period. The human capital model explained about 60 per cent of the variance in the black/white male earnings differential over time, the institutional model about 90 per cent. In the model combining both sets of variables, the human capital variables did not achieve statistical significance. Thus, Keifer and Philips conclude that the institutional model provides a better explanation than the human capital model of the narrowing of the black/white male earnings differential over time.

Reich (1988) argues that the most important lessons regarding the black/white male earnings differential over time derive from examining differences in the periods when the differential narrowed and when it did not. Such an approach indicates what kinds of activities are likely to be successful in

---

variables can be either labor market variables or societal variables, or both. Also, in terms of policy, institutional economists and radical economists often make the same recommendations. On the other hand, most institutional economists do not use the Marxist framework for their analyses, and it seems worth preserving that distinction in the categories that we use.

further narrowing the differential. Reich concludes that political movements are the most important explanatory variables in determining the degree to which the black/white male differential narrowed over time.

The female/male earnings differential. As indicated in Table 1, in 1981, among full-time, year-round workers, women's annual earnings were 59 per cent of men's. In 1981, among all full-time workers (regardless of weeks worked), women's usual weekly earnings were 65 per cent of men's. Recent work by Blau and Beller (1988), which uses earnings of all workers and corrects them for time inputs and selectivity bias, indicates that during the seventies the female/male earnings ratio increased for whites by between 9 and 17 per cent (the latter figure includes the correction for selectivity bias) and for blacks by 11 per cent. A decomposition of this increase indicates that change in the educational attainment between men and women did not play much of a role in increasing the female/male earnings ratio. Change in the *return* to educational attainment contributed to a *decline* in the female/ male earnings ratio, especially among whites. The increase in women's potential experience (age) relative to men's made a small contribution to the decline in the earnings ratio for both whites and blacks. For whites, change in the return to potential experience contributed to a decline in the earnings ratio and the total effect of potential experience (the effect of the change in means plus the effect of the change in coefficients) was to contribute to a decline in the earnings ratio. For blacks, the total effect of experience was to contribute (slightly) to an increase in the ratio.

Also contributing to a decline in the female/male earnings ratio was the total effect of variables reflecting the gender composition of occupations. Blau and Beller (1988) found that "although women increased their representation in male jobs and integrated jobs, the *return* to such employment decreased for women relative to men" (p. 528). Outweighing the effects of changes in education, potential experience, and the gender composition of occupational variables, however, were the effects of decreases in the constant term in the regression, which Blau and Beller interpret as a decline in discrimination over the period, and a decrease in the gender differences in the return to being married with spouse present and, for whites, in the effect of children on earnings.

Despite the authors' ambitious and painstaking work, the implications of their findings for human capital theory and its critics are not clear and illustrate the problems involved in testing the alternative explanations of earnings differentials.[10] First, because of the lack of available data, the

---

[10] Blau and Beller make it very clear that their work is not designed to test the alternative explanations (p. 518).

experience variable is not truly an experience variable but a measure of potential experience, i.e., age. Next, the constant term may be considered to proxy discrimination, but in fact it is simply a measure of all the variables not included in the equation. Finally, although the variable measuring the gender composition of an occupation is interpreted by institutionalists as an institutional variable, it is interpreted by human capital theorists as a human capital variable, a measure of the extent to which women have chosen occupations that do not penalize them for intermittent labor force participation. These difficulties in interpretation render the verdict on the explanatory power of the alternative theories a loud and clear "draw."

If empirical resolution of the central debate remains elusive, somewhat greater success has been achieved around the edges. For example, Madden (1987) looks at workers displaced in 1983 and compares their salary losses to a control group who were not displaced during that year. She hypothesizes that if after controlling for education, experience, and length of service, women invest less in specific human capital than men, then women would be expected to incur lower wage losses than men as a result of displacement. However, if women workers face discrimination after being displaced, they would be expected to earn less than their male counterparts who had equivalent pay in their original jobs, are equivalently qualified, and engaged in equivalent amounts of search. Madden found that women experienced a greater wage loss than men as a result of displacement and she suggests that these results score a point for the discrimination explanation.

The argument that women are paid less because they work less intensively than men has been seriously undercut by analysis of the Michigan time-use data, which show that, as compared to men, women spend less time in coffee breaks and regularly scheduled work breaks, less time relaxing at work, and less time at lunch. After adjusting the female/male earnings ratio for time spent in breaks and relaxing, Stafford and Duncan (1980) find that the ratio decreases by three percentage points (from .62 to .59). That is, the ratio usually quoted understates the actual differential because women's work intensity is greater than men's.

Similarly, Blau and Kahn (1981) and Osterman (1982) have shown that it is incorrect to assume that women's lower earnings are caused by their higher quit rates. Rather, it may be that women's higher quit rates are caused by their low earnings and poor prospects for promotion. Blau and Kahn found that holding constant occupation and industry, women's quit rates are no higher than men's and in some instances are lower. Osterman demonstrates that women's quit rates are lower in industries with a high prevalence of affirmative action plans than they are in other industries.

Finally, there has been some closure on the issue of the size and duration of the penalty women pay for intermittent labor force participation. Corcoran, Duncan, and Ponza (1984), using PSID data, find that women who leave the labor force have lower real earnings when they return than they did at the time they dropped out. As predicted by human capital theory, in the first few years back at work, their wages tend to rise. The overall loss from having dropped out seems to be small. On the other hand, in managerial and certain professional jobs, the penalty for dropping out can be quite large. For example, see Strober (1981) regarding the penalty for MBAs.

Occupational segregation. The debate about the causes of occupational segregation remains heated, as evidenced in the exchanges between the two leading protagonists, Polachek and England.[11] England *et al.* argue that the human capital view, that women prefer to forego investment in on-the-job training and instead take jobs with high starting salaries, is not confirmed in the empirical literature: "No analysis has found the higher starting wages in female occupations that the theory predicts; to the contrary, starting wages are lower in female than male occupations requiring the same education" (p. 545). Nor, they insist, does research confirm that predominantly female occupations have lower depreciation rates than do male occupations for women who have dropped out of the labor force. England *et al.* also provide disconfirming evidence for Filer's (1986) contentions that women choose jobs that are less onerous than the ones that men choose and that part of the reason why men earn more than women is that men receive "compensating differentials" for the more onerous aspects of their work. England *et al.* find that even after holding constant skill demands and working conditions (in addition to human capital variables), those who work in occupations with more women earn less.

Polachek argues that human capital theory is nonetheless vindicated because human capital variables explain about half of the variance in the female/male earnings differential while the per cent female in an occupation explains only 5 per cent. He also thinks that for econometric reasons the variable per cent female is not a good proxy for the degree of intermittency of employment associated with particular occupations.

A different type of evidence in favor of the institutional explanation of wage differentials is found in Gregory *et al.* (1989), whose work compares changes in the female/male earnings ratio between 1969 and 1976 in Australia, Great Britain, and the United States. Over that period, the American earnings ratio remained constant but the Australian ratio increased by 30

---

[11] Polachek and England review the issues in their latest papers (Polachek, 1987; England *et al.*, 1988).

per cent and the British ratio increased by 20 per cent. The authors conclude that human capital variables do not explain the differences in the behavior of these ratios. Rather, the differences are explained by the fact that in Australia and Great Britain wages are set more centrally and in both countries specific policies for increasing the female/male earnings differential were adopted during the period under consideration.

Strober's work on occupational segregation is less directly critical of human capital theory. Using microdata from the 1960, 1970, and 1980 Censuses, Catanzarite and Strober (1988) construct a measure of occupational attractiveness to white men. The measure is a ratio in which the numerator is white men's actual mean earnings in an occupation and the denominator is the earnings that would be predicted based on the mean human capital of white male occupational incumbents. Human capital is represented by number of years of education, hours worked, age, and age squared. Separate measures of attractiveness are calculated for each of the Census years.

Catanzarite and Strober find that in all three years there was a positive correlation between the attractiveness of an occupation and its percentage of white male incumbents. Moreover, except for black men in 1980, where the correlation between attractiveness and the percentage of black men was insignificant, in all three years the measure of occupational attractiveness was significantly *negatively* correlated with the percentage of black women, white women, and black men. The authors also found that over the 20-year period there was no change in the degree of positive correlation between attractiveness and white men's occupational representation. And, except for black men between 1970 and 1980, there were no changes in the negative correlations between attractiveness and the percentage representation of black women, white women, and black men. Catanzarite and Strober argue that these results suggest that white men are at the head of a labor "queue" and that the degree to which they are pre-eminent did not change during the 1960–1980 period. The findings are consistent with the argument that white men are given first choice of occupations and that they choose those occupations that are high in attractiveness relative to other occupations.

Conclusion

What economists learn from a reappraisal of human capital theory depends upon their separate world views. Although economists consider their discipline a science, there is a good deal of "belief" involved in the profession. Because of the difficulty of designing and carrying out empirical tests that definitively "prove" one theory or another, several theories continue in contention over long periods of time. Empirical work that seems convincing to one denomination often has no persuasive power for another. Not surprisingly, then, the debates are often characterized by the half-full/half-empty syndrome. If human capital variables explain half of the variance in an earnings regression, the human capital advocates cheer for the victory of the human capital variables. On the other hand, opponents of the human capital view, institutionalists as well as radicals, are quick to point out that half of the variance in earnings is explained by variables other than education and experience.

Scholars often make their mark in academia by becoming associated with a particular position and entering into frequent doctrinal debates while stubbornly defending their particular orthodoxy. After all, to the extent that academics measure their own and others' success by the number of entries in the citation index, it pays not necessarily to be right, but to be clearly identified with a particular position and then to be attacked and to counter-attack frequently. Academics often gain little from seeking commonalities among denominations or building bridges across sects.

Managers, on the other hand, gain success from making "good" decisions, from incorporating valuable insights into their decision-making regardless of the particular school of thought from which the insights derive. Managers are rewarded for integrating ideas. With respect to decisions about recruitment and hiring, setting wage differentials, and achieving desired employee tenure, human resources and industrial relations managers have much to learn from both human capital theorists and from their critics.

For managers, there are two key lessons to be learned from this review. The first is that human capital theory is basically a supply-side theory, and that, as all economists are taught (although the retention on this point is often brief), prices are determined by demand as well as supply. Human capital theory by itself explains some of the variance in earnings, but not all of it. The second lesson issues from the institutionalists, and especially the internal labor market theorists: managers have real power. Firms operate under certain economic constraints, but wages are not set simply by impersonal market forces. Moreover, from a public policy point of view, managers probably have less to fear from government "interference" in wage setting than they perhaps imagine. Affirmative action processes often turn out to be good business practice and even pay equity adjustments seem to be compatible with employers' continued economic strength.

The U.S. economy is likely to face a labor shortage in the not-too-distant future and it will become more important than ever to fully utilize existing labor. Human resources and industrial relations managers will need all of the insights they can get from existing theories and empirical work as they begin to restructure jobs, provide in-house training, and place women and minority men into occupations and jobs that have been closed to them. For their part, economists who study labor markets and education will have much to learn from the behavior of managers and workers under these new labor market conditions.

The Economics of Internal Labor Markets

MICHAEL L. WACHTER and RANDALL D. WRIGHT[*]

Our essay focuses on the economics of long-term contractual relationships between a firm and its employees, referred to as the internal labor market. We review the economics literature on match-specific investments, risk aversion, asymmetric information, and transaction costs. We argue that an integrated treatment of all four factors is needed in order to apply implicit contract theory to internal labor markets. Integrating the topics also highlights the tradeoffs created among these factors. Our discussion stresses contract enforcement mechanisms, including self-enforcing contracts and third-party enforcement.

THE INTERNAL LABOR MARKET (ILM) consists of a set of explicit or implicit, more or less long-term agreements between a firm and its workers.[1] These agreements include implicit and explicit rules governing wages, hours of work, promotion opportunities, and grievance procedures. The manner in which the agreements are to be enforced, including self-enforcement and third-party enforcement mechanisms, are delineated as well. The terms of the contractual relationship also may be contingent on exogenous future events, such as changes in the firm's product market conditions or changes in the macro economy.

* The authors' affiliations are, respectively, Department of Economics and Institute for Law and Economics, University of Pennsylvania, and Department of Economics, University of Pennsylvania and Hoover Institution, Stanford University. Valuable research support was provided by the Institute for Law and Economics of the University of Pennsylvania. We thank Costas Azariadis, Harold Cole, Ronald Ehrenberg, Morris Kleiner, Ed Nosal, John Pencavel, Sherwin Rosen, and Mahmood Zaidi for their helpful comments.
1 Long-term employment relationships are empirically important. Hall (1982), for example, finds that the median completed tenure for workers in the U.S. is 7.7 years, and that 28 per cent of workers are currently in jobs that will last at least 20 years. Much job turnover occurs among younger workers before they establish long-term attachment (see Mincer and Jovanovic, 1981). Furthermore, Feldstein (1976) and Lilien (1980) find that over 70 per cent of layoffs are temporary, indicating that short-term separations usually do not end the long-run employment arrangement.

The analysis of internal labor markets began during the fifties when Kerr, Dunlop, and others developed the idea that the textbook market of supply and demand analysis could only accurately describe the external market for new hires, or the internal market of a few industries, such as agricultural labor and construction.[2] These scholars also first described the institutional realities of internal markets, their implications for the overall economy, and the "ports-of-entry" through which the external market influenced the internal markets. The resulting models were interdisciplinary, incorporating organizational behavior and legal aspects of the markets.[3]

This pioneering literature did not explicitly integrate the ILM into the neoclassical economic model. Consequently, it was sometimes assumed that a primary effect of the ILM was to reduce the importance of economic forces such as optimizing behavior. The early pioneers did not, however, take an anti-efficiency approach. Instead, they primarily attacked the uncritical application of the textbook model of supply and demand to the ILM.

The efficiency aspects of the ILM were first explicitly stressed in the seventies. Doeringer and Piore (1971) made the initial steps in developing some areas of compatibility between the ILM and the neoclassical model. Williamson, Wachter, and Harris (1975) and Okun (1981), among others, applied the developing contract literature to the ILM and consciously stressed the efficiency aspects of the ILM. Freeman and Medoff (1984) placed the role and impact of labor unions in a neoclassical perspective.

More recent economics literature has emphasized the efficiency theme in a more formal theoretical framework designed to isolate the central behavioral features of the ILM. Each potential behavioral assumption is separately modeled, in an effort to test the extent to which any single factor can provide a simple theoretical explanation of the employment relationship (see recent reviews by Flanagan [1984a], Rosen [1985], and Parsons [1986c]). This labor contracts literature has made great strides in developing a theoretical structure for the ILM, but the results remain incomplete. While factors such as risk aversion and specific training can explain important

---

[2] See, for example, Dunlop (1958) and Kerr (1954) and their recent retrospective reviews, Dunlop (1988) and Kerr (1988). This literature is extensively reviewed in Doeringer and Piore (1971).

[3] In reviewing the early ILM literature, Dunlop (1988, p. 50) noted, "An understanding of labor markets and compensation requires a recognition that the work place is a social organization, at least informally, and that labor markets take on significant social characteristics that do not characterize commodity and financial markets and that are not readily encapsulated in ordinary demand and supply analysis." The interdisciplinary nature of the ILM literature is evident in leading casebooks and monographs. In labor law, see for example, Cox, Box, and Gorman (1986); and in labor relations, Kochan, Katz, and McKersie (1986).

attributes of the ILM, no single element can do all of the work itself. As a consequence, this theoretical literature has not provided an integrated model of the ILM that might be useful to labor relations specialists and practitioners.

In this paper, we survey the diverse aspects of the current labor contracts literature in an attempt to bridge the separate strands of the theoretical literature and the more traditional interdisciplinary approach. We identify four factors—match-specific investments, risk aversion, asymmetric information, and transaction costs—which must be brought together to explain the full range of institutional rules in the ILM. We argue that the main contribution economic analysis can make to an interdisciplinary vision of the ILM is to identify how contract rules serve the optimizing goals of the firm and its workers. In moving toward a more integrated view of the contract that underlies the employment relationship, we focus on the enforcement aspects of the relationship. Enforcement problems are complex because the contract is designed to be long term but is also often incomplete. Nevertheless, these problems suggest ways in which the theoretical model can be applied to current issues.

Our main concern is with efficiency aspects of the ILM, and we spend less time on distributional issues. One of the strengths of the economic approach is that it allows the two to be separated. Thus, within the ILM there will generally exist a set of contractual arrangements (referred to as the "contract curve") that imply different divisions of the surplus created by the parties' joint profit-maximizing behavior. Any of the points on the contract curve will be characterized by the same qualitative efficiency conditions. However, many of the ILM issues which previously have been viewed as distributional are actually subsumed in an efficiency model which allows for asymmetric information, transaction costs, and sunk investments. For example, strategic behavior between workers and the firm, motivated by an interest in redistributing the ILM surplus, are treated as constraints whose costs the parties attempt to minimize by creating contractual mechanisms that reduce inefficient, rent-seeking behavior.

The paper is organized as follows: We begin by comparing the internal labor market with the standard textbook or external market. Then we discuss and attempt to integrate the contributions of specific capital, risk aversion, asymmetric information, and transaction costs. Next, we analyze contract enforcement, describe the contractual terms included in the implicit or explicit agreement to make the contract self-enforcing, address various forms of third-party contract enforcement, and discuss distributional issues. We close the paper with a summary and concluding comments.[4]

---

[4] The literatures we review are voluminous; our discussion is necessarily selective. We

The Internal Labor Market Compared to the External Market

Before analyzing the complexities of the internal labor market, it is useful to compare it briefly with the simple textbook model of labor markets, a model which effectively describes the labor market external to the firm. The external labor market (ELM) has two components. First, many firms participate in the external market when hiring new workers. Although these markets are segmented by the general skill of the workers (ranging from unskilled workers without a high school education to corporate administrators), they cover wide geographical regions and contain large numbers of workers and firms. In such broad markets, the potential for monopsony power by firms or monopoly power by workers is limited.[5] Second, certain industries maintain labor markets that are primarily external. The literature often cites unskilled labor markets in agriculture and retail trade as examples, but some highly skilled markets, including the construction trade and some professional occupations, are also close to the ELM norm.

In the textbook model of the labor market, firms and workers make few investments in the job or in the relationship. Hence, firms can discharge workers, and workers can quit at little cost. In the extreme case, sunk investments are zero, so the parties lose nothing by terminating their relationship.

The distinguishing characteristic of the internal labor market, on the other hand, is that firms and workers incur substantial sunk cost investments. Since these investments are not portable across firms, job immobility results. If workers were to switch jobs or firms were to discharge workers, the sunk investments would be lost. Minimizing these sunk cost losses encourages the parties to maintain their ongoing relationship.

The external labor market is the benchmark for any analysis of the ILM. It provides the opportunity costs of alternative employment for workers, and of alternative workers for firms. Workers in the ILM always have opportunities to find jobs with other firms, and these external opportunities

---

must, for example, omit much of the empirical literature attached to the models we review. In many cases, we reference other surveys which the interested reader may consult for more extensive bibliographies.

[5] The ELM model of perfectly competitive labor markets can be broadened to include localized monopoly power. ELM imperfections arise, not from the traditional source of few competitors, but from costly search due to imperfect worker information. The result is a distribution of equilibrium initial wages (discounted to present value over the life of the contract) rather than a single price. As long as the relevant information is too costly for the firms to provide to workers, the price differences will prevail and firms will have local monopoly power over workers. The existence of wage distributions rather than a single wage has been widely documented, beginning with Dunlop (1958).

provide limits below which their rewards cannot fall. Similarly, firms can hire new workers from the ELM and discharge workers who fail to meet work standards. Although the wages and other terms and conditions of employment are set administratively by the firm, they must ultimately rest on the opportunities for hiring new workers into port-of-entry ILM jobs from the external market. Hence, ELM economic pressures on the ILM are not repealed; they are simply rechanneled through these port-of-entry jobs.

The Nature of Internal Labor Markets

In this section, we describe four central economic factors that affect an ongoing employment relationship: (1) firm or match-specific training, (2) risk aversion, (3) asymmetric information, and (4) transaction costs. Our thesis is that all four of these factors need to be considered simultaneously in order to provide a view of the ILM that is consistent with the broad "stylized facts" of ongoing employment relations. Although all of these factors have been extensively analyzed in isolation, we believe this to be the first attempt to tie them together in an analysis of internal labor markets.

Match-specific capital. The central rationale for long-term attachments rests on firm-specific investments. Narrowly defined, these refer to investments in training that make workers more productive with their current firm than with alternative firms.[6] In the polar case, such training only increases the marginal product of workers on their current job and has a zero impact on their productivity with other firms. The result is an incentive to continue the employment relationship.

Match-specific investments is a somewhat broader category. It refers to firm-specific investments in human capital via on-the-job training, learning-by-doing, etc.; to worker-specific investments; and generally to the case in which a firm and a worker may simply have formed a "good match." This match implies a greater expected "surplus" than would result if a new random worker was inserted into the slot, or if the worker was assigned a new random job.[7]

The surplus consists of the firm's profit derived from its current

---

[6] These could also be "worker-specific" investments where, for instance, the employer designs programs, compensation packages, etc. to meet the needs and desires of a particular group of workers, making it costly for the workers to move to another job.

[7] Classic references include Becker (1964), Mincer (1962), and Oi (1962) for on-the-job training, and Arrow (1962) for learning by doing. Models of matching that do not explain in detail why some partnerships yield a greater surplus, but investigate the implications of the fact that the surplus can differ across worker-firm matches include Jovanovic (1979) and Mortenson (1985).

employees over and above what could be earned by recourse only to an external labor market, and the utility of the workers from the employment compensation package over and above what they could derive on the external market. The goal of the worker-firm coalition is to maximize this surplus subject to constraints imposed by technology, information, and other features of the environment.[8]

Workers enter a firm with general (i.e., portable across firms) training. However, productivity often benefits from match-specific investments, so the size of the surplus becomes a function of the return on those investments. The first investments in the match are the expenditures on hiring and screening that allocate workers to jobs in which their productivity is likely to be highest. Specific training can then be undertaken at a level which maximizes the value of the match.

A difficulty with match-specific investments is that although the ILM is disciplined *ex ante* by the usual market forces, *ex post* there is a lock-in effect due to the investments that have been sunk into the relationship. This makes the *ex post* ILM a bilateral bargaining situation. In this context, inefficient rent seeking is possible. A particular problem involves quits or discharges designed to prevent a party from recouping past investments. To encourage joint surplus maximization, rather than self-interested or counter-productive rent seeking, the ILM must design enforceable contractual arrangements to deal with such turnover.[9]

Given these turnover costs, why do we not observe contracts that simply prohibit or directly restrict such occurrences? For example, workers (firms) would sign contracts that prohibit quits (discharges), eliminating the potential for the other party's loss of its share of the investment. The existing economics literature has not satisfactorily answered this question.

The usual explanation is that laws against worker servitude make such contracts unenforceable, but this cannot be the whole answer. The only contracts that would involve indentured servitude are those that require "specific performance," meaning that the breaching party must fulfill the specific terms of the contract. Few commercial contracts are enforced in this way; instead, the breaching party pays damages. This damage remedy could also be used to compensate a breach of match-specific investments.

A second explanation rests on the fact that future events, such as changes in tastes or skill, could make fixed employment contracts inefficient; that is, not all turnover is inefficient, *ex post*. Such contingencies, however,

---

[8] Although distribution (i.e., how to divide the surplus between firms and workers) is important, we choose to give it less attention here.

[9] Studies on the implications of the specific-training model for turnover include Hashimoto (1981), Mortenson (1978), Parsons (1972), and Pencavel (1972).

could be handled by writing the relevant contingent-claims contract which would delineate job tenure and related employment issues as a function of future events. A difficulty with this solution is the transaction cost of writing contingent-claims contracts (a subject we address later in this paper).

The ILM's answer to turnover is to deal with it *indirectly* through wage or compensation policy. In his seminal study on human capital, Becker (1964) suggests that rent-seeking behavior (quits or discharges to gain a larger proportion of the surplus) could be reduced if both parties shared in the investment costs, with the goal of making their contract self-enforcing. For example, workers would invest in their own specific training to the extent that their current wage (w) is lower than their opportunity wage (ow) in the external market. The firm's investment is similarly measured by the difference between the worker's marginal product (mp) and w. The worker would be deterred from quitting, and the firm would be deterred from laying off the worker because such behavior would result in the loss of future returns on these investments.

Thus, a central result of the specific-training literature is a wedge between the marginal product and the wage (the firm's investment) and between the wage and the opportunity wage (the workers' investments). The wedge reflects the fact that the returns on investments occur later than the investment costs. A continuing pattern of such investments produces the familiar upward-sloping age-earnings profile. Internal promotions can similarly be explained by this investment pattern.

Although the parties primarily set the efficient level of turnover indirectly through compensation policy, recent legal innovations have tilted toward third-party enforcement for certain types of quits or discharges. For example, firms are increasingly relying on "key-employee" or "noncompetition" clauses that prevent workers from trading on their industry-specific knowledge. This most often affects managerial workers, the group that might be expected to receive the greatest amount of match-specific training (e.g., see Closius and Schaffer, 1984). Workers, on the other hand, are more actively pursuing court redress for losses due to "wrongful discharge." This trend raises broader issues which we discuss further below. (See also Krueger, 1988.)

Risk aversion. The "implicit contract" literature that began with Azariadis (1975), Baily (1974), and Gordon (1974) was not based explicitly on training or specific capital, but on risk allocation between employers and their workers. Whether due to better access to financial capital markets or simply to different attitudes toward fluctuations in income as stressed by Knight (1921), employers are assumed in these models to be typically less risk averse than workers.

Efficient risk sharing thus requires that compensation be smoothed. Smoothing means that mp will vary by more than w, and at any point in time mp need not equal w. Hence, the risk-sharing model, like the match-specific investment model, predicts divergence between mp and w.[10] This divergence has different implications in the two models in terms of the sequencing of pay. Only match-specific investments explain why wages increase with age. However, the profile could also exhibit a high variance. Indeed, absent risk aversion on the part of workers, wages may vary as much as profits.

Risk aversion converts the firm-worker partnership into a partnership in which workers effectively become a "limited partner" or a "secured creditor" whose payment is guaranteed against fluctuations in output or job performance. Hence, risk aversion must be added to match-specific investments to explain an age-earnings profile that is smoothed as well as upward sloping. Both factors are needed to account for the empirical regularities.

Still, risk aversion *in itself* cannot be the single basis for a continuing employment relationship, given that much of this insurance function could be accomplished outside of a firm's ILM. Insurance policies, including those concerning life, health, disability, and unemployment could, in principle, all be written by private carriers. Similarly, as is currently the case with social security, all retirement plans could be run by agencies outside of the firm or through spot market contracts.

Yet there may be reasons for incorporating risk sharing into the ILM once an ongoing relationship is in place. For example, using the ILM to perform parts of this function within the firm may reduce transaction and some other costs of insurance contracting, including monitoring. That is, whether or not risk sharing is a primary reason for the initial emergence of the ILM, once the ILM is in place, it is likely to be a cost-effective method for income smoothing.

There are tradeoffs, as well as complementarities, between match-specific investments and risk aversion. The deferred compensation that is used to make contracts self-enforcing conflicts with the goal of smoothing workers' income (unless deferred compensation can be perfectly insured against future exogenous events). The presence of these tradeoffs illustrates the importance of an integrated view. Additional tradeoffs between risk aversion and asymmetric information are discussed below.[11]

---

[10] Several implications of the divergence between w and mp in the implicit contract model are discussed in detail in Wright (1988).

[11] It is now widely accepted that contract theory based on risk aversion does not clarify inefficiencies or unemployment based on wage rigidities. Unemployment results in these

Asymmetric information. A critical problem in the ILM is the presence of asymmetric information. Asymmetric information exists when it is relatively more costly for one of the parties to observe or monitor the quantity and quality of either inputs or outputs or the state of technology and demand. In the polar case, one party's information is entirely private and unverifiable by the other party.[12] Two classic examples are: (1) workers having asymmetric information advantages in determining their work effort and (2) firms having an advantage in determining the state of the product market and technology.

If both parties cannot observe work effort or product market conditions at equal cost, cost minimization suggests allocating the collection of such information to the low-cost party. Although it seems efficient to simply have that party report the results, incentive problems arise because the party with the informational advantage can use that information to achieve opportunistic aims. For a contract to be efficient, it must resolve this dilemma: It must not only assign the information gathering to the low-cost party, but also provide a mechanism which prevents the information from being used strategically. We call a contract that resolves this dilemma a self-enforcing contract or an incentive compatible contract.[13]

Contracts that control workers' strategic behavior. It is generally assumed that workers know their own work effort, while the firm can only learn about the quality of the workers' input through costly monitoring. Since workers prefer leisure to work, they have an incentive to overstate their effort if left to monitor it themselves. Modeled as a principal-agent problem, consider a worker (agent) who produces output (y) according to the function $y = f(e,x)$, where e is effort and x is a random variable. Neither x nor e is observed by the firm (principal), although we will assume that it can observe y. If e (or x) is public information, then assuming the worker is risk averse and the firm is risk neutral, the optimal contract would have the worker expend a certain efficient level of effort in return for *constant* wage w. The effect is to make w independent of y.

---

models because labor is assumed to be indivisible (see Rogerson, 1988). Such unemployment may or may not be "involuntary," but it is nonetheless efficient (see Rogerson and Wright, 1988).

[12] There are models which explicitly account for verification by the other party at a positive, but finite cost. See, for example, Townsend (1979).

[13] Sometimes the efficient outcome which is subject to informational constraints is referred to as the "second best" result, indicating that it is only "best" given asymmetric information. Because informational constraints are, in principle, no different from the constraints imposed by the production function or any other aspect of the environment, we will simply refer to the outcome as efficient while recognizing that all economic decisions are made subject to constraints.

When information is distributed asymmetrically, however, an opportunity arises for strategic behavior by the worker. The worker is able to put forth a very low level of e (assuming leisure is preferable to hard work) and claim that the resulting low level of y is due to a bad realization of x, so she/he is entitled to the same level of w. Hence, there is no incentive to supply the correct effort.

The optimal contract in this case (under certain fairly mild regularity conditions) sets w as an increasing function of output, $w = w(y)$, $w' > 0$. This provides incentives for more appropriate effort, although it also exposes the worker to uncertain income, which is a problem if she/he is risk averse. This illustrates an important tradeoff between allocating income risk and providing the correct incentives in contracts. It is the extension of this simple model that leads to the broad problem of motivating work effort through incentive pay.[14]

Another approach is a variant of the law-enforcement model first developed by Becker and Stigler (1974). Suppose the worker has the opportunity to shirk on the job. Let b denote the benefit of such cheating to the worker. Given a level of monitoring, let p be the probability of detecting him/her in the act. Then if we make the worker post a bond of size B, as long as $pB \geq b$ there will be complete compliance.[15]

We do not, however, often see workers actually post a bond. Many workers are "credit constrained" in the sense that they cannot raise the required amount, B (see Azariadis, 1988). Consequently, the bond may take more complex forms that circumvent the credit constraint. Such bonds are descriptive of a range of actual personnel practices. For example, internal promotion hierarchies, pension plans, and other deferred reward systems can be interpreted as partial solutions to the monitoring problem. Such mechanisms are not used more broadly because, although they may provide appropriate incentives for work effort, they may also conflict with the efficient allocation of income over time, based on insurance and other smoothing considerations.

The bonding involved in the work effort problem is different from deferred compensation in the specific-training model. In particular, in the specific-training model, increased skill means that pay is sequenced so that workers' mp > w in later periods; in the work monitoring problem, the bond implies

---

[14] There is a vast literature on principal-agent models of contracting. See Hart and Holmstrom (1987) for a state-of-the-art survey with many references.

[15] Harris and Raviv (1979) study the more complicated case where the monitoring technology is imperfect; see Parsons (1986) for a discussion of these and some other models. Lazear (1981) discusses how bonding mechanisms might work over time via back-loaded wages. See also Akerlof and Yellen (1986) and Holmstrom (1983).

that w > mp in later periods (these differences are discussed in Hutchens [1987] and Medoff and Abraham [1980]).

Contracts that control firms' strategic behavior. There are also models in which firms have the informational advantage, usually with respect to the state of product demand or technology. Two general models are worth discussing. Appropriate work incentives would encourage workers to work harder when product market conditions are favorable and mp is higher. But if w were constant due to income smoothing, the firm would have an incentive to misreport the product market as being favorable, hence forcing greater work effort. As above, the misreporting problem is alleviated by making compensation (as in bonuses or profit sharing) vary with work effort. Such contracts have important self-enforcing properties because the firm does not gain by misreporting product market conditions. Here again, however, income smoothing is traded off against appropriate work incentives (see Green and Kahn, 1983; Hart, 1983; and Cooper's [1987] survey).

A second problem relates to the sequencing of w and mp (mentioned above). In this case, workers (but not firms) are in the recoupment phase on their sunk investments in later years (with w > mp). By misreporting its product market conditions as unfavorable, a firm could seek to discharge workers who are recouping on their deferred compensation. One solution is to restrict the way in which a firm can adjust to changes in product market conditions. Seniority schedules are partly a response to this problem. When the firm is investing in workers, forcing it to lay off workers according to a seniority schedule means that it must accept a loss on investment in junior workers before senior workers (with w > mp) can be laid off (see Riordan and Wachter, 1982).

The asymmetric information literature leads one to expect to find complex state-contingent contracts including self-enforcing mechanisms developed to control strategic behavior. Such contracts would specify what happens in the face of potential exogenous changes in technology or in the demand for the firm's output, and hence inputs. Combined with risk aversion and match-specific investments, such contracts would also describe the parties agreed-upon tradeoffs between income smoothing and the provision of appropriate incentives for correct reporting of asymmetric information.

The problem with this prediction is that we do not observe such complex contracts, at least not in the nonunion sector, where over 80 per cent of the work force is employed. In fact, we often observe the opposite—incomplete contracts.

Transaction costs. The puzzle concerning the absence of detailed contracts is solved by one of the factors which explains why the relationship is brought inside the firm in the first place—transaction costs. If the parties inside the firm attempt to maximize the coalition's surplus, they must obviously attempt to reduce transaction costs as much as possible (or, more accurately, as much as it is efficient to do so). Since negotiating, writing, and enforcing contracts often incur high transaction costs, complex state-contingent contracts might not be joint profit maximizing.[16]

In place of this state-contingent contract, the parties could reach an understanding on general principles, but not on specifics. This agreement could be either implicit or explicit, although in most nonunion firms it is entirely implicit. In this contracting framework, the parties deal with new events by rolling over their general understanding to these new factors.[17]

Incomplete contracts might seem to worsen problems of asymmetric information. Absent detailed, state-contingent contracts, what factors prevent opportunistic behavior by either of the parties? Perhaps the most important disincentive for strategic behavior is the repeated nature of the ILM relationship. Repeated transactions are less subject to opportunism than are short-run relationships. An opportunity for gain that results in a breakdown of the relationship is not likely to be pursued if there is much surplus to be lost or significant fixed costs to be incurred in terminating or restarting the relationship. Long-term relationships sometimes can reduce opportunities to misrepresent the outcomes of stochastic events due to the application of the law of large numbers; it is simply not acceptable to report that a certain

---

[16] Williamson, Wachter, and Harris (1975) emphasize that efficiency dictates the use of incomplete contracts and that long-term relationships are designed to economize on the real resources that are required for negotiating, writing, and enforcing agreements, as well as for adapting efficiently to certain exogenous changes in the economic environment.

[17] It is useful to underline the distinction between an implicit contract and an incomplete one. Both share the distinction of being unwritten and, therefore, both save on certain transaction costs. However, in an implicit contract, a "meeting of the minds" has in fact occurred. The contract is two-sided, showing the "consideration" which may be sufficient to make the contract enforceable. Seniority provisions (in the nonunion sector) and income smoothing over the business cycle are examples of implicit contract terms. Implicit contracts are not unique to internal labor markets—most commercial contracts are at least partially implicit. Moreover, the courts have no difficulty in enforcing such contracts. In an incomplete contract, there has been no meeting of the minds. Incompleteness may involve contingencies which had not arisen before or which could be construed as unforeseeable (e.g., the liability of successor firms to honor the implicit contract agreed to by a liquidated firm). A final consideration concerns explicit terms that are not meant to be enforceable, such as a current controversy involving firms' employment handbooks that purport to describe the rights of workers in the plant. Until recently, these explicit terms were not thought to be enforceable in court, and not considered part of any contract. This is changing, particularly in the area of wrongful discharge.

advantageous outcome has occurred too often.

Reputational considerations are also frequently cited as critical in restraining strategic behavior. Obviously firms are more likely than workers to acquire reputations in the external labor market. To the extent that firms engage in strategic behavior at the cost of workers, their reputation in the external market will suffer. These firms will have to pay higher wages to attract new workers or will find it more costly to continue the contract provision that requires the workers to post a bond in the form of deferred compensation.[18]

A second control over strategic behavior is the potential for retaliation by the other party. Firms can obviously discharge workers. The more difficult issue concerns redress for workers. By deciding to shirk in response to perceived unfairness, workers can prevent a firm from realizing profits generated by strategic behavior. In the extreme, workers can engage in sabotage. Using such methods, however, clearly reduces the joint profits of the parties.

Perhaps the most powerful redress available to workers is to insist that their contracts be made more explicit and more enforceable by third parties. This effectively means that the workers will become unionized. Third-party enforcement generates transaction costs that reduce the joint profits generated by an employment relationship. Moreover, when the underlying issue is one of misreporting asymmetric information, third-party enforcement would necessitate that any asymmetric information be provided to the third party.

Summary. We have identified four factors—match-specific investments, risk aversion, asymmetric information, and transaction costs—that are important in shaping the ILM. As each of the factors explains some, but not all of the observed characteristics of ILM behavior, they must be considered collectively. An important example is that risk aversion as well as specific investments are needed to explain wage patterns that are smoothed as well as increasing with tenure.

In this integrated framework, tradeoffs and conflicts between the ILM's responses to these factors become apparent. For example, risk aversion conflicts with the fact that the wage should be an increasing function of output under asymmetric information. A second example is that the desire for detailed state-contingent contracts conflicts with transaction costs. The job of the ILM is to resolve such conflicts and tradeoffs. We would expect observable ILMs to resolve these tradeoffs differently depending on the preferences of the workers and the technology of the firm. Since these are

---

[18] These arguments have merit, especially with respect to the effects of reputation. See Carmichael (1984) and Bull (1987).

similar to the tradeoffs that economists analyze in their study of resource allocation, the economic model can be used to illuminate the precise tradeoffs as well as to describe the choices made by particular firms and workers.

Third-Party Enforcement: The Role of the Legal System

In this section, we discuss the methods of third-party enforcement and their efficiency properties. The types of contracts we consider include: (1) contracts in the external market (ELM contracts), (2) contracts in ILM union markets, (3) contracts in ILM nonunion markets, and (4) contract terms introduced through statutory or common law.

Commercial contracts in the external labor market. An analysis of labor contracting in the external market provides a useful benchmark for understanding ILM contracts, because of the similarity of the economic relationship in the two markets. Of special interest are ELM relationships with considerable match-specific investments, such as contracts involving personal services, subcontracting, franchising, and exclusive dealerships and distributorships.

Contracts in the external market fit a prototype of detailed, state-contingent contracts predicted by the theory involving asymmetric information. These contracts include explicit formulas for dividing the surplus dependent on stochastic events, as well as enforcement methods. The parties bargain under a regime of freedom-of-contract, so that there are no mandatory standards.[19] The assumption is that the parties themselves know best 'what types of clauses fit their needs. Finally, these ELM contracts make considerable use of third-party enforcement.

Third-party enforcement is treated within the law governing commercial contracts. The extensive law and economics literature in this area finds that contract law is broadly consistent with economic efficiency. In cases involving contract breach, courts act to enforce the terms of the contract. Legal precedents serve as "default settings" that tell the parties how the law will interpret the contract if it is silent on the subject being contested. The default settings make it possible for the courts to enforce contracts without complicated case-by-case litigation. Similarly, standard-form contracts, which reflect industrial practice, evolve in these markets. Such "off-the-shelf" contracts are complex, but are inexpensive to use. Default settings and

---

[19] There are a few statutory restrictions on the freedom-of-contract. For example, in a number of states, statutory regulations may require exclusive dealerships to run for some minimal time period.

standard-form contracts reduce the transaction costs associated with contract formation.

In an ELM contract, the rules governing termination of the relationship usually are explicit. Most often the contract has a minimum duration but is terminable at will (at discrete intervals) by either party after that period. Terminating the agreement within the minimum period would involve a penalty related to the monetary value of the sunk investments. In other words, match-specific investments are protected by joint consent.

If the contract is silent on termination, the default setting is that the contract is terminable at will only after a "reasonable duration." (This is true particularly in contracts involving exclusive dealerships or franchises.) If the contract is terminated before that point, the breaching party must pay damages. Here again, the damages are frequently the value of the match-specific investments. However, an exception is made if the court finds that the breach was opportunistic, in which case penalty damages are assessed.

Detailed contracts in the union sector. As is true in ELM contracts, union contracts are relatively detailed, explicit, and state contingent.[20] Moreover, they typically provide for an arbitration process that fills in many of the gaps in the explicit contract.

The differences between ELM contracts and union contracts involve restrictions on the freedom-of-contract, including (1) a requirement that the parties bargain over "mandatory topics"; (2) a set of rules governing the use of "economic weapons" if the parties bargain to impasse over the mandatory topics; and (3) a process that allows for union certification. These standards are inalienable in that the firm cannot require as a condition of employment that workers or their union bargain away these rights. On the other hand, all of the restrictions involve process; there are no mandated outcomes. So, after bargaining to impasse on the mandatory topics, the firm can, as one of its weapons, hire permanent replacement workers who might then petition for the union to be decertified.

An interesting question is why the National Labor Relations Act (NLRA) makes substantial use of inalienable entitlements. Many traditional labor law scholars maintain that the NLRA attempts to foster industrial peace and democracy by giving workers greater bargaining rights and a guaranteed voice in the employment relationship. The assumption is that if the rights were alienable, the inequality of bargaining power in favor of the firm would

---

[20] Since the union sector is analyzed elsewhere, we only briefly discuss the points that are relevant to our focus on the efficiency of alternative contracting rules. For an early treatment of labor unions, see Rees (1962). For a recent general survey, see Farber (1986).

result in workers giving away those rights under duress (see Atleson, 1983).

From a purely economic perspective, it is always difficult to defend inalienable rights. The restrictions on the bargaining process would have to be based on the presumption that the government knows the efficient process and that the parties themselves would not use the same process because of some failure in the bargaining power. This argument seems strained today, but it may have made more sense during the thirties.

The efficiency argument for labor unions is that there are potential gains in having workers choose an exclusive agent-auditor to represent them in bargaining with the employer. In this context, unions lower the transaction costs by replacing worker-by-worker bargaining with a single agent. The agent also acts as an auditor who monitors the firm's use of its (asymmetric) information and reduces the potential for inefficient rent seeking. This view of unions has been stressed by Freeman and Medoff (1984).[21]

Unions and the NLRA have recently become an active topic of research in the law and economics literature. The traditional interpretation is that of the Chicago school, which argues that the intent of the NLRA was to cartelize the labor market, resulting in successful rent-seeking by workers (see Posner, 1986).

Wachter and Cohen (1988) analyze National Labor Relations Board and court decisions regarding specific contract rules. In this work, the contract terms and the NLRB and court interpretations of those terms are judged against a standard of efficiency. The conclusion is that these rules are broadly consistent with the self-enforcing contracts described above. A particularly important issue for our topic involves job tenure and the mobility of capital in the union sector. In this area, NLRB decisions leave firms with considerable unilateral freedom to determine employment levels, to relocate work across plants, and to sell assets to other firms. This is compatible with firms having an asymmetric information advantage with respect to product market conditions and technology. On the other hand, firms do not have unilateral freedom to change wage rates, a rule which is also in accord with the setting of information asymmetries. To limit strategic behavior, however, the NLRB also infers a broad obligation on the part of the firm to bargain over the effects of the decision. This mandatory bargaining would address such factors as seniority, within and across plants, and severance pay.

These legal rules are similar in substance, although not in process, to the implicit rules in nonunion contracts. In nonunion contracts, firms obviously

---

[21] Freeman and Medoff (1984) recognize both the positive and negative roles of unions. A recent literature suggests that the primary empirical effect of unions is successful rent-seeking in the form of high union wage premiums. See, for example, Hirsch and Addison (1986), Addison and Hirsch (1989), and Linneman and Wachter (1986).

retain decision rights over total employment levels and capital mobility, but frequently accord workers protection through informal seniority provisions and relative wage stability. (See also the discussion below of the Plant Closing Act.)

In terms of process, the grievance procedure in most union contracts gives union workers greater protection with respect to termination than that found in the nonunion sector. Union workers can contest a dismissal using the grievance process, while in the nonunion sector an inference of employment-at-will means that there is no formal recourse against a dismissal. (However, see the discussion below on wrongful discharge suits under common law.)

The efficiency of NLRA contract law in the union sector has implications for the long-run market shares of unions. The NLRA left considerable room for workers to remain in nonunion firms where contract rules are very different. The result has been, and continues to be, competition between union and nonunion firms and even between union and nonunion subsidiaries of the same firm. The competition pits the legal process rules of the NLRA, the resulting detailed explicit contracts in the union sector, and any noncompetitive contractual outcomes against the nonunion contracts which we describe below.[22]

Incomplete contracts in the nonunion sector. As discussed above, in most internal labor markets in the U.S., contracts are largely incomplete and, where provisions exist, they are typically implicit. This fits with the predictions of the transaction costs model, which views ILMs as promoting the joint surplus through savings on contract costs.

The bipolarization of the incomplete contracts in the nonunion ILMs versus the detailed state-contingent contracts observed in ELM contracts and in the union sector is puzzling. Analyzed from the perspective of the nonunion contract form, three explanations merit attention.

First, the degree of incompleteness may reflect the underlying rationale for creating internal labor markets. As stressed above, a comparative

---

[22] An obvious question for contract theory to explain is why some sectors become unionized and write very detailed contracts while others remain nonunionized and write almost no contracts at all. Part of the answer is almost certainly historical. The craft and industrial unions formed during the thirties were in the more mature manufacturing, construction, mining, and transportation industries. Other service-producing sectors were less important during that time period and largely remained nonunionized. The only significant sector that became unionized after the fifties was the government sector. Presumably the choice between unionizing or not would also reflect the industry-specific costs and benefits of unionizing. These are typically described as the Hicks-Marshall conditions. (See, for example, Ehrenberg and Smith [1988].) Unfortunately, little attempt has been made to analyze whether these conditions make sense in the broader context of labor contract theory.

advantage of organizing activities inside the firm is to save on the transaction costs that occur in writing explicit ELM contracts. From this perspective, it is not the incomplete contracts in the nonunion sector that require explanation but the detailed contracts in the union sector.

A second factor is the NLRA rule that makes it unlawful for employers to dominate, assist, or interfere with the formation or administration of any labor organization. If a firm in the nonunion sector were to *negotiate* a contract with its workers, it would be an unfair labor practice, and the activity would be enjoined. The outlawing of company-dominated unions reflects the opinion during the thirties that such unions only serve to thwart true collective bargaining. In today's environment, it is certainly intriguing to ask whether the nonunion sector would be "more organized" without these legal restrictions.[23]

Finally, bipolarization may arise from the difficulty of writing very partial contracts. If a contract is to be enforceable, it must be specific enough to enable the courts or the third-party arbitrator to draw guidance from the terms to apply to the area in dispute. Contracts that are largely incomplete, but contain a few enforceable clauses, are vulnerable to misguided rulings. If the parties are to write a contract, it is thus likely to be detailed.[24]

The duration of the employment relationship in the nonunion sector is based on a default setting of employment-at-will. Under this doctrine, an employer has complete freedom to terminate an employee for any reason. Recently, dents in that precedent have occurred as discharged workers have sought relief through a claim of wrongful discharge. Under wrongful discharge, a plaintiff can request reinstatement or damages if the court finds that an implied contract exists between the parties. In such cases, the court attempts to learn the terms of the unilateral contract signed by the employee upon joining the firm. In particular, it looks for evidence (sometimes from employee handbooks) that the firm appears to be offering a long-term

---

[23] Of course, employers can still draft explicit contracts. This can be accomplished by bargaining with individual workers over their specific terms and conditions of employment. However, to devise a contract covering many workers, the agreement could not reflect bargaining between the parties. Rather, employers would unilaterally write a contract to which the workers would effectively agree by accepting the offer of employment.

[24] Contract breach often occurs over an event whose consequences were unforeseen at the time of contract formation. If the event is neither explicitly nor implicitly covered by the contract terms, the court may decide the outcome by filling in the gaps in the contract. The court attempts to determine how the parties themselves would have dealt with the event if they could have foreseen it during the contract formation. When a contract is largely incomplete, the court is less likely to be able to fill in the gap. The result is that the contract cannot be enforced by the court, or if enforced, might be prone to errors and hence inefficiencies.

contract.[25]

Laws regulating union and nonunion ILMs. Prior to the seventies, Congress was reluctant to intervene in the employment relationship, beyond its broad support of unionization through the NLRA. In part, this stance was based on the assumption that labor unions were the law's solution to employment contracting problems. Having chosen collective bargaining as the mechanism to resolve ILM difficulties, further statutory intervention in the form of explicit contract terms or outcomes was avoided. (See Gross [1974] for an extensive history of the NLRA.)

Statutory regulation of all ILMs, whether union or nonunion, began in earnest in the seventies when it was clear that the majority of U.S. workers would remain nonunion. The Occupational Safety and Health Act (OSHA), which established health and safety standards in the workplace, was the first attempt to regulate aspects of the employment relationship. In 1974, authority for establishing standards for pension plans was established under the Employee Retirement Income Security Act (ERISA). In 1988, the Worker Adjustment and Retraining Notification Act (referred to as the Plant Closing Act), provided standards that firms must fulfill before they can close or relocate a plant.

These statutory measures, which apply to both the union and nonunion markets, put in place the kinds of complex, state-contingent contract terms envisioned by contract theory. However, in a turnaround in policy toward the ILM, the parties themselves were not permitted to draft their own terms; instead, standards were set by third-party regulators.

There is a considerable literature on the efficiency aspects of OSHA (see Viscusi, 1979) and ERISA (see Ippolito, 1986). It can be shown, for example, that if the government agency knows both the workers' preferences and the firm's offer curve, it can set the optimal contract terms. Moreover, if the government knows this better than the parties themselves, such intervention would be necessary to reach the optimal contract. But it seems implausible

---

[25] The debate over employment-at-will should be differentiated from the issue of freedom-of-contract. Nonunion contracts, like other commercial contracts, operate under a broad mandate of freedom-of-contract. That freedom allows the parties to adopt whatever terms are mutually advantageous. In most areas of contracts, the law allows the parties to reach agreements, with the courts only serving as a mechanism for enforcing those private agreements. Currently, most nonunion contracts, with the exceptions mentioned above, do not explicitly indicate whether the courts should allow for wrongful discharge. Hence, in the debate over wrongful discharge, at issue are the terms that the court should infer when the contract is silent. That debate is not of great import for the long run unless the courts were to decide that their default settings were nonwaivable by the parties.

that a regulatory agency would know individual preferences better than the individuals themselves; it is slightly less implausible that an agency would know better the risks, and hence, the true offer curve of the firm. A stronger efficiency argument for standards is that they reduce transaction costs, since the parties themselves need not deal with the issues. The standards are *minimum* standards; they are akin to default settings that can be raised, but not lowered. In this sense, they are akin to minimum wage laws, overtime pay, and other forms of protective labor legislation.

The Plant Closing Act is particularly relevant to this paper since it alters the manner in which the ILM contract may be terminated (see Ehrenberg and Jakubson, 1988; 1989). The Act's provisions comport closely with NLRB and court rules regarding plant closings in the union sector. The rule as formulated by the NLRB is that firms have a unilateral right to make the *decision* to close or relocate. However, the firm must bargain with the union over the *effects* of the closing. Under the Plant Closing Act, firms have the unilateral right to decide to close a plant, but they must give prior notice of that closing to the workers. The Act will thus lead to discussions (nonunion) or bargaining (union) over the effects of the decision on workers. In either case, the parties have recourse to certain economic weapons.

Common law and statutory law regulating ILMs reduced the bipolarization that has characterized union and nonunion contracts in the past. How far this trend continues will certainly remain an important topic in labor economics. Our argument is that such laws can usefully be analyzed using the principles of economic efficiency described above.

Distributional issues. Whereas we stress the efficiency aspects of the ILM contract, an alternative view argues that contract rules are primarily about battles over income distribution (or the surplus created by the contract). This is often combined with a related point that contractual terms are more about "fairness" than efficiency and that ILMs are frequently inefficient given the high transaction costs, worker immobility, and potential for strategic behavior. In the older neoclassical literature, these concerns would indeed appear as inefficiencies and about battles for income shares. This view of the ILM is most frequently found in the literature that developed around the initial work of Doeringer and Piore (1971).

In current modeling, however, efficiency is defined as a surplus maximization contract where the maximization includes constraints imposed by asymmetric information, transaction costs, and match-specific investments, in addition to the more traditional constraints imposed by technology and endowments. In other words, some of the presumed sources of inefficiency are now incorporated into the maximization process itself. Hence, when the ILM parties design rules to control each other's potential strategic behavior, they can be viewed as primarily acting to maximize the surplus. However, typically there is no unique, efficient ILM contract. Instead, within the ILM there is generally a set of contractual arrangements (the contract curve) that imply different divisions of the surplus.

Legal and statutory rules, as distinct from private contractual terms, are less likely to be about efficiency and more likely to be about income distribution. Legal rules can change the initial entitlements of the parties, thereby altering the final income distribution. Moreover, although competitive market discipline drives the parties toward efficient behavior, the same discipline does not necessarily drive legal rules. In fact, there is a considerable literature which argues there is a "market" for statutory rules, and that the demand for such rules is derived from rent-seeking behavior by interested parties who lobby for the legislation. Even in these cases, however, the rules cannot have *long-run* distributional effects in voluntary contracts of a repeated nature. Since each party is motivated to achieve at least the market rate of return on its investments, it will shift resources out of sectors with below-market outcomes. The only exception arises when the legal rule is both inalienable and governs the entire relevant labor market. Of course, in the ILM contracts with extensive match-specific investments, the short run can last for a long time.

As noted above in the discussion of union labor markets, for example, the Chicago school views the NLRA as primarily an attempt by unionized workers to redistribute income in their favor and away from capital and nonunion workers. Hence, the literature on bargaining outcomes has determined that most unions achieve a premium wage above the competitive market. Moreover, this premium has persisted for several decades. On the other hand, the long run may be approaching, as unions lose market share to the nonunion sectors of the labor market (see Linneman and Wachter, 1986).

Conclusion

In this paper, we have analyzed the functioning of internal labor markets, emphasizing the efficiency aspects of the implicit and explicit contracts that govern the relationship. In our model, the ILM exists because it furthers the utility and profit maximizing goals of the parties.

To summarize, firms and workers make sunk firm-specific or match-specific investments, such as certain types of worker training, that effectively lock them into an ongoing relationship. Due to workers' risk aversion, the parties agree to income smoothing, so much of the stochastic variation in the surplus is borne by the firm. At the same time, however, the existence of asymmetric information introduces some of the most complex problems that threaten cooperation in the ILM. Since strategic false reporting implies an advantage, neither party can rely on the other always to report their information truthfully. The result is to encourage the parties to adopt self-enforcing contract terms. The analysis of such terms represents an active area of economic research that can be applied to the analysis of actual ILM contracts. Finally, what is required to explain actual ILM contracts is the additional assumption that agents can more efficiently bring the inputs inside the ILM, rather than purchase them on the external market. This follows from transactional cost savings. More specifically, contracts can be made less explicit and less complete.

Contracting inside the firm poses difficult questions of enforcement. The parties themselves recognize and limit the potential for strategic behavior by agreeing to terms that have important self-enforcing properties. We have suggested that these self-enforcing contractual terms include many of the stylized features of actual ILM structures.

The alternative to using self-enforcing mechanisms is to write contracts that can be enforced by third parties. Use of third-party enforcement varies considerably across labor markets. For example, while union contracts and labor contracts in the external market (e.g., personal service or subcontracting) make substantial use of third-party enforcement, nonunion contracts are designed to be almost entirely self-enforcing.

There are important tradeoffs in dealing with the four factors and the related enforcement issues. On the one hand, in order to provide the correct incentives for joint profit maximization, contracts might involve investment cost sharing, deferred compensation, and compensation that depends on performance. However, such incentive terms might conflict with the goal of efficient risk bearing. A second tradeoff exists between the need for complex contingent claims contracts and the transaction costs of writing such contracts. The result of this tradeoff is a bimodal distribution of contract forms. In the nonunion sector, contracts are largely incomplete and almost entirely implicit. In union contracts and in external labor market contracts, contracts are largely explicit and reasonably complete.

Economic analysis of the ILM should be useful in evaluating specific firm contracts that are developed by the parties themselves. Also, by creating a benchmark of efficient contracting, economic analysis assists in determining the effects of regulation on the employment relationship and on the welfare of the parties. This highlights the nature of the factors that shape the ILM and the potential tradeoffs they create. Since economic analysis is designed to examine such tradeoffs, it can usefully be brought to bear in the study and in the operation of the ILM.

Pensions and Deferred Benefits as Strategic Compensation

EDWARD P. LAZEAR*

This paper examines labor-oriented aspects of pensions and deferred benefits. Recent work has embedded pensions in the framework of optimal compensation schemes that induce workers to behave in certain ways. Most pension formulas present workers with securities that look like options, the value of which depends on exercise time. This view reconciles the tendency for turnover rates to fall as vesting approaches, even though there has been no change in the naive valuation of pension accrual. The paper also discusses the use of pensions as severance pay and notes that the various pension formulas have different incentive effects.

IT IS ONLY IN THE PAST FEW YEARS that pensions and deferred compensation have become an important part of the economics literature on compensation. Analysis of these institutions previously was assigned to accountants and financial experts, who viewed pensions and other forms of deferred compensation as tax-free saving accounts (e.g., see Black, 1980; Tepper, 1981). While it is clear that tax implications are important for the choice of compensation method (Miller and Scholes, 1982), there are labor-oriented aspects of pensions and deferred benefits that must be understood.

Pensions and deferred compensation play a crucial role in affecting incentives and labor supply. My analysis of mandatory retirement (Lazear, 1979) finds that the use of a performance contingent pension is essential to ensure that workers continue to perform in their final years on the job. Not only does the pension motivate workers to work hard, it also affects their desire to remain on the job. Turnover rates generally, and retirement ages in particular, are fundamentally influenced by the structure of pension plans and deferred compensation. Pension formulas can be modified to act as a substitute for mandatory retirement, which is almost entirely barred under

* Graduate School of Business, University of Chicago, and Hoover Institution, Stanford, California. Financial support from the National Science Foundation is gratefully acknowledged.

current law. Finally, human capital investment depends on the structure of deferred compensation because workers will be unwilling to bear the costs of investment if they cannot capture the returns.

Private pension plans differ significantly across and even within firms in the United States. The provisions of the plans induce workers to behave in particular ways. Some are efficient; others seem to create adverse incentives. Understanding the effects of these provisions is essential.

Turnover

Elsewhere, I have argued that defined benefit pension plans can be interpreted as severance pay (Lazear, 1983a) because the expected present value of pension benefits declines with age of retirement beyond some point. For example, a typical plan for blue-collar workers specifies that the worker will receive

$$P = (\$X)(\text{years of service})$$

where P is the annual pension received for each year that the worker lives after retirement and X is some number negotiated by unions and management. Suppose that a worker will die at age 86 and that he or she began employment with the firm at age 35. Table 1 gives the present value (in age 55 dollars) of his (her) pension benefits as a function of age of retirement.

Although the pension flow per year increases with additional years of service, the present value of those benefits declines, primarily because postponed retirement means fewer years during which to collect the pension. Present value increases until age 56 and then declines. While there is a $177 pension gain associated with working the year between age 55 and age 56, there is a pension loss of $390 associated with working the following year. The loss rises to $3,431 if the worker chooses to work until 65 instead of retiring at age 64. Things may not decline so dramatically if X is adjusted through ad hoc increases at each round of negotiations, but the point still remains valid. Eventually, the present value of the pension declines.

The "penalty" associated with retiring later can be rephrased: The firm is willing to buy the worker out by offering a higher pension if he/she retires early. The amount by which the pension is increased for retiring earlier is severance pay. The evidence reveals that implicit severance pay is widespread. The data in my study of pensions as severance pay (Lazear, 1983a) relate to plans that account for approximately 25 per cent of all covered workers in the United States. Most defined benefit plans in the sample[1] have the feature

---

[1] Most workers are covered by defined benefit plans since large firms tend to use them. Some make ad hoc adjustments to workers who continue; this tends to reduce the rate at which present value declines. Kotlikoff and Wise (1987) also find declines in present value beyond some age, usually before 65.

TABLE 1

PRESENT VALUE OF PENSION BENEFITS AS A FUNCTION OF RETIREMENT AGE[a]
(IN AGE 55 DOLLARS)

Age of retirement	Pension per year	Number of years	Present value	Pension loss[b]
55	$7,500	15	$116,946	
56	$8,000	16	$117,123	-$177
57	$8,500	17	$116,734	$390
58	$9,000	18	$115,826	$908
59	$9,500	19	$114,445	$1,381
60	$10,000	20	$112,633	$1,812
61	$10,500	21	$110,430	$2,204
62	$11,000	22	$107,871	$2,559
63	$11,500	23	$104,990	$2,880
64	$12,000	24	$101,820	$3,171
65	$12,500	25	$98,388	$3,431
66	$13,000	26	$94,723	$3,665
67	$13,500	27	$90,849	$3,874
68	$14,000	28	$86,789	$4,060
69	$14,500	29	$82,565	$4,224
70	$15,000	30	$78,197	$4,368
71	$15,500	31	$73,703	$4,494
72	$16,000	32	$69,100	$4,603
73	$16,500	33	$64,403	$4,697
74	$17,000	34	$59,627	$4,776
75	$17,500	35	$54,786	$4,842
76	$18,000	36	$49,890	$4,896
77	$18,500	37	$44,951	$4,938
78	$19,000	38	$39,980	$4,971
79	$19,500	39	$34,986	$4,994
80	$20,000	40	$29,977	$5,009
81	$20,500	41	$24,961	$5,016
82	$21,000	42	$19,945	$5,016
83	$21,500	43	$14,936	$5,010
84	$22,000	44	$9,938	$4,997
85	$22,500	45	$4,958	$4,980
86	$23,000	46	$0	$4,958

[a] Interest rate = 5%; X = $500; age started work = 40.
[b] Pension loss = P(t − 1) − P(t).

that beyond some age earlier than 65, the present value of pension benefits declines with the age of retirement.

The choice of pension formula provides firms with an alternative to mandatory retirement. Although mandatory retirement is essentially illegal, pension formulas have not been constrained in ways that eliminate the severance pay feature. Thus, firms can induce workers to retire at the appropriate ages by using pensions strategically.[2]

The data show that pensions do affect turnover, but the strength of the effect has only recently become clear. In the past, the empirical specification of the independent variable usually has been incorrect. The argument, which is spelled out in Lazear and Moore (1988), is that it is neither the current pension value nor even the pension accrual in a particular year that is the appropriate variable. Instead, it is the "option value" of working the additional year that matters. The following example makes the point.

The military awards a substantial pension to individuals who remain in the service for 20 years or more, but those who leave before 20 years receive nothing. This extreme form of cliff vesting has tremendous effects on turnover. Once a soldier has been in the service for eight to ten years, the chances that he/she will stay for 20 are high. Of course, many leave right at 20 years because the value of staying on beyond that is much smaller than the value of serving the 20th year. A simple view of the pension variable could not explain this phenomenon. If $P(t)$ is defined as the present value of the pension of a soldier who leaves with t years of experience, then a stylized version of the military pension is

$$P(t) = 0 \qquad \text{for } t < 20$$
$$P(t) = Z \qquad \text{for } t = 20$$
$$P(t) = Z + (t\text{-}20)X \text{ for } t > 20$$

where X is the annual accrual value after the soldier is vested. Further, define $D(t)$ as the change in the pension value associated with serving the tth year. Given $P(t)$,

$$D(t) = 0 \text{ for } t < 20$$
$$D(t) = Z \text{ for } t = 20$$
$$D(t) = X \text{ for } t > 20$$

Figure 1 shows $P(t)$ and $D(t)$; Figure 2 shows the likely turnover pattern.

Consider an analysis of data composed solely of individuals who have less than 20 years experience. If turnover is shown as in Figure 2, then a regression of their turnover rates on either $P(t)$ or $D(t)$ is unlikely to yield any significant results. Although the pension clearly is affecting turnover rates, it will not show up in a regression of those rates on pension value or even on that year's accrual. This example of cliff vesting illustrates the pitfalls of using accrued pension or changes in it to explain turnover. The correct approach recognizes that the value of working today is not just the pension accrual today, but the value of the right to accrue next year. There is an option value of working during that year that is being ignored and it

---

[2] See Pesando and Gunderson (1988), who find that pension plans are not good substitutes for mandatory retirement in Canada.

FIGURE 1

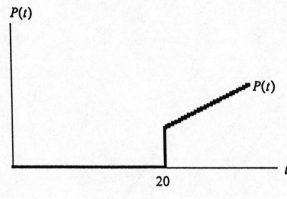

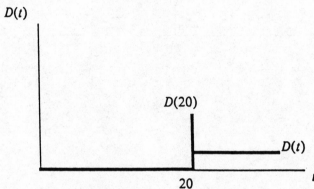

is the option value that affects behavior.

The option value approach. Formally, the value of working in year t (ignoring the wage) can be shown (see Lazear and Moore, 1988) to be given by

(1) $V(t) = M(t) - [P(t-1)](1+r)$

where $M(t)$ is defined recursively as

$$M(T) = \max\{P(t), M(t+1)/(1+r)\}$$

and where

$$M(T) = P(T).$$

Equation (1) makes clearer why soldiers rarely leave the military in their 18th or 19th years. Here, since $P(19) = 0$,

$$V(19) = \max\{0, P(20)/(1+r)\} - 0$$
$$= P(20)/(1+r)$$

The reason is the discounted value of waiting from now to year 20 to receive pension $P(20)$. In general, for $t < 20$, $P(t) = P(20)/(1+r)^{(20-t)}$. It has the

FIGURE 2

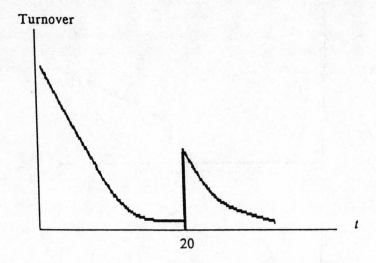

FIGURE 3

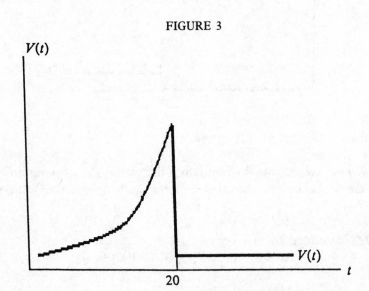

shape shown in Figure 3.

A regression of turnover rates on V(t) will give a very nice negative relation, as expected. When the value of remaining with the firm for one more year is high because it brings the worker close to the date at which he/she will become vested, turnover is low. When that value is low, as at the vesting date, turnover is high. Not only is the option value approach more satisfying theoretically, it allows us to deal with issues that cannot be addressed by the work-leisure method. Specifically, the timing of work over the life cycle, rather than merely the total amount of work, can be predicted. Additionally, uncertainty is easily incorporated. Also, the decision to leave is not always a decision to take leisure. This is easily taken into account in the option value approach.

The option value approach has demonstrated strong effects of pensions on turnover. Wolf and Levy (1984) found some weak evidence of the effect of vesting provisions on turnover. In Lazear and Moore (1988), large effects of pensions on turnover are estimated. Turnover rates are predicted to be twice as high for workers without pensions as for those with the average pension. Additionally, an increase of 10 per cent in the option value would reduce the probability of turnover for older workers by 22 per cent.[3]

In a refined version of the option approach, Stock and Wise (1988) estimate the effect of pensions on retirement dates. Their results are extremely impressive. Their model is able to predict accurately the large jumps in retirement rates at ages 55, 60, and 62 that are found in the data. No previous model had been successful at picking up these kinds of discontinuities. Further, at older ages, Stock and Wise's model predicts almost exactly the proportion of employees who have left the firm. They conclude that firm pension plans have a much greater effect on employee retirement decisions than the incentives inherent in the social security system.[4]

Pensions and deferred compensation (which can also be analyzed using the option approach) have a profound effect on turnover rates. Far from being merely variations of a tax-free savings account, most pension formulas influence the entire age-tenure structure of the firm.

Plan Structure and Worker Behavior

Pension plans vary significantly in their provisions. Some are defined contribution, some are defined benefit where pension value depends directly on the salary, and some are defined benefit where only years of service has a direct effect on pension flow. The various plans vest their workers after a different number of years of service.[5] Analogously, deferred compensation

---

[3] Hurd (1988) points out some weaknesses of this approach.

[4] Additionally, Ippolito (1985;1987) argues that pensions decrease labor mobility. His findings are corroborated by those of Allen, Clark, and McDermed (1988). Gustman and Steinmeier (1987) simulate the effects of pension changes on mobility.

[5] Ellwood (1985) finds that the value of vesting is substantial for those 45 years and older.

in the form of stocks, stock options, or other fringes have different contingencies associated with them and may place restrictions on the recipients. Not all of these restrictions are efficient and the choice of provision can have dramatic effects on worker behavior.[6]

Let us consider the most common kind of pension plans, those that specify defined benefits. These plans can be classified into two types—conventional and pattern. The conventional plans, which cover white-collar workers primarily, most frequently make pension flow an explicit function of some average of final years' salaries. While the reason for doing this is unclear, one reasonable conjecture is that it enables one plan to cover a large range of workers with varying salaries. It also indexes the pension to inflation since the salary average and prices will be correlated. This indexing is a major advantage of a conventional plan, but the formula has implicit in it some disadvantages. In particular, tying pensions to final salary creates an incentive to work hard and long during the final years. Motivating workers is generally applauded. In this case, though, the incentives are too strong: They induce workers to put out more effort and hours than is efficient. Before this proposition is demonstrated formally, the point can be understood by the following anecdote.

A few years ago, a subway train collided with another that was stopped at a station, and many people were injured. The investigation that followed revealed that the driver of the offending train was asleep at the wheel. He was 64 years old and had been working 60 hour weeks for a period of time because the pension that he would soon receive depended on this final year's compensation, including overtime. Since he was senior, he exercised his option to a large number of overtime hours and apparently carried it to excess. The pension plan motivated him to work, but it was too effective. In fact, it created an inefficiency. The social value of sleep exceeded that of work, but because of the pension structure, the train engineer chose work. Put more technically, the worker's alternative use of time during those last few hours each week exceeded the value of his marginal product at work, but the pension formula meant that the implicit wage (which included the change in pension benefits) exceeded his alternative use of time. As a result, the worker chose to drive even though doing so was inefficient.

This can be shown formally as follows. A worker can choose the amount of time he/she works over his/her life, H, and the amount of effort or human capital that he/she puts into each year, K. Thus, the worker's lifetime product is

$$(J + K)H,$$

---

[6] The analysis in this section is based on Lazear (1985).

where J is the value of raw labor.

A conventional pension plan has the form

$$P = \gamma HW,$$

where W is the salary on which the pension is based.

In competitive equilibrium, the firm pays workers their output on average,

$$WH + P = (J + K)H$$

or

$$W = J + K - \overline{P/H}$$

where $\overline{P/H}$ is the amount that the firm implicitly subtracts from annual salary in equilibrium to cover pension costs. The wage function is then equal to marginal product minus pension cost. This means that

$$\frac{\partial W}{\partial K} = 1.$$

The worker's problem is to choose K and H to maximize lifetime utility

(2) $\underset{H,K}{\text{Max}}\, WH + P - C(K) - L(H)$

where C(K) reflects the disutility of effort and L(H) reflects the disutility of hours.[7]

The first-order conditions are

(3a) $\dfrac{\partial}{\partial H} = W(1 + \gamma) - L'(H) = 0$

$\qquad\qquad = J + K - \gamma W + \gamma W - L'(H) = 0$

$\qquad\qquad = J + K - L'(H) = 0$

and

(3b) $\dfrac{\partial}{\partial K} = H + \partial P/\partial K - C'(K) = 0$

$\qquad\qquad = H + \gamma H - C'(K) = 0$

$\qquad\qquad = H(1 + \gamma) - C'(K) = 0.$

It is straightforward to show that efficiency requires

(4a) $J + K - L'(H) = 0$

and

(4b) $H - C'(K) = 0.$

---

[7] Separability is assumed.

FIGURE 4

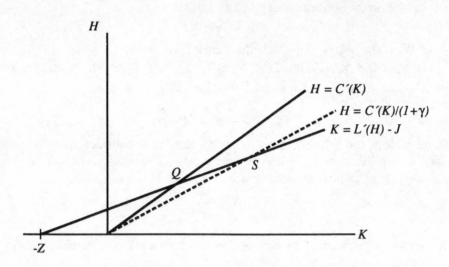

The logic is that workers should set the marginal cost of an hour equal to its (social) value, $J + K$, and the marginal cost of effort equal to its (social) value, H. Thus, for

$$\gamma > 0,$$

i.e., whenever there is a conventional pension, (3a) and (3b) deviate from (4a) and (4b).

The direction of the inefficiency can be determined by examination of Figure 4. The solutions to (4a) and (4b) are shown at point Q. For any $\gamma > 0$, (3b), written as $H = C'(K)/(1 + \gamma)$, is flatter than the function $H = C'(K)$. The optimum is at S.

Both H and K are larger when $\gamma > 0$. The pension induces the worker to work harder and to work longer because the pension formula inflates compensation for work above the marginal product so that the worker's incentives are too great.[8] This is what accounts for the long hours worked by the subway train engineer.

While defined benefit plans that tie pensions to final salary create an inefficiency by exaggerating incentives, the same is not true of pattern plans. Pattern plans tie worker pensions to years of service, but not (explicitly) to

---

[8] Of course, if the wage function were appropriately deflated by γ, the inefficiency could be offset. But it is doubtful that firms optimally adjust the response of wages to human capital as a function of pensions.

final salary. Because the pension is independent of the amount of effort and work time (within a year) that the worker puts forth, incentives are appropriate.[9] What the worker receives in pension benefits is exactly offset by the decrease in the wage. This leaves the marginal effect of time and effort exactly equal to the worker's product, which induces efficiency.

Formally, the worker's maximization problem is the same as it is in (2), but the pension formula is different. Now, it is

$$P = \beta H.$$

and is independent of final salary. As a result, first-order conditions are

$$(5a) \quad \frac{\partial}{\partial H} = W + \beta - L(H)$$

$$= J + K - P/H + \beta - L'(H) = 0$$

$$= J + K - \beta \overline{H}/H + \beta - L'(H) = 0$$

$$= J + K - L'(H) = 0$$

and

$$(5b) \quad \frac{\partial}{\partial K} = H \frac{\partial W}{\partial K} + \frac{\partial P}{\partial K} - C'(K) = 0$$

$$= H + 0 - C'(K) = 0$$

$$= H - C'(K) = 0.$$

Equations (5a) and (5b) are identical to (4a) and (4b) and guarantee efficiency. The pattern plan ensures that what is given by one hand in the form of pension benefits is exactly offset by what is taken by the other hand. As a result, it implies optimal retirement as well as efficient choice of effort.

Other things equal, this means that workers who have pattern plans will retire earlier and will work less hard than those with conventional plans. While this is not likely to have been the desire of those setting up the plans, it is the effect. Human resources administrators often resist the idea that pensions can be used to affect incentives. Even personnel people think of pensions and other deferred compensation as a fringe with few effects other than enhancement of the recipients' income. Nevertheless, the choice of

---

[9] To the extent that pensions do vary in a predictable way with years of service through ad hoc adjustments, the argument that such pension formulas are efficient loses its force.

pension formula does have very definite effects on worker behavior. Ignoring the effects will not cause them to disappear.[10]

Vesting. Surely, if there is any provision that has clear incentive effects, cliff vesting must be it. As noted earlier, military cliff vesting has clear effects on turnover. But the military example is not fully revealing because military compensation does not evolve in a fully competitive environment. Since vesting affects pension accrual, it must be offset by wage reduction in a competitive market. The two effects taken together will influence worker effort and turnover, but in somewhat subtle ways that may or may not be understood by bargaining parties.

Without going through the detailed analysis (but see Lazear, 1985), the major conclusion is that vesting tends to bifurcate the population. Individuals who remain beyond the vesting date spend too long on the job and expend too much effort. Those who leave early in their careers leave even earlier and work less hard than they would otherwise. This is because the expense of pension benefits must be covered. Those who leave early receive a wage that falls short of the value of their effort and those who leave beyond the vesting date receive a wage greater than that value. Thus, short-term employees are even worse off then they would be in the absence of a cliff-vested pension plan.

From the point of view of industrial relations and human resource management, it is important to point out that the interests of "leavers" and "stayers" diverge in their desire for cliff vesting. While it is no surprise that those who expect to leave the firm early prefer immediate vesting, it is less obvious that stayers actually prefer cliff vesting to immediate vesting. Cliff vesting implies a transfer from leavers to stayers. Thus, cliff vesting leads an employer to prefer his long-term employees over shorter term ones.

Finally, defined contribution plans, which vest immediately, are always efficient and have no obvious, adverse incentive effects. Such plans most closely resemble the tax-free savings account that is the view held of pensions by some finance economists. Since the account is the property of the worker, and since the equilibrium wage is reduced by exactly the amount of the contribution, there are no distortions introduced by defined contribution plans. That they are less effective at worker retention is often noted as a defect of such plans. The empirical point that incentives for worker retention are less pronounced under defined contribution is correct. But conventional plans imply too little turnover; defined contribution plans do not imply too much.

---

[10] Mitchell and Fields (1984) find that economic variables, particularly base wealth and the value of continued work, do explain retirement behavior.

Recent statistics have revealed that there is a move toward more coverage by defined contribution plans (see Ippolito and Kolodrubetz, 1985). Part of that may reflect the desire of a more mobile labor force (with two earners), but part may merely reflect the growing importance of supplementary retirement benefits. Most supplemental plans are defined contribution so it is difficult to determine whether these plans are replacing conventional ones because of their efficiency effects, or whether the increase in defined contribution plans is incremental.

Defined contribution plans do reduce flexibility. It has already been argued that a severance-pay-like pension structure is a substitute for mandatory retirement. But since a defined contribution plan creates an account, the expected value of which cannot decline with time, defined contribution plans do not offer the same ability to buy workers out. As a result, the elimination of mandatory retirement is a reason for moving toward defined benefit plans and reversing the trend, if there is one, toward defined contribution.

Pensions versus Other Deferred Compensation

Pensions are widespread, but so are other forms of deferred compensation. Some deferred compensation is explicit. For example, after a worker is with a firm for a long enough period of time, he/she may be entitled to receive some of the company's stock or to participate in some form of company savings plan. But deferred compensation may be less obvious. When wages rise more rapidly than worker productivity, this is a form of deferred compensation. A worker who remains with the firm for a significant amount of time receives as a "bonus" wages that exceed his productivity and, presumably, his alternative use of time. Why select one form over another?

Pensions and implicit deferred compensation have more in common with one another than they do with deferred stock or stock options as motivators, but there are some differences. First, pensions are not received until the individual retires, whereas the benefits of deferred compensation may begin to be enjoyed well before retirement. In a world of perfect capital markets, this consideration would be unimportant. It is the hand-to-mouth aspects of consumption that may create a preference for the timing of deferred compensation over that of pensions.[11] If borrowing and lending are costly to undertake, so that workers alter their consumption based on their current income, then two schemes which yield the same expected income may yield

---

[11] See Rosen (1985) for a discussion of capital markets and implicit contracts.

very different utility.[12]

Another advantage of using deferred compensation in the form of altered experience-earnings profiles is that it offers somewhat more flexibility. In particular, earnings profiles are not as vulnerable to government constraints as are pension benefits. ERISA (and the courts even in the absence of ERISA) places significant restrictions on what employers and employees may voluntarily contract to do with pension benefits. Not only are there restrictions on how pension funding must occur and on how those funds must be invested, but there are also constraints on provisions of the plan, most notably, vesting formulas.[13] Deferred compensation is subject to review of the courts if a worker opts to sue his/her firm, say, for age discrimination. But those constraints are less likely to be binding than those imposed by a law as explicit as ERISA.

This last point is also a benefit of pensions over deferred compensation. To the extent that it is easier to write enforceable pension contracts than it is to create binding deferred compensation agreements, transactions costs are reduced and efficiency is served. Thus, if the courts are a relatively cheap enforcement agency, and if an explicit pension contract is easy to enforce, then this may permit trades to occur that otherwise would have failed to take place. But this is really an argument in favor of explicit contracts over implicit ones, rather than for pensions over deferred compensation. There is no reason why an explicit contract cannot be written which prescribes the exact terms of deferred compensation in the same way that such contracts determine pensions.

One advantage of a pension is that it is not paid until retirement. Although this may imply reduced utility to the worker, it also provides better incentive effects during the final years. In fact, it is necessary to have some (discrete) payment at retirement in order to solve the end-game problem during the worker's final years (see Lazear, 1981). While deferred compensation that is paid before retirement allows the worker to consume in a time pattern that is more to his liking, already paid rewards exert no influence on worker behavior. Thus, pensions provide more incentives during the final years,

---

[12] There is evidence that current income affects consumption. For example, Hausman and Paquette (1987) find that food consumption falls after retirement, even if the retirement is anticipated. Since food is a necessity, they take this as evidence of significant effects on standard of living.

[13] Fischel (1984) argues that these restrictions on labor transactions deviate from standard legal practices and often are contradictory. The protective laws, by focusing on a narrow component of compensation and ignoring other aspects, often work against the interests of those workers whom the law was designed to protect.

simply because they are to some extent contingent on final performance.[14] Of course, an inappropriately structured pension plan may provide too much in the way of incentives, as argued above.

Let us now compare pensions and direct deferred compensation as a set to deferred stock and stock options as an incentive device.[15] Just as pensions and direct deferred compensation can be lumped together, for the most part, stock can be viewed as a special case of a stock option. Stock is an option with an exercise price of zero so that the worker is always in the money. Thus, most of the following discussion refers only to options.

If worker output or effort is easily observed, then deferred compensation and pensions are superior to options. Options have the disadvantage that ownership in the firm is diluted so that a worker captures only a very small part of the value from his/her effort. This is the standard free-rider problem in a partnership, where the worker captures only $1/N$ (N being the number of partners) of the output he/she creates. Deferred compensation need not be constrained in the same way. It is true that workers cannot get more than the full value of the firm, but with deferred compensation, worker A is not entitled to any of the output produced by worker B, so the adding-up restriction is not problematic.[16] The free-rider effect by itself would be sufficient to argue in favor of pensions and deferred compensation as a motivating device over options were it not for other considerations.

One major consideration is default by management on its promise to workers. This point has already arisen in the comparison of deferred compensation to pensions. But the difference between deferred compensation as a class and options is even greater. Options have superior nondefault properties when compared with deferred compensation. In order for management to default on its promise to pay workers pensions or deferred compensation, the firm need only renege. Defaulting on an option already owned by a worker requires making that option valueless, which can be accomplished only by reducing the value of the stock below the exercise price. To do so implies a devaluation of the assets of the firm and means that other shareholders, including the principal owners of the firm, are hurt by the default. In other words, it is more costly to breach an options contract

---

[14] The ability to make pensions contingent on final performance has been circumscribed by ERISA because workers who fail in their final years are still likely to be successful in forcing their employers to give them almost their full pensions.

[15] The discussion is based on Jackson and Lazear (1988).

[16] There are two qualifications: First, team motivation effects produced by a profit-sharing plan implicit in option ownership may push toward using options (see Kandel and Lazear, 1989). Second, Carmichael (1983) argues that tournament incentives, which are a modified form of deferred compensation, act as efficient motivators when there is a large number of agents.

with a worker than to breach a deferred compensation contract that promises the worker the same benefit. Thus, the self-enforcing features of options dominate those of deferred compensation and pensions. The logic of this argument implies that the probability of management default on options used to motivate workers increases with the proportion of stock held by nonmanaging owners. This suggests that start-ups, where a large fraction of equity is held by the operating manager, should use stocks and options as motivators over pensions and other forms of deferred compensation. Casual observation suggests that this is borne out by the data.

One way to view a pension is that it is a put.[17] A worker has the option to "put" his/her services to the firm in return for a pension. Thus, the worker is long and the firm is short the put. When traditional options are given to workers, workers are long call options rather than short put options. That is, the worker has the right to buy the firm's stock at a predetermined exercise price. There is an incentive for the worker to do well if he/she believes his/her performance will help the firm, which will be reflected in the stock price. The higher the stock price (above the exercise price), the more he/she makes on his/her option. But similar incentives are generated when workers are short puts. This is analogous to saying that we can either tax undesirable behavior or subsidize desirable behavior. A worker can be paid to be short a put. This means that the firm has the right to sell a worker stock at some predetermined exercise price. The cost to the worker increases as the price of the stock falls since the firm sells him stock at a high price which is worth an amount that decreases in its spot price. Thus, the worker is penalized for poor performance that is reflected in the price of the firm's stock.

What is the difference? Mainly, it is a question of risk. It is well known that the value of a call increases in variance of returns. This gives a worker who is long calls an incentive to take chances, by adopting riskier projects. Conversely, a worker who is short puts prefers to see the value of the call, now held by the firm, decrease. He/she will therefore tend to adopt safe, low variance projects. To the extent that workers behave in a fashion that is too risk averse, they should be made long calls. To the extent that they are too anxious to take risk, they should be short puts. The evidence and casual observation suggest that workers behave too conservatively, reflected in the rarity of being short puts.

Risk factors also affect the choice between deferred compensation (including pensions) and options as motivators. Deferred compensation often

---

[17] Abowd and Manaster (1985) make extensive use of this language in a labor market context.

seems less risky than stock options. While this may be true, it is far from automatic. Deferred compensation can be made a function of random variables, such as the firm's earnings, the CPI, or average wages in the occupation. There is a great deal of flexibility inherent in deferred compensation so that the risk can be varied significantly. The same can be said of options, however, since different combinations of shares and exercise prices can achieve a given expected present value with differing degrees of risk. There are situations where deferred compensation is significantly more risky than options. For example, the Japanese (large firm) labor force receives a significant portion of its compensation in the form of bonuses which are conditioned on firm performance. This form of deferred compensation is quite risky and might actually introduce more variance into a worker's earnings than would giving him/her some combination of options with varying exercise prices.

A similar point relates to defined benefit versus defined contribution pension plans. The casual observer might conclude that defined benefit plans shift the risk toward the firm and insulate the worker, whereas defined contribution plans place the risk with the worker. Although defined benefit plans may be less risky in nominal terms, they are likely to be more risky in real terms. To the extent that the nominal value of the defined contribution portfolio moves with inflation as a result of interest rate adjustments, the defined contribution plan offers the worker benefits that are indexed. Defined contribution plans, which are fixed in nominal terms, introduce more real risk. Only ad hoc adjustments keep defined benefit plans moving with inflation. This argument has even more force after the retirement date. Defined benefit plans, by definition, cannot be cashed out. Thus, the nominal value is fixed at retirement date, which introduces a significant amount of real variation.[18]

Conclusion

Many of the points discussed above are counterintuitive and have only begun to be understood by economists. Incentive effects of various pension schemes are subtle and the behavior induced often deviates from what would be predicted by a naive view of pensions and deferred compensation. What this means for human resource management is that personnel managers, vice presidents of human resources, and vice presidents of finance need to recognize that their actions often have unanticipated and dramatic effects. Several have been mentioned in this analysis. Other things equal, conventional

---

[18] See Green (1985) for a discussion of pension plan risk.

plans induce more work and later retirement than pattern plans. Cliff vesting makes short-term employees too anxious to leave and long-term workers too anxious to stay. Pension formulas have implicit in them incentives to retire at particular ages. Manipulation of these formulas can act as a good substitute for mandatory retirement.

Executives often argue that they do not want to use their pension (and sometimes even deferred compensation) plans as incentive devices. They frequently take the position that pensions are for worker security in old age and that other compensation schemes should be used to motivate workers. These statements reveal a complete misunderstanding of incentives. Desires of management are irrelevant. Implicit in pension formulas and deferred compensation plans are incentives that affect worker turnover and worker effort as well as old age security. The incentives do not disappear simply because management chooses to think of pensions as providing only old age security. The major challenge for human resource managers is to integrate their thinking on incentives with that on financial aspects of deferred compensation and to make a convincing case to their firms that the two are inseparable.

Labor Market Analysis and Concerted Behavior

LLOYD ULMAN*

In the first part of this paper, the importance of concerted behavior by workers emerges from examination of some prominent theories which set out to explain wage rigidity in the face of declining demand or excess supply without abandoning key elements of competitive theory. In the second part, the importance of certain Keynesian and satisficing behavioral postulates in motivating concerted worker behavior is suggested by the shortcomings of some contemporary economic models of the trade union which assume expected utility maximization and accurate knowledge of market conditions under ordinary circumstances.

CONTEMPORARY ECONOMIC ANALYSIS has been generating models which make unorganized labor markets behave, in some important respects, as if they were unionized, or which make unions behave, in some important respects, as if they were not. Models of the first variety have been invoked to explain the phenomena of rigid wages and unemployment in the face of a slump in demand; they can be found in the literature on Keynesianism, human capital, implicit contracts, and efficiency wages. These theories and those of market segmentation have made important contributions to the analysis of labor market behavior. But none has succeeded convincingly in reaching their common (if implicit) objective: to explain gross market failure without recourse to concerted behavior by workers or restrictive regulation by public authority.

Concerted behavior is the essence of modern trade unionism, but it is also antecedent to unionism and it can be found in its absence. As

* Department of Economics, University of California at Berkeley. The author acknowledges the generous support provided for this study by the Economic and Social Research Council (Corporatism and Accountability Program) and the Institute of Industrial Relations, University of California at Berkeley.

"continuous" (Webb) or "permanent" (Marx) associations, trade unions enhance the bargaining power of their constituents by accumulating strike funds as well as reserves of negotiating expertise and business knowledge, and also by entering into continuing bargaining relationships which can generate a credible threat of striking as a cost-effective substitute for the deed itself. As national (or marketwide) organizations, they aim to "take wages out of competition" and thus reduce the incentive for individual competing firms to take strikes or to remove the "whipsaw" advantage enjoyed by multi-establishment employers vis-a-vis isolated workplace groups of employees.

Nevertheless, concerted behavior by ad hoc associations need not evolve into formal institutions in order to pack an economic punch. Slowdowns and petty sabotage may not be as efficient as strikes in reducing the employer's cash flow, but they do maintain some cash flow for the workers. Localized job action is well suited to establishing or protecting restrictive work practices ("negotiating the production function"), even under collective bargaining. And, as noted below, despite the absence of an institutionalized strike threat, the uncertainty generated by the ever-present potential of workplace groups to coalesce in response to shared stimuli can elicit preemptive behavior by the nonunion employer.

Theories of Wage Rigidity and Unemployment

Keynesian workers. Although critics successfully disputed Keynes' strong claim that involuntary unemployment could not be eliminated by a reduction in the general level of money wages (which would be matched by a fall in prices), Keynes had also maintained that it would be virtually impossible to obtain such a reduction under a regime of decentralized determination of money wages. Since "there is no machinery for effecting a simultaneous reduction" (Keynes, 1963 ed., p. 247), the individual worker perceives a prospective cut in his or her own money wage to be a cut in his or her relative wage; and this "is a sufficient justification...to resist it" (*ibid.*, p. 14). But how effective could isolated resistance be, given the availability to the employer of replacements in the form of involuntarily unemployed workers who, by definition, are willing to do the work at a lower wage? To be effective, resistance would have to take the form of collective action, which could oblige the employer to balance the gain from a wage cut against the costs of a shutdown or slowdown which would have to be incurred to secure the wage cut. Concerted behavior is required as the necessary means whereby the individual employee's propensity to resist could be translated into an observed stickiness of money wages.

Trade unionism also can be regarded, in part, as endogenous to the interaction between adverse market pressures and worker propensities as described by Keynes.[1] But subsequent economists who have sought to explain wage rigidity under competitive conditions as well as adverse market conditions have hypothesized situations under which it might be accepted by employers, absent the fear of collective employee resistance.

Human capitalists. This problem has been addressed by human capital theory in an attempt to explain, not equilibrium unemployment, but temporary labor hoarding—i.e., employment in excess of labor demand at the going wage. This theory holds that firms would retain some employees whose training is highly specific to their operations during temporary downswings in demand, not only as long as revenues attributable to their work cover their wages, but even after they fail to do so (Becker, 1964). Hoarding these workers would protect the employer's investment in their training by minimizing the risk of losing them permanently. Therefore employment in excess of currently depressed demand at current wages might be preferable to layoffs and/or wage reductions.

At the same time, however, this explanation of labor hoarding during recessions can be regarded as consistent with layoffs. For, according to the theory, employers protect their human capital investments by offering workers with more firm-specific training higher wages in order to deter them from quitting. A wage high enough to preclude or significantly reduce the probability of quitting should also ensure a high recall rate. Thus, the firm should be able to temporarily lay off these workers as well as more generally trained employees. Moreover, the employer should be able to link a layoff policy with reductions in wages and still rest secure in the expectation that all (or most) souls departed will faithfully return to the fold when demand picks up. What attracts the specifically trained worker to the job for which he or she is best qualified is the premium which his or her wage commands over the reward for such alternative employment opportunities as the more general component of his or her training fits him or her for. Since wages for general training (in which employers make no investment, under competitive conditions) should fall during a downswing in overall demand, wages of the more specifically trained workers can also decline without reducing the premiums and hence the incentives to remain on—and return to—the jobs in question. But wage flexibility combined with layoffs does

---

[1] Keynes evidently distilled this part of the General Theory from his observation and sympathetic interpretation of the behavior of established unions and labor unrest in Britain's interwar period (Renshaw, 1975).

not generate involuntary unemployment (in a static and perfectly competitive economy). That is freely acknowledged by human capital theorists (Oi, 1962), but it is the result that Keynesian and most other rigid-wage models have been driving at.

Implicit contracts. According to a theory widely accepted in the seventies, a combination of rigid wages and equilibrium unemployment can result from "implicit contracts" between employers and their employees, whereby the former insure the latter against the risk of wage reductions in bad times. Workers pay for this insurance in the same coin in which they supposedly pay for the acquisition of general, or transferable, skills—by accepting lower wage levels over the long haul than they might have secured if (in this case) they were less risk-averse (Azariadis, 1975; Baily, 1974; Gordon, 1974). Implicit contract theory appears to reach Keynesian conclusions more effectively than the original analysis: it ranges employers on the side of wage rigidity rather than in opposition; and it credits workers with conventionally "rational" decision-making, while its own special psychological assumption of differentially greater risk aversion appears plausible.

Nevertheless, some have claimed that there is less to this model than meets the innocent eye. I don't pretend to follow the tortuous trail blazed by the critics, but two of their objections can be readily appreciated. First, why would not the firm be willing to offer the risk-shunning worker protection against reductions in employment as well as—or even in preference to—wages (Akerlof and Miyazaki, 1980)? Second, if it is assumed that management knows more about the true state of business than its workers do, why could it not take advantage of such "private information" to cheat the latter; and, if it could, why would the workers buy insurance from such double dealers?

Two theoretical counterrebuttals have been filed in reply to the first criticism. Employers, it is claimed, would be reluctant to guarantee both wage rates and jobs against cyclical decline because a guarantee of the wage bill would shift all of the variability in the firm's income to profits. And while workers may seek to minimize the risk of (downward) variation in their incomes, the willingness of employers to take risks has limits of its own. (The assumption of differential risk aversion is thus weakened.) As for the workers, they might be unwilling to buy a contract which precludes reductions in employment while allowing wages to vary if their employers cannot be prevented from taking advantage of their ignorance by falsely claiming that business is worse than it really is and then proceeding to reduce wage rates. Since employers would not gain any advantage by reducing employment under a wage-only contract in the same situation, the wage-only guarantee would appear to be rehabilitated (Grossman and Hart, 1983). Under the latter, however, employers may require that their employees work more hours in good times than in bad times, so they now have an incentive to claim that business is *better* than it really is and proceed to make their employees work more hours than they would wish. The upshot seems to be that such a constant-wage contract is associated with "overemployment" and hence can't explain involuntary unemployment (Azariadis and Stiglitz, 1983; Green and Kahn, 1983).

The existence, at least in the U.S., of long-term employment relationships which offer workers significant elements of security along with sticky wage rates in downswings, but which also permit temporary layoffs, is well known to observers. The incidence of these arrangements has been highest in large-scale firms located in the more oligopolistic sectors of the economy. When the latter become subjected to more intensely competitive pressures—which are assumed in this theory—their guarantees are often weakened or even abandoned. Moreover, wage levels have tended to be relatively high, not low, which might suggest that the workers involved have not been paying (or not paying much) for insurance and that employers have not been selling it. The arrangements have depended for their observance on what Okun (1980) called the "invisible handshake," backed by the firm's concern for its reputation as an employer. Finally, breaches have occurred under adverse conditions, recognized as such by both sides; and when employees have sought more binding instruments of enforcement, they sometimes (notably in the thirties) turned unionist in an effort to replace implicit contracts with explicit contracts.

Efficiency wages. A less conventional theory of sticky wages and involuntary unemployment—but one of long standing—holds that employers are reluctant to reduce wages when confronted by a downswing in demand because they fear that doing so would reduce worker efficiency. According to a recent version of this theory (Shapiro and Stiglitz, 1984), the individual worker is deterred from "shirking" only by the probability that he or she will be caught and fired from a job that pays more than he or she could hope to receive elsewhere. If employers wish to reduce wages, they must spend more on "monitoring" (supervision) to prevent increased shirking and loss of productivity; if, instead, they hold the line on wages, shirking will be restrained by the resulting increase in unemployment throughout the economy and the consequent fear of job loss.

In this theory, then, the degree of wage stickiness and the level of unemployment depend in part on the cost of monitoring to the firm; but this conveys an exaggerated impression of the importance of detection of employee inefficiency by shrugging off or ignoring some well-known facts of plant life. Shirking includes absenteeism and tardiness; neither is costly to detect. Workers with bad work habits can be detected and weeded out during short probationary periods. Moreover, discipline is "graded" and applied "progressively," depending both on the gravity of the offense and the number of individual infractions. Hence the probability of dismissal—which is the ultimate punishment and the bottom line for the worker in this model—can be increased even if the probability and cost of detection are not.

Under a different and older version of what is now called the efficiency wage hypothesis, the worker is viewed as regarding a lower level of wages not as a new equilibrium to which he or she will adjust with a correspondingly reduced level of effort, but as a disequilibrium situation which he or she aims at rectifying by an instrumental and temporary withdrawal of efficiency. This response is triggered by a common feeling of inequity and resentment over the breach of an implicit contract, not by a lessened fear of losing a job which appears to have suffered a loss in its relative attractiveness. It takes the form of concerted action, and management's defenses against concerted withdrawals of efficiency are weaker than are its defenses against individual infractions of discipline. Detection is not the primary problem when everyone is breaking rules. Potential economies of exemplary discipline (singling out ringleaders) are restricted in the presence of group cohesiveness; and the cost of multiple replacements is "lumpy" (Ulman, 1987).

Still, restriction of output by unorganized workers has its limitations as a wage-earner weapon. It may avert wage reductions, but the threat of strikes by continuous associations, established over wider competitive areas, is better able "to exact higher wages or more favorable working conditions" (Slichter, 1920, p. 38, n. 1). Informal and ad hoc collective action has not infrequently given way to full-fledged trade unionism and collective bargaining. That sequence, however, is neither inevitable nor irreversible; nor could refusal by employers to reduce wages in bad times always be taken as evidence of a credible threat of unionization. Nevertheless, as Hicks argued in 1932:

> ...even in a market where labour is still unorganised, the principal check of this sort on the action of employers is generally their fear that reductions will stimulate combined resistance (1964, p. 137).

Segmented markets. Some factors that have been assigned causal roles in explanations of unemployment and unresponsive wage levels have also been cited in attempts to account for unresponsive wage structures which mark the boundaries separating labor markets containing good jobs at good wages from labor markets containing bad jobs at low wages. Instead of exerting downward pressure on the higher sectoral wages, the excess supplies of labor available to the "primary" market exert downward pressure on the "secondary" markets. How can this economically perverse result be explained?

Doeringer and Piore (1971) attributed high wages in internal markets in major part to the "tremendous amount of power" (p. 32) conferred on workers who possess job-specific skills (or human capital) and on whom enterprise managers must depend for the training of junior employees. These authors also assigned to "custom" a role in motivating employees to resist changes in wages and other conditions which they had come to regard as established under the terms of an implicit contract. But what was to prevent competition among job applicants (attracted from the secondary sectors) from holding down entry-level wages sufficiently to equalize rates of return on human capital investments and present values of career earnings among the different sectors?

A obvious candidate was trade unionism, which became a ubiquitous feature of these high-wage sectors in the United States after the mid-thirties; or, before that, the threat of unionism in large-scale oligopolistic firms, often with relatively high rates of growth in productivity (Gordon, Edwards, and Reich, 1982; Reich, 1984). Slichter (1929) traced the origin of internal labor markets to big corporations' attempts to preclude a return to unionism by maintaining wages relative to prices in the depression of 1920–1921, a move which "compelled [employers] to make their men more efficient" (p. 40l). This they did "by developing a stable work force and maintaining the good will and cooperation of the men" (*ibid.*) through benefit programs, promotion ladders, and other paternalistic devices which collectively came to be known as "Welfare Capitalism." These same devices made it more feasible for employers to invest in the development of those firm-specific skills that were later assigned a causal role in the analysis of wage differentiation and market segmentation. The imposition of high wages for these reasons meant that individual workers were denied the competitive option of paying for the acquisition of general, or transferable, skills by bidding down entry-level wages; but low rates of turnover resulting from the high wages—and other features of welfare capitalism—presumably made it worthwhile for their employers to finance general as well as specific training. Hildebrand and Delehanty (1966), on the other hand, attributed excess supplies of unskilled labor in the fifties and sixties mainly to the role of collective bargaining in maintaining and increasing relatively high entry-level wages in high-wage jurisdictions.

A more recent analysis views unionism less as a cause of economically inefficient market segmentation than as a beneficent by-product, generated in reaction to and as a preventive of "opportunistic" exploitation of individual monopoly positions by workers endowed with firm-specific expertise. This approach has contributed importantly to information and organization theory; but as an implicit theory of unionism, I find the theory of "idiosyncratic exchange" less convincing than the Keynesian and the historically based models. It is not readily reconciled with the high adversarial content of union-management relations. It may, as well, impute too much individual monopoly power to members of blue-collar work forces, so many of whom hold jobs which are designed to be mastered by semiskilled production workers. Nevertheless, this panglossian model could claim kinship (more or less extended) with more explicit theories which present the union either as improving an otherwise imperfect economy in the course of its collective efforts on behalf of its own members or as ultimately unable to prevail against salutary competitive forces.

Institutional Realities vs. Academic Models

While some economists, who believe that wages tend to be relatively unresponsive to declines in demand, have been trying to explain that phenomenon in the absence of unionism (or other institutional restraints), others have been trying to explain whether, how, or why unions can act "rationally" in opposition to competitive market forces. Ever since the clash between those two ideological Titans of the nineteenth century, the Wages Fund theory and the Lump of Labor cum Purchasing Power theories, differing assessments of the elasticities of labor demand and supply have underlain differences in the assessment of both the economic strength of trade unions and their social utility. Mainstream economists ultimately wriggled out of the strait jacket in which Wages Fund had confined them; and Marshall (1928 ed.) even derived special theoretical conditions (monopsony) under which unions could raise wages (of low-paid and immobile workers) at the expense of profits rather than jobs. But he also warned that normally and in the long run, union power would be subject to restraint by strong forces of competition, substitution, and mobility. A union could find it possible to raise wages significantly and "permanently" only where specified conditions combined to make the demand for the labor of its members "stiff and inelastic" (Marshall, 1927 ed., p. 385) and, further, only where the supply of such labor was also inelastic—lest "interlopers find their way in" (Marshall, 1928 ed., p. 350) and undermine the union wage. However, this early analysis ignored the possible existence of barriers to entry consisting of fixed set-up costs and also of costs of resisting organization with which the level of the union's wage "premium" might vary directly.

Friedman (1951), applying the Marshallian analysis to postwar conditions in the U.S., argued that unionists favored by conditions of inelastic demand were largely confined to a relatively small minority in skilled crafts and that "In many cases, so to speak, unions are simply thermometers registering the heat rather than furnaces producing the heat" (p. 222). For a time, this model of the weak union influenced economists strongly. Most subsequent empirical studies, however, estimated that in the seventies the wages of union members were significantly and substantially higher than those of nonunion members in otherwise comparable circumstances; nor were these differentials (mostly between 15 and 25 per cent) neutralized by favorable differentials in productivity. On the other hand, these postwar premia might be interpreted as a (slowly) passing phenomenon. They were associated with a steep decline in the degree of union organization in the U.S., and this could be taken as evidence that the unions had been helping to put themselves out of business by attracting "interlopers" (foreign as well as domestic) and by making it more worthwhile for established nonunion firms to resist organization.

Analogy to the firm. Acceleration of the decline of American unionism in the eighties was matched by an upsurge in the production of academic models of the union which assumed its ability not only to set wages at premium levels but often to set them at levels of its own choosing. This work had been anticipated by Dunlop's (1950) pioneering model. Analogizing to profit-maximizing by the firm in monopoly theory, he postulated the wage bill as the union's maximand. This was less satisfactory to most of his fellow institutional labor economists and other students of industrial relations than to later economists in the conventional mode.

The institutionalists. The institutionalists, led by Ross (1948), maintained that union wage policy is driven by internal political considerations, instead of conforming to the contours of the relevant economic environment. A more up-to-date institutionalist model might view the union's target wage as a function of the employment position of the membership, but also and more importantly, as a function of such Keynesian variables as relative and real wages, and also of the employer's profitability. Employment can be a political variable (each job is a vote), but it may carry less weight as a determinant of wage policy—owing to the myopia of unionists who ignore the long-run effects of wage increases on employment via substitution by employers and consumers, or to unionists' reliance on their employers to keep employment high by keeping settlements sufficiently below union demands (Mitchell, 1972), or to wishful thinking or willingness to incur risk of job loss (in contrast to the high risk aversion conventionally imputed to the individual wage earner). As a result, unionists have been regarded as prone to view changes in wages and changes in employment as largely independent events. This tendency has prompted the adoption of policies of "nonaccommodation" to adverse market conditions.

On the other hand, the union may also be regarded as a "satisficing" institution which will not always exploit its potential bargaining power to the fullest extent. When economic stagnation or decline threaten what its members regard as minimally acceptable—and equitably imperative—levels of wages or employment, it may well push for the latter to a point where the costs of striking exceed obtainable gains. But in times of economic growth or recovery, the union may be content with settlements which equal or exceed the expectations of the membership while permitting profits, output, and employment to expand. Thus, while unions can be called forth by conditions of stringency which disappoint expectations held by working people, it is economic growth which supplies the lubricant conducive to the continuing viability of collective bargaining.

The "new utilitarians." The payroll maximization model, on the other hand, can be regarded as a special case of the new conventional theory which assumes that the union maximizes the expected utility of its "representative" member. Utility varies directly with the level of the union wage and the probability of being employed at that wage. It also varies directly with whatever compensation (including nonpeuniary satisfaction) the individual can obtain when not so employed; but it varies inversely with the remaining probability of not being employed at the union wage. The union is also assumed to have accurate knowledge of the elasticity of the demand for labor—to recognize that in raising (lowering) its wage it reduces (raises) the probability of employment at the union wage, and by how much. Thus the wage level chosen by the union varies inversely with the elasticity of labor demand, and it varies inversely with the members' degree of risk aversion. In view of the rather high values normally imputed to both variables in conventional analysis, the union wage yielded by these assumptions might be lower than the wage generated by institutionalist models—but this result also reduces the plausibility of the initial assumption of union wage-setting power.

More recent models have attempted to uncover alternative sources of aggressiveness in the presumed ability of the unions to affect either employment or membership independently of their effect on wages. They purport to have identified institutional mechanisms or market conditions that might make the elasticity of employment of most union members low even if the elasticity of demand for labor is high. The former is a more inclusive concept than the latter. The elasticity of membership employment can be taken as the product of (a) the elasticity of employment in union jobs with respect to the union wage (which includes labor demand elasticity as one of its own components) and (b) the elasticity of membership with respect to employment. The first component can reflect certain nonwage activities of unions which could prevent or minimize loss of union jobs in response to higher union wages. The second component is intended to cover the possibility that a loss in union jobs need not result in an equivalent reduction in employment of all or a key subgroup of union members and consequent inhibition of union wage policy. Below, the essential features of the Voice, Efficient Contract, and End Game models are reviewed as an example of the first component. The Insider-Outsider, Competitive, and Seniority models are discussed as examples of the second component.

Keeping Jobs While Raising Wages

A voice or an echo? In adapting the "exit-voice" theory to industrial relations, Freeman (1976, 1980) and Freeman and Medoff (1979) argue that unions can offset their negotiated wage increases by negotiated grievance procedures which, by providing employees with an alternative to quitting and a source of heightened dignity and morale, reduce turnover costs, encourage employer investment in training, and increase productivity and the demand for labor. In its strongest form, this theory suggested that cost increases generated by wage determination under collective bargaining would be neutralized by productivity increases generated by "voice" mechanisms although it did not specify any institutional means of linking wage determination to the grievance procedure. Initial claims that unions exerted as strong a positive effect on productivity as they exerted on wages were dropped as the result of later empirical work, leaving a diminished economic role for the voice mechanism. Nor is there agreement that unions have raised productivity: some econometric studies point to positive impacts; some point to negative effects; some suggest that in certain industries the effect may have changed direction from one period to another (Brown and Medoff, 1978; Clark, 1980, 1984; Allen, 1984, 1986, 1988).

The ambiguity of these results reflects inherent limitations of available data and analytic technique (Hirsch and Addison, 1986); this lack of clarity is also understandable in view of the diversity of union bargaining objectives and techniques. If the informational and motivational virtues of the grievance procedure are conducive to greater productivity, unions' pursuit of historic nonwage objectives—including job security and reduced effort—can produce lower productivity. And these objectives can be pursued through the grievance procedure itself, especially when the alternatives of formal negotiations and authorized striking are barred for the duration of a fixed contract period.[2] The grievance process may function as an informational voice, but it is an adversarial procedure. (When nonunion firms install grievance procedures, they invariably omit the final stage of arbitration by an impartial outsider.)

According to another view, the flip side of increased productivity associated with unionism by the voice theory consists in more onerous or otherwise undesirable conditions of work. The latter might be taken as given and elicit unionism as a way to secure compensatory wage differentials for the workers involved, transforming the union voice into a market echo. Alternatively, poorer nonpecuniary conditions of work can be regarded as adjustments made by employers to offset wage increases wrested from them by union muscle (Duncan and Stafford, 1980). Evidence on the qualitative nature of nonpecuniary conditions of work, however, has tended to be tenuous and contradictory. Moreover, this argument ignores the fact that, at the same time that unions have bargained over pay, they have often sought to reduce required effort or increase security by "bargaining over the production function." Thus instead of a combination of poorer working conditions and higher productivity, collective bargaining could be associated with a combination of favorable working conditions and lower productivity. In contrast with both of these possible outcomes, the voice theory envisions a combination of better conditions and higher productivity. But whatever its shortcomings, this theory has the merit of focusing attention on some of the nonwage bargaining activities of the union.

Efficient contracts and restrictive practices. If the voice theory suggests that unions, through devices like the grievance procedure, make it profitable for employers to hire more labor at the union wage, efficient contract theory asserts that unions oblige employers to hire more labor than they would wish to at that wage. However, the economist regards the outcome of this double-barreled deployment of union monopoly power as "efficient" because, unlike wage-only bargaining, it is not characterized by a level of employment which would simultaneously leave the employer wanting to hire more labor and the members of the work force wanting to sell more labor at some lower

---

[2] According to two studies, lower quit rates in unionized firms reflect the greater availability of strikes to their employees as well as other factors (Pencavel, 1970; Ulman and Sorensen, 1984).

wage.[3]

Collective agreements, however, have only rarely specified minimum overall levels of employment or total wage bills, which Leontief (1946) had anticipated. Nevertheless, McDonald and Solow (1981) suggested that the same result might—although it need not (Ulman, 1955)—be approximated via the large variety of working arrangements which have been frequently negotiated or protected under collective bargaining. Like the voice theory, these models take important nonwage bargaining activities of unions into account. But it is ironic that arrangements which are labeled in everyday life as "restrictive practices" because they result in the wasteful deployment of labor should be classified by economists as "efficient contracts" because they prevent management from employing too little labor. Such efficiency must be recognized to be a very narrow and private concept and can indeed make for inefficiency in a global context. By obliging firms to employ too much labor in the production of a given level of output, unions may raise unit costs—which would result in the production of too little output and ultimately the employment of too little labor overall in the unionized sectors of the economy.

End game—a silver lining? A recent application of Marshallian demand analysis found a source of lower elasticity of labor demand and hence increased union bargaining power in *declining* levels (or growth) of demand in the seventies. Lower (or in some cases zero) investment in more modern labor-saving plant and equipment could be counted on to reduce management's ability to substitute capital for labor and therefore to encourage the unions to press for higher wage increases (Lawrence and Lawrence, 1985). It has been widely presumed, on the other hand, that as demand for the output of these U.S. manufacturing industries declined under the stimulus of increased foreign competition, it became more elastic; and increased price elasticity of product demand *per se* would make for increased wage elasticity of labor demand. Thus if labor became relatively more essential in production, its output became less essential to its employer's customers. Moreover, even if labor substitutability in production is assumed to be a more important influence than product substitutability in consumption, the argument implies that negotiated wage increases should decline during periods of industrial growth, as the authors themselves observe. It might then be more plausible to argue that unions, having demonstrated a persistent

---

[3] One example of such an efficient contract would occur if the firm agreed to employ exactly as much labor at the union wage as it would have at a competitively determined wage (Hall and Lilien, 1979).

tendency to underestimate employers' capacity to substitute capital for labor in better times, happened to get things right in bad times; and that, in any event, they could distill short-term bargaining power from employers' financial and even competitive weakness.

Counting Heads While Losing Jobs

Insiders and outsiders. Another theory, based on the relationship between "insiders" and "outsiders," has also regarded economic decline as a source of union-imposed wage increases, but only when that decline is unanticipated and comes as a "shock" (Blanchard and Summers, 1986). The union is regarded as intent on setting the highest wage for its current members that is consistent with their continued employment. If it anticipates a decline in demand, it would reduce the wage by enough to induce the employer to leave the level of employment unchanged, provided labor demand is sufficiently elastic, or responsive to a wage cut. But if the decline in demand comes as an unanticipated "shock," the employer makes the first adjustment by reducing employment. Because membership is conditioned on employment in the bargaining sector, reducing employment reduces the current membership. After employment has been cut, the union would not seek to reduce wages in order to regain its former level; indeed, if demand for output is expected to recover following the shock, the union would press for a higher wage that would preclude an increase to the pre-shock levels of employment and membership. Yesterday's employment is yesterday's membership is history. Thus, the reduced level of employment tends to perpetuate itself (i.e., "hysteresis") by inducing the surviving insiders to ratchet up their wage.

The hypothesis that the union would not seek to restrain its wage in the interests of those beyond the pale of membership has been invoked to help explain the concentration of unemployment among new entrants to the labor force (mainly school-leavers and women) under centralized bargaining in European countries in the second half of the seventies (Flanagan, Soskice, and Ulman, 1983). And this theory, with the inclusion of the shock hypothesis, has been used to explain the persistence of high levels of unemployment in the major European countries since the early eighties (Lindbeck and Snower, 1986; Blanchard and Summers, 1986).

However, the usefulness of the first proposition—that the union *would* restrain its wage in the interest of its current membership when adverse conditions are anticipated—is problematical. Given that assumption, the occurrence of a shock is required to explain subsequent wage rigidity or advancement. But why would not an employer feel encouraged to respond to an adverse shock by requesting a wage cut, or similar "concession," from a union which he knows to have been "normally" congenial to such an action before he decides whether to pass out the pink slips? This model denies that option to the employer because it assumes that the union has the exclusive power to set wages. Therefore the union must act as if in unilateral conformity with a Doctrine of the Immaculate Concession, under foreseeably adverse conditions. In real life, of course, concession bargaining typically originates with employer requests. When adversely impacted employers do *not* approach unions before laying off their members, it is presumably because they are deterred by the belief, based on accumulated experience, that such a quest would be futile (or too costly). The union snub would have issued from an ingrained belief in the inelasticity of demand and hence the suspicion that wage restraint is a highly dubious venture, as well as one in which those who bear the costs stand to reap little or no gain. And if unions do not subordinate their wage policies to the job security interests of their own members, it should come as no surprise that they fail to subordinate their wage policies to the employment interests of other workers.

Nor does union rejection of wage flexibility as a means of maintaining or increasing employment necessarily imply a lack of concern about unemployment; neither does it connote a lack of determination to reach that objective by other means. Hiring of outsiders may result from a variety of make-work and share-work rules and incentives.[4] Unsurprisingly, the outcomes of these incentives, which increase unit costs, have often disappointed their sponsors. Their effectiveness in maintaining or increasing employment is likely to be greater in the short run than in the long run, when demand becomes more elastic—just as the effectiveness of wage flexibility is likely to be greater in the long run than in the short run.

The hiring of outsiders also may serve the interests of those already in the union. I have discussed how a union (modeled on institutionalist lines) might realistically settle for a wage which permits expansion of output and employment provided that it can thereby satisfy some "externally" generated conditions of acceptability to the membership. And in so doing it could reduce not only the probability of occurrence or probable duration of a strike but also (via an increase in membership) the per capita fixed costs of unionism. Thus, the implication of insider-outsider theory that a union will necessarily exploit an anticipated growth in demand by raising wages to

---

[4] For example, the introduction of "penalty pay" for overtime in the U.S. was originally intended to induce the hiring of additional shifts. Recent negotiated reductions in the length of the standard work week by major German unions have also been designed to reduce unemployment.

levels high enough to preclude growth in employment must be rejected. Similarly untenable is Simons' (1944, p. 132) classic precursor of contemporary insider-outsider theory, according to which a labor leader, "should...seek, controlling prices via labor costs, to restrict production as rapidly as consistent with decline of my membership by death and retirement...." Since the last surviving member happily rakes in a handsome pot, I have dubbed this model of institutional suicide the Cheshire Cat theory.

Finally, we might ask whether the restrictive membership assumption—at the heart of insider-outsider theory—is in fact a significant determinant of union wage policy. It has been suggested (in part as a policy spinoff of this theory) that the unemployed outsiders in an industry be permitted to vote in union elections on strikes and collective bargaining outcomes. The presumption is that they would vote against wage changes that would preclude their re-employment. But even if they did so—and even if labor demand is assumed to be elastic and accepted as such by all the voters involved—the unemployed voters normally would be heavily outnumbered by the employed voters (who theoretically should always press for the highest wage consistent with the maintenance of their status as job-holders). Thus, it makes little if any difference whether those currently jobless are excluded as outsiders or included as insiders.

The competitive theory: counting those on the outside in. According to this model (Lazear, 1983b), workers are displaced by the imposition of a union wage on their employers, but, instead of becoming unemployed, they are hired by nonunion firms in the same sector, as the latter find it profitable to resist the union and pay a lower wage. Thus the union's bargaining power is determined, among other things, by costs of nonunion operation. The model, however, includes employees in nonunion firms as members of the union, whose welfare varies directly with the level of the *nonunion* wage as well as the union wage. The union must make the best of a wage-wage instead of a wage-employment tradeoff: it will set the union wage high enough to induce the formation of a nonunion sector within its jurisdiction, but not one so large that it will make the probability of working at that wage too low or that it will induce too low a *non*union wage for which some of its members must work.

In depicting the economy as a group of partially organized sectors, this theory accords with the reality of much of the contemporary American scene. And if more unions were to allow their wage policies to be more influenced by nonunion competition, they might begin to achieve a state of equilibrium in their current environment. But in most cases, of course, membership in a union does not extend beyond the territory occupied by its collective bargaining contracts. And even in jurisdictions where the duration of the job is short and members may go in and out of nonunion work, unions typically have rationalized their wage policies on the belief— or in the hope—that "the best organizing weapon is a good contract" and that raising the union wage might shrink the nonunion sector rather than their own domain.

Seniority: counting some on the inside out. Another theory finds the key to union wage behavior in the institution of seniority, combined with majority rule (e.g., Oswald, 1987; Blair and Crawford, 1984). This combination should result in the determination of a wage level that causes a loss of employment which is concentrated in a large minority of lower-seniority employees. Presumably the wage will be set low enough to accommodate the continued employment of the "median voter" in the union and high enough to terminate the employment of the minority with lower seniority. This model is a more cold-blooded variant of the insider-outsider model— one in which some of the insiders (as well as outsiders) are excluded from employment by a wage voted on by the majority of insiders in full knowledge of its probable employment consequences. It betrays the same tendency to institutional suicide characteristic of the Cheshire Cat model: each successive wage-setting leaves a smaller (and more senior) work force in its wake.[5]

American unions have pushed very hard for the seniority principle, primarily because it has served as the most tangible embodiment of their historic objectives of job security and "equity." In this respect, however, they have viewed it primarily as administering *temporary* layoffs in the course of a continuing and long-term employment relationship, and they have invariably combined layoff seniority with recall seniority. In this capacity, layoff seniority could command the support of short-service as well as senior employees, because the former could "see a reasonably good prospect of soon becoming members of the preferred group" (Slichter, 1941, p. 129). The younger worker could expect to enjoy the gains from a current settlement over a longer period in the future than could an older worker. And while the younger worker must accept a greater chance than the older one of being laid off after a given settlement, his or her costs of layoff will be lower because wages foregone will be lower, both in absolute terms and relative to income from alternative sources. Thus, the layoff cost of a settlement that is demanded by the more senior and secure members of a union would not necessarily be regarded by their lower paid and less secure junior

---

[5] This has been regarded as "a disturbing implication" by two proponents (Blair and Crawford, 1984, p. 556).

colleagues as unacceptably high.

Hence, the divergence of economic interests between workers with greater and less seniority is probably smaller than would be suggested by the difference between their average layoff probabilities. Nor is there reason to believe—as this theory would suggest (Blair and Crawford, 1984)—that the wage policies of unions that ration work through rotary hiring halls (which conform to the usual theoretical assumption that all members face the same probability of employment) have been any more restrained than the wage policies followed by seniority unions.

Conclusions

The importance of concerted behavior by workers and the importance of equitable comparison, feelings of injustice, and economic shortsightedness in motivating such behavior are suggested by the inadequacies of some of the leading models of labor market activity which rely on more academically conventional behavioral assumptions. One reason why unorganized markets sometimes behave as if they were unionized is that unorganized workers sometimes behave like unionists, seeking to maintain their wage rates by concerted action. I do not claim here that these workers can succeed invariably or indefinitely in the face of declining demand or excess supply of labor. (Nor do I deny that involuntary unemployment might occur when wages fall flexibly.) But other phenomena—prospective cuts in relative wages, specific human capital, implicit contracting, the difficulty and cost of detecting individual shirkers—are not convincing *per se* as deterrents to downward wage flexibility, although they may perform other important functions.

The second part of my double-barreled proposition levels a general charge of unreality against contemporary academic models of the trade union. In this paper, we have come across unions that increase the ability of employers to pay the wages that they negotiate (Voice theory), but we have also encountered unions that oblige employers to hire more labor than they would wish at negotiated wages (Efficient Contracts). We have made the acquaintance of unions that set their wages with an eye to controlling the wages set by nonunion firms in the same industries (Competitive theory), of unions that would raise wages in declining industries and by the same token lower wages in growing ones (End Game), of unions that would keep their wages at higher levels when unemployment is high and membership low than when unemployment is low and membership high (Insider-Outsider), of unions that would always keep their wages low enough to provide work for the older majority of their members and high enough to exclude the younger minority from employment, thereby continuing to raise wages as employment and membership shrink, in a process of institutional suicide (Seniority).

Two factors might account for this diversity and distortion. Diversity and distortion can result when different economists, at work on different problems (or on different approaches to the same problem), assign different roles to the trade union and are satisfied with single-purpose models which may or may not accord with essential features of institutional reality. Eliciting institutional behavior in the solution of some wider economic or social problem can provide new insights into the nature of the institution itself, particularly when the investigators hold perspectives different from those held by specialists in industrial relations. But such models should incorporate or accommodate generally accepted performance characteristics of the union.

The proliferation of incongruities to which this paper has directed attention has also stemmed from the manifest unwillingness of economists in the contemporary neoclassical mode to relax their traditional behavioral assumptions of individual utility maximization and rational expectations, which have been borrowed from theories of atomistically competitive markets, in order to accommodate elements of discretion and satisficing, equitable comparison, and economic myopia, which have been traditional components of institutionalist explanations of union behavior. To the contemporary neoclassicists, the assumption of utility maximization possesses the virtues of simplicity and universality: it is the driving force in capital and product markets; it motivates employers and workers in their individual decision-making; it overrides cultural differences and is impervious to historical change. But a price has had to be paid for ignoring some of the awkward but stubborn evidence provided by the historical record, specialist observation, and behavioral science. It has taken the form of ad hoc models which in some instances have featured sharply divergent behavioral characteristics and have caricatured institutional reality. Some of the economists who pioneered in the development of basic analytic concepts declined to sacrifice what they accepted as institutional reality on the altar of theoretical consistency or analytic convenience. Some of them even sought to account for a wider range of motivation in their analyses of individual behavior, and, in so doing, helped to soften the distinction drawn between individual and group behavior in labor markets. As some contemporary efforts along these lines attract more support and encouragement, they should empower the construction of more recognizable and useful models of trade unionism and other forms of concerted behavior. And if comparative and historical studies of labor relations can proceed with an eye to their wider economic significance, the economists should be provided with more sharply defined standards of institutional relevance.

The Economics of Unions and Collective Bargaining

ROBERT J. FLANAGAN*

This paper reviews recent research on the economics of unions and collective bargaining, emphasizing the implications for human resource management. Research findings on the impact of unions, strategic union avoidance behavior by management, strategic use of labor law by unions and employers, and conflict and conflict resolution in labor relations are discussed. The paper highlights unexploited connections between research on union impact and research on strategic behavior.

RESEARCH INTO THE ECONOMICS of unions, collective bargaining, and labor-management relations has grown, even as the coverage of unions has declined in the United States and some other Western countries. This paper explores the implications of some major research developments for human resource management and notes some unexploited research opportunities.

There have been two general branches of research into the economics of unions and collective bargaining in the past decade. One, in addressing the outcomes associated with the presence of unions, has developed sharper factual profiles of union and nonunion employment settings; the other has explored the nature of strategic behavior by the parties to collective bargaining, working out how labor and management respond to and influence union-related outcomes. Although the two branches are logically connected— rational strategic behavior occurs in response to actual or expected outcomes associated with unions—research on outcomes and strategy has generally proceeded independently. This paper develops some of the connections between the two branches and examines their implications for human resource management.

---
* Graduate School of Business, Stanford University. The author thanks Janet Spitz for research assistance and the Graduate School of Business, Stanford University for research support.

Lessons from Studies of Union Impact

Research on the outcomes of unions and collective bargaining has undermined any notion that nonunion human resource managers passively follow and adopt employment practices established under collective bargaining. During the eighties, studies have continued to document and extend the list of significant differences in outcomes associated with unionism.

Compensation. Union wage effects is one of the most frequently investigated topics in empirical economics. In finding that union workers received a wage premium of 10 to 15 per cent over "equivalent" nonunion workers, Lewis (1963) virtually "invented a field of study."[1] His study occurred before the development of large and detailed microeconomic data bases and the techniques to analyze them. However, in a recent evaluation of over 200 econometric studies of union-nonunion pay differentials, Lewis found a similar average wage impact of unions, even after controlling for many other influences on wages and after considering the effects of advances in research methodology since the publication of his earlier study (Lewis, 1986). The new study and the papers that it analyzes also reveal considerable dispersion of union wage effects by sector, by demographic group, and over time. The union wage gap "...is greater for black workers than for white..., for nonmanufacturing than for manufacturing,...for blue-collar than for white-collar workers, for laborers than for operatives, for operatives than for craftsmen, for the South than for the Northeast region, for small cities than for large, for private than for government employees, for hazardous than for other work, for other marital status than for the married" (*ibid.*, p. 8). The gap also increased during the seventies.

Despite its vastness, the literature on union wage and compensation effects offers almost no discussion of why these measurements are of interest either generally or from the perspective of human resource management. Clearly, unions are able to use bargaining power to raise wages in most instances, and just as clearly, nonunion employers do not fully match union wages in some general reaction to a union "threat." Beyond this, the exercise in measurement has been accompanied by very little interpretation.

There are at least three potential uses of measurements of union relative pay effects. First, and most broadly, the measurements may be used to assess the allocative efficiency losses attributable to union wage bargaining.

---

[1] The phrase is Reder's (1988, p. 139). Interestingly, this new field of study was limited to North America and the United Kingdom. In other countries, more comprehensive bargaining arrangements or the legal extension of collective bargaining provisions to nonunion firms limited interest in the question.

The last use of estimates of union relative wage effects for this purpose seems to have been over 25 years ago.[2] Union relative wages increased during the seventies, but union relative employment declined. The net effect of these changes is unknown, since no new estimates of the allocative efficiency losses have been published, perhaps because during the eighties attention turned toward the direct effects of unions on productivity.

The other two potential uses of union relative wage measurements—research into the reasons for and the effects of the variance in union relative pay effects—are more pertinent to human resource management. There have been surprisingly few attempts to explain the variance in wage outcomes associated with unionization. Why does the presence of a union in one sector produce a relative wage effect two to three times larger than in some other sector? What accounts for variations in union and employer bargaining power? Why do union wage effects vary over time? The only efforts to answer such questions are in studies of the relationship between bargaining structure and union wage impact. These studies find that after controlling for the characteristics of industries and workers, wages tend to be higher under multi-employer bargaining units in local product markets than in single employer units, and that unions achieve more generous contracts in company-wide bargaining units than in industry-wide bargaining units, at least in national product markets (Hendricks, 1975; Hendricks and Kahn, 1984; Feuille, Hendricks, and Kahn, 1981).

Human resource management could also benefit from studies of the effects of union-nonunion pay differentials on labor relations behavior. The fact that differentials of this size and variability should influence the strategies of management and labor in all aspects of labor relations has received little attention until very recently. (Studies discussing the economic responses to unions are discussed later in this paper.)

Productivity. For years, anecdotal evidence of restrictive production practices by some unions in the construction, printing, and transportation industries fueled the belief that unions tended to reduce productivity while raising relative wages. For example, one student of the impact of unions on labor markets observed over 25 years ago that losses from "direct restrictions of output through control of manning requirements, the work pace, and work practices, often called 'featherbedding,'... probably exceed the social losses from relative wage effects" (Rees, 1963, p. 75). In fact, the anecdotal evidence contained significant ambiguity, as nonunion firms provided some

---

[2] Using Lewis' estimates, Rees (1963) concluded the loss in real output attributable to union wage effects to be 0.14 per cent of gross national product in 1957.

of the earliest examples of the informal development of group production norms and restrictive practices by workers (Matthewson, 1931).

Systematic studies of the relationship between productivity levels and unionization have appeared only in the past decade, and they have produced the most provocative findings of research into the effects of unions: Labor productivity appears to be higher in unionized settings. Cross-sectional studies of manufacturing and construction find average productivity differentials of approximately 20 per cent associated with the presence of unions, although in construction the union advantage appears to emerge mainly on larger objects (e.g., see Allen, 1984, 1987; Brown and Medoff, 1978). In the one (small) panel study comparing labor productivity in several plants before and after unionization, the effect of unionization was also positive, but about one-third the size of the effect measured in the cross-sectional studies (Clark, 1980). Nevertheless, its persistence across several studies in different settings suggests that the result is not a statistical artifact.

As with studies of union impact on compensation, these studies have been more effective in measuring differentials than in explaining their source. Many control for the effects of differences in capital intensity and labor quality, for example—important factors that human resource managers might adjust in response to union pay pressures—before measuring the relationship between union representation and productivity. What else could be at work? Some have conjectured that the union productivity effect reflects such factors as improved morale from the establishment of systems of industrial jurisprudence (grievance procedures and other contractual constraints on supervisory discretion), the morale effects of high wages (and the lower quit rates that result), and increases in firm-specific skills in response to higher union wages. Research on the connections between specific industrial relations practices and productivity is slim. One study of a multi-plant company indicates that the unionized plants (each with a grievance procedure) have higher labor productivity than the company's one nonunion plant, but productivity declines as the grievance rate increases. Nevertheless, productivity at union plants with high grievance rates exceeded productivity in nonunion plants (Ichniowski, 1986). There is very little additional evidence available.

The productivity studies present two paradoxes. First, despite statistical evidence that unions are associated with higher productivity, they are not accepted by employers as highly valuable management consultants. Indeed, there is ample evidence, addressed later in this paper, that most employers oppose demands for recognition by unions and that employer associations oppose proposed labor law reforms that might aid unionism. One reason is that the combined union productivity and wage effects may produce little gain in unit labor costs. The evidence that profits are lower in union settings confirms this possibility (Freeman and Medoff, 1984; Voos and Mishel, 1986) and raises the second paradox: Many of the practices conjectured to account for higher productivity in union establishments could be implemented unilaterally by nonunion managers without incurring an offsetting union wage effect, but in general such changes are not undertaken.

Here the difficulty appears to be a principal-agent problem. Some of the practices that raise productivity in union settings may place constraints on the prerogatives and discretion that managers value in a nonunion setting. Managers may oppose such practices in order to protect their power and discretion. This is done at a sacrifice of profit, and it is not clear whether the market disciplines this deviation from value maximization. Shareholders clearly associate unions with lower profits (Ruback and Zimmerman, 1984), but it is not known whether a failure to adopt union employment practices without the union results in falling share prices. The market for corporate control appears to be the main device for disciplining this principal-agent problem.

Collective choice and union outcomes. If research into union outcomes shows that nonunion human resource managers do not mechanically emulate employment practices that accompany unionization, it also poses the question of why personnel practices established through collective bargaining should differ from those established in nonunion bureaucratic settings. In modern terminology, why do explicit employment contracts codify different practices than implicit employment contracts? Remarkably, formal theories of unions provide no guidance. Not only do these theories fail to predict the difference in contract arrangements between the union and nonunion sectors, they fail, as well, to predict major new developments within the union sector, such as the spread of concession bargaining in the eighties and the particular forms that concession bargaining has taken.[3]

The difficulty appears to be that the structure of formal economic theories of unions bears little resemblance to decision-making in unions. The theories are logical extensions of models of consumer or firm behavior. But unions are more like governments than firms, and most important decisions affecting union policy—e.g., the election of officers, the ratification of collective bargaining agreements—are determined by voting. It is well-known that in a world of voting, the notion of a "typical union member" or a "union utility function" is not well-defined. Indeed, the resolution of the conflicting

---

[3] Farber (1986), Oswald (1985), and Pencavel (1985) provide throughful reviews of this literature.

objectives of union leaders and union members, a standard challenge to union organizations, is assumed away in formal economic models of unions.

Because most major decisions in unions are made by a vote of the membership or their elected representatives, union objectives are more likely to be governed by the objectives of the median union member. On the other hand, the policies of human resource managers in nonunion settings are more likely to be governed by the interests of the marginal employees. Thus, union contracts are more likely to reflect the interests of older, more senior workers than are nonunion employment arrangements, and many differences in union and nonunion employment arrangements can be rationalized through this argument (Freeman and Medoff, 1984). For example, fringe benefits comprise a comparatively large proportion of union pay, and seniority is given much greater weight in allocating employment opportunities in the union sector.

The median voter argument also provides insight into the incidence and form of union wage concessions. When layoffs are determined by seniority, a fixed-wage policy amounts to income insurance for the median (seniority) union workers as long as fluctuations in demand are moderate. When substantial business declines threaten the job security of the median voter, as occurred in some industries in the early eighties, wage concessions and a shift to more flexible compensation arrangements (e.g., profit sharing) can survive a ratification vote (Flanagan, 1984b). The preference for adopting two-tier wage structures (providing a lower rate for new employees) rather than a general rate reduction also is easily rationalized by self-interested voting by current union members. It seems likely that further progress in predicting union behavior could be made through further analyses of unions as collective choice organizations.

Strategic Behavior in Labor Relations

Bargaining and strategy are at the heart of relationships between organized labor and management. Yet, not only did the earlier literature on the measurement of union outcomes fail to explain the variations in measurements, it also often neglected the effects of differences in union and nonunion outcomes on the strategic behavior of management and labor. Research into the nature of strategic behavior in labor relations has increased since the seventies, as economists have attempted to understand the extent to which the unprecedented and precipitous decline in unionization is tied to behavioral choices by the parties to labor relations.

Economic theory stresses that changes in unionization will result from three kinds of responses to changing incentives—changes in the spending patterns of consumers, changes in the production methods and human resource policies of firms, and, given the voluntary nature of most unionism in the United States, changes in worker demand for union representation.

Adjustments by consumers. When union productivity effects do not offset union relative wage effects (and they generally do not), the relative price of union-produced goods and services should increase, inducing some consumers to shift their purchases elsewhere, and thus tending to reduce union employment. Important shifts in consumer spending patterns to products produced in less unionized industries in the United States and to products produced abroad have occurred since the rise of the union relative wage in the seventies. (Moreover, the latter shift was enhanced by the rise of the dollar in the first half of the eighties.)

Nevertheless, the earliest research into the decline of unionization in the U.S. established that shifts in the distribution of jobs between industries with high and low degrees of unionization explained only a small fraction of the decline in unionization (Farber, 1985). These studies indicate that the more important issue is why the degree of unionization has declined in *every* industry. Some part of this is attributable to consumer substitution from union to nonunion output within the same industries. The number of domestic nonunion alternatives grew substantially: In a few industries, deregulation reducing important barriers to entry was followed by the expansion of largely nonunion activity; in other industries, nonunion alternatives were increased by the union avoidance activities of firms.

Union avoidance by firms. Company strategies leading to expansion of the nonunion sector of an industry or company have only begun to receive research attention. The elements of a firm's union avoidance strategy include decisions regarding future investments, plant location, adoption of internal human resource management policies, and stance toward labor relations laws. Of these, the study of internal human resource management policies has been left by default to specialists in organizational behavior. The issue of compliance with labor relations law has received substantial research attention and is reviewed below. Research cited below indicates that the other investment decisions have increasingly been used as central elements of union avoidance strategies.

Investment decisions present unionized firms with an opportunity to choose among (1) expanding an existing unionized facility, (2) negotiating with the union over the establishment of a new facility with union representation (e.g., the Saturn plant of General Motors), or (3) opening a new nonunion plant. Each alternative has both advantages and disadvantages.

Option (1) may offer the possibilities of economies of scale along with union costs and contractual rules. Option (2) retains union representation but may offer advantages if, as in the case of the GM Saturn agreement with the United Automobile Workers, it provides the opportunity to negotiate a novel labor relations system. Option (3) provides the opportunity for a company to implement flexible work systems unilaterally and to locate a new plant in an area where the odds that workers will choose union representation are low. The growing cost associated with being unionized during the seventies and the increased intensity of competition should have tilted the choice toward investing in nonunion operations, and survey evidence indicates that this did occur (Kochan, McKersie, and Chalykoff, 1986). Despite suggestive case studies (e.g., Verma, 1985), however, there has not yet been a systematic economic analysis of this aspect of a company's strategic labor relations choices.

Worker demand for unionization. Survey evidence indicates that while most union members are satisfied with their representation, the fraction of nonunion workers desiring union representation has decreased. Increased job satisfaction and increasing doubts that unions can improve wages and working conditions play a role in declining demand. This development raises strategic issues for unions that have received little attention. If the dramatic layoffs of union members that occurred despite efforts to preserve union jobs with wage concessions raise doubts among unorganized workers that unions can improve working conditions, how should unions evaluate potential concessions? Do unions find it increasingly difficult to differentiate their product because social legislation that they support covers union and nonunion workers alike? Or does social legislation raise the demand for unions to monitor the application of social regulations by government agencies? Research findings on these issues are few and they are inconsistent (Neumann and Rissman, 1984; Freeman, 1987). In the face of aggressive resistance to union organizing, should unions spread their resources thinly or concentrate on the most likely targets? Interestingly, in the face of a hostile National Labor Relations Board during the mid-eighties, unions petitioned for many fewer elections, but they began to win a higher per cent of them. This raises the general question of strategic use of labor relations laws.

NLRA strategy. The easiest way to appreciate the general confusion that exists regarding the effects of the National Labor Relations Act (NLRA) on labor relations is to consider three arguments that have been advanced to support some degree of deregulation of labor relations. The oldest deregulation argument urges abolition of the NLRA because it facilitates cartelization of the labor market. This argument assumes that the Act has produced superior outcomes for unionized labor. More recently, however, some representatives of labor have argued that deregulation would assist unions because the administration of the Act by the NLRB now results in worse outcomes than would be obtained under deregulation. Finally, some academics and practitioners, noting that many NLRB regulations do not contribute to the objectives of the NLRA, have argued for at least partial deregulation of labor relations.

Increased regulatory conflict occurred into the early eighties. Between 1955 and 1980, the annual number of unfair labor practice charges grew by 38,000, and charges against employers from 4,300 to 31,200 per year.[4] Remedial awards by the NLRB also increased significantly. Over the same period, unions lost an increasing proportion of representation elections; and even when they did win elections, unions had more difficulty in concluding collective bargaining agreements. The correlations with the decline in union membership are so dramatic that casual empiricism is almost irresistible.

Research has shown that the connection between regulatory conflict, labor relations outcomes, and union membership trends is more tenuous than commonly assumed. There are two reasons for this. First, the results of representation elections have only a small bearing on the growth of union membership. Membership also varies with cyclical and secular changes in the employment level at organized plants, with plant closures, and (for a given success rate in representation elections) with the intensity of union organizing activity. All of these factors have contributed to the decline in union membership (Dickens and Leonard, 1985).

Second, the connections between illegal behavior and election outcomes are not well-determined. Estimating the effect of illegal activity on representation election outcomes has proved difficult because many factors other than regulated campaign behavior also influence voting behavior. Workers are not uninformed voters, swayed by each new campaign promise or tactic. Most enter a union representation campaign with fairly strong predispositions about how they will vote on the basis of their knowledge of employment conditions, job satisfaction, and expectations of likely union influence (Getman, Goldberg, and Herman, 1976). A few economic studies of union membership have carried this idea to an extreme by assuming that the tactics of a union representation campaign have no bearing on workers' assessments of the net benefits of union membership (Farber and Saks,

---

[4] Unfair labor practice charges also increased in Canada, which takes a similar approach to regulating labor relations.

1980; Lee, 1978).

If general studies of union representation rarely consider the effects of campaign behavior, studies of union elections go to the other extreme by rarely controlling for noncampaign influences before testing for the effects of noncampaign behavior. The implicit assumption of these studies, that the unionization choice would be random in the absence of regulation, is not supported by the broader analyses of union representation. When noncampaign factors in union elections are controlled for, the impact of specific unfair labor practices is uncertain and controversial (Getman *et al.*, 1976; Dickens, 1983). Underlying the controversy is the behavioral question of whether increased employer resistance thwarts unionization by raising the costs of establishing unions or assists unionization by convincing workers that the only way to counter employer power is by forming collective organizations. Studies of representation elections produce wide agreement, however, that delays in holding elections, whether due to procedural maneuvers or to congestion in the adjudication system, reduce the probability that a union will win an election.

The compliance choice. Compliance with the NLRA is no more assured than with other laws and regulations. The puzzle is why legal conflict under the Act grew sharply into the early eighties and then declined. In a field as contentious as labor relations, it is all too easy to attribute observed changes in the behavior of the parties to unobserved changes in ideology. Such explanations fail to address a basic question: If it was in the interests of employers to resist unions in the seventies, why was it not in their interest to do so in the fifties? Although employer noncompliance receives most attention, the interests of both management and labor are pertinent, for regulatory noncompliance is not observed unless it is challenged by the filing of unfair labor practice charges by a union or worker. If rational employers consider the benefits and costs of noncompliance, rational unions and workers consider the benefits and costs of challenging employer behavior by filing unfair labor practice charges. The volume of regulatory litigation depends on both. Moreover, the parties act strategically in the sense that they choose with knowledge of the likely response of their adversary.

Recent economic analyses of strategic behavior in labor relations show that behavior sometimes viewed as ideological is in fact a response to changing compliance and enforcement incentives (Flanagan, 1987, 1989). Primary among these incentives is the growth in the difference between the cost of union labor and the cost of nonunion labor during the seventies, which provided incentives for employers (who had more to lose) to violate the Act and to unions (who had more to gain) to file charges claiming noncompliance with the Act. Findings such as these show that litigation under the Act is often driven by incentives that are beyond the sphere of regulatory influence. Even if the Board were permitted to fashion punitive remedies, their effect could be overwhelmed by economic incentives, such as changing relative union labor costs, that are beyond the direct influence of the NLRB.

These observations help to explain the reversal in the trend in unfair labor practices charges during the eighties. First, the volume of activity subject to regulation declined with a fall in the annual number of representation elections as unions became more selective about their organizing targets and more discriminating in their use of the strike. Second, beginning around 1982, there was a reversal in one of the main influences on the growth of regulatory litigation during the seventies. After 13 years of growth, the union relative wage began to decline, in the face of concession bargaining. Third, the rulings of the NLRB indicated that in many areas of regulation, charges by unions would receive a less sympathetic hearing than previously. With declining odds of success, unions had less incentive to file charges, although the same development would have encouraged employers to adopt more tactics at the borderline of the law.

In comparison to other countries, the responses of American management to changing incentives may appear extreme, but unionized American employers are not as insulated from (domestic) competition by the broad bargaining structures found in many European countries. The choices and accidents of labor history that have produced a comparatively decentralized collective bargaining system have conditioned the sharp management responses to changing market incentives.

Many unexploited opportunities remain for the application of strategic analysis to labor relations. To date, research has focused on one or another element of the strategic choices facing employers or unions. Broader choices facing human resource managers, such as that between opening nonunion plants or union resistance via noncompliance with labor relations law, have not yet received careful attention but can be analyzed with the techniques that have been applied more narrowly in early work.

Conflict and Conflict Resolution

Research in several of the social sciences has extended our understanding of the mechanisms of conflict and its resolution. Because of the central role of work stoppages in collective bargaining, conflict can be observed directly and studies of strikes, lockouts, and arbitration can be used to evaluate alternative theories of the sources of conflict and alternative approaches to conflict resolution.

Strikes produce agreement because they impose costs on both parties to a negotiation. The parties to collective bargaining therefore have an incentive to avoid these costs by developing arrangements that minimize strike costs (Reder and Neumann, 1980), and most negotiations settle without a work stoppage. Strikes result in only 15 to 20 per cent of collective bargaining negotiations in North America.[5] Strikes may be avoided by mutual acceptance of certain protocols—such as the Experimental Negotiating Agreement adopted in steel negotiations between 1974 and 1980 in which unresolved national bargaining issues were referred to an arbitration board for resolution. Alternatively, high strike costs may encourage the use of other means, such as the regulatory system, to achieve objectives. Unions in a strong bargaining position rarely need to allege violations of the duty to bargain, for example.

Sources of conflict. Why does conflict occur? Until recently, discussions of strikes foundered on the Hicks paradox—if both parties understand the costs of conflict in advance, they should adopt the terms of settlement in advance, thereby sharing a pie that is larger by the avoided costs of conflict. It is hardly satisfactory to label the relatively few stoppages that do take place as mistakes—particularly when many occur in long-standing bargaining relationships conducted by experienced negotiators. Moreover, it is difficult to attribute certain empirical regularities in strike behavior to negotiating "mistakes." Both the incidence and settlement rates of strikes are procyclical, for example. (Strike duration is counter cyclical.) Due to the effects of heterogeneity, in the United States and Canada the probability that a strike will settle declines as the strike continues (Wilson and Kennan, 1988). Much of the modern strike literature seeks to address the Hicks paradox and make sense of the empirical regularities.

The leading explanations of bargaining impasses and strikes among rational negotiators rest on uncertainty, misinformation, and miscalculation. For example, strikes can result from asymmetric information, which occurs when one negotiating party is uncertain about the ability of the other to grant its demands. If a union is uncertain about the employer's ability to pay, it make take a strike to elicit accurate information. By increasing the cost of bargaining, a strike increases an employer's incentive to reveal its true position sooner, thus producing a quicker solution (Hayes, 1984). The theory implies a negative relationship between wage settlements and strike duration since a profitable firm can avoid strike costs by accepting a high union wage proposal, while a relatively unprofitable firm will endure the strike until the

---

[5] See Kennan (1986) for an excellent review of the earlier literature on strikes.

union is convinced that the firm can only afford a lower wage. There is limited evidence of such a relationship in the United States (McConnell, 1989). Increased uncertainty about an employer's ability to accept union proposals should increase both the probability that a strike occurs and the duration of a strike, and empirical evidence indicates that both the incidence and duration of strike activity are higher in firms with more variable profitability (Tracy, 1986, 1987). Uncertainty about general economic conditions, such as inflation, can also lead to strikes when contracts fail to provide contingent adjustments (Gramm, Hendricks, and Kahn, 1988).

Several other game theoretic approaches, including wars of attrition, signaling, and reputation models have been advanced during the eighties. One lesson of the recent proliferation of game theoretic models of bargaining is that there may not be a single explanation of strikes (conflict) that applies to all situations. Nevertheless, these models are some distance from the "anything goes" approach of *post hoc* rationalization, for the more recent models of conflict give explicit predictions for large classes of stoppages and settlements.

Contract structure and conflict. Can the parties to an employment relationship alter the likelihood of future conflict by their choice of personnel policies? Recent research on strikes approaches this issue by asking whether the parties to collective bargaining can alter the probability of future work stoppages by their choice of contract characteristics. To date, only the influence of contract duration and date of expiration have been explored.

One view of the relationship between contract duration and strikes might hold that longer contracts produce fewer strikes because there are fewer opportunities to strike. Thus, bargaining relationships with long duration contracts should be less prone to conflict. By this argument, unionized employment relationships should be less conflict-prone than nonunionized relationships, in which wage and other terms of employment are adjusted more frequently (i.e., at least once a year).

The true relationship is more complicated because the probability of a strike may be a function of contract duration. The leading reason is that longer conflicts confront greater uncertainty and may be less able to adjust to unanticipated events than nonunion arrangements that are typically adjusted more frequently. This is consistent with findings cited above of a relationship between strikes and uncertainty. Efforts by labor and management to establish contingent arrangements apparently are not fully effective, for recent evidence shows that the probability that a strike will occur in fact rises with contract length and that contract reopening clauses, which reduce the effective contract length for some issues, reduce the odds of a work stoppage (Card, 1988). Within the unionized sector, the number of strikes per period appears to be independent of the length of an agreement. The broader implication for human resource management is that conflict is unlikely to be reduced by lengthening the period between adjustments in personnel policies unless a broad range of contingency arrangements is established.

Arbitration. Other research has addressed the strategic behavior of labor and management under interest arbitration. Arbitration raises both positive and normative questions. Perhaps the foremost positive questions are whether the introduction of an arbitration option into collective bargaining alters either the likelihood of a negotiated settlement or the terms and conditions of employment. Tied to this is a longstanding normative concern that institutional arrangements should encourage privately negotiated settlements on the grounds that these are more likely to be enforced by the parties than solutions that are established by a third party.

If the specter of strike costs encourages negotiated settlements in most of the organized private sector, interest arbitration will encourage settlements in the public sector to the extent that its use imposes costs on the parties. Two types of costs seem to serve this function—the direct costs of using an arbitration procedure and the uncertainty of an arbitrator's award when the parties to collective bargaining are risk averse (Bloom, 1986; Farber and Katz, 1979).

Absent uncertainty, the negotiating party who expects to gain more from an arbitration award than from collective bargaining will create an impasse. Arbitration procedures in which the arbitrator's award is highly predictable will therefore tend to undermine meaningful collective bargaining. These would include procedures requiring an arbitral award to be based on easily observed criteria, such as a cost-of-living index or a fact-finder's report. Arrangements with predictable arbitral awards are not inconsistent with negotiated settlements, but the availability of (predictable) arbitration in general will change the terms of the negotiated settlement (to approximately the award) as long as either party can follow a course of action that takes the dispute into arbitration. Another implication of this line of argument is that if an arbitrator's award becomes more certain over time (with exposure to the arbitrator and the decisions), the use of arbitration (or the undermining of collective bargaining) may increase.

On the other hand, awards based on multiple criteria considered with unknown and shifting weights create considerable uncertainty and would stimulate genuine negotiated settlements among risk-averse negotiators, who would be willing to settle for less than the expected value of an arbitral award. There is some experimental evidence that arbitrators consider a variety of criteria and attach some weight to both the actual offers of the negotiating parties as well as independent factors that apparently influence arbitrators' notions of fairness (Bazerman and Farber, 1985).

To what extent do the decision rules used by arbitrators influence the degree of uncertainty and therefore the extent to which arbitration undermines collective bargaining? The classic claim is that arbitrators are likely to "split the difference" or otherwise strike a compromise between the positions of labor and management and that this type of award does not encourage the negotiators to make the concessions needed to reach a negotiated agreement. This view of arbitrators has been criticized as being observationally equivalent to a scenario in which labor and management forecast the arbitrator's decision and then locate their demands and offers around that forecast. The research cited above indicates that the offers themselves have some bearing on the award, however.

An alternative decision rule, advanced by Stevens (1966) and now adopted in several public sector jurisdictions and professional sports is to require arbitrators to select either the final offer of the union or the final offer of management, usually without modification. The premise is that this rule will produce greater uncertainty that the parties will try to avoid by reaching a negotiated settlement. The use of this decision rule apparently does raise the frequency of negotiated settlements (Feuille, 1975).

Influence on the contract. As noted earlier, studies of unions and wages find that union wage differentials in the public sector are smaller than in the private sector.[6] The availability of arbitration could therefore produce higher wage outcomes through arbitration itself to the extent that arbitrators use criteria applied in the private sector as a frame of reference. The availability of interest arbitration as an impasse resolution mechanism may also produce higher bargained settlements if labor and management recognize the likely outcome of an arbitration and adjust their expectations and final offers accordingly. Thus, it is the availability rather than the actual use of arbitration that should influence the outcomes of public sector collective bargaining.

Feuille and Delaney (1986) find mixed evidence on the effects of arbitration in a study of police salaries between 1971 and 1981. Although arbitration appears to have a positive association with salaries in relatively simple tests, it turns out that police salaries were relatively high *(ceteris paribus)* in several

---

[6] The smaller wage impact is consistent with the illegality of strikes in the public sector and the generally lower level of strike activity by public unions.

states before arbitration statutes were passed. Feuille and Delaney's tests indicate no significant influence of the actual use of arbitration, once its availability is controlled for.

Studies of final-offer arbitration in New Jersey find that unions win two-thirds of the cases by submitting relatively conservative final offers, while employers win only one-third by low-balling. When employers win an award, however, the outcome is superior to the average collectively bargained outcome for employers, while unions do only about as well in arbitration as in collective bargaining (Ashenfelter and Bloom, 1984).

Conclusions

Research into the impact of unions on employment conditions has produced a vast body of work, much of which falls under the heading of "measurement without interpretation." This body of work is available to those who wish to refocus research from "What do unions do?" to "How and why do they do it?" The latter questions now appear to be most important for both scholars and human resource managers in both the union and nonunion sectors. Research into the strategies adopted by labor and management in different aspects of labor relations has only begun during the eighties, but it appears to be a most promising line for pursuing the how and why questions.

The New Institutionalism: What Can It Learn from the Old?

SANFORD M. JACOBY*

The new institutional labor economics is a promising development, but it has faults that could be remedied by an infusion of theoretical and methodological insights from the old institutional approach. This claim is illustrated by a critical analysis of three key concepts: asset specificity, deferred rewards, and opportunism. The essay concludes with a set of methodological precepts to guide future research.

OVER THE YEARS, economics has persistently expanded the range of phenomena that it seeks to explain. Among recent expressions of this theoretical expansiveness is the "new efficiency-oriented institutional labor economics" (NEO-ILE), of which the papers in this symposium are an excellent sampling. The NEO-ILE takes efficiency-oriented concepts derived from neoclassical theory—human capital, agency theory, transactions costs—and applies them to the analysis of various real-world institutions, chiefly those that support employment relations in organizations. Yet many of these institutions had been identified and analyzed by an earlier generation of labor economists, whose approach can be called simply "institutional labor economics" (ILE). Thus, the NEO-ILE has a mixed parentage. It has roots in the ILE approach, but it draws more heavily on neoclassical theory and is more rigorously analytical than was the ILE.

This cross-breeding has resulted in great variation in the kinds of research produced by those working on NEO-ILE topics. Some of it has a strong empirical, policy, and interdisciplinary orientation. Its use of theory is eclectic and realistic, as with efficiency wage theory. This strand of the

* Anderson Graduate School of Management, University of California at Los Angeles. The author is very grateful for comments and criticism received from Phil Beaumont, Peter Cappelli, Stanley Engerman, Bruce Kaufman, Paul Osterman, Michael Reich, and Keith Sisson. All usual disclaimers apply.

NEO-ILE has generated research that is at least as good as (and in some cases better than) that produced by the ILE approach. Other parts of the NEO-ILE research corpus are more problematic. There is a tendency to rationalize employment practices in functional or efficiency terms without regard to their historical-causal (how did the practice arise?) or empirical (how do we measure theoretical constructs and how much variation do they explain?) complexities. Noneconomic factors are either ignored or derogated as transitory or secondary phenomena. As elsewhere in the discipline, modeling is favored over facts and empiricism, which can and sometimes does lead to theories that are based on wrong or garbled facts, and are of little use for policy.

In this essay, I argue that the institutional tradition still has much to offer modern labor economics. Some labor economists know that and borrow in various ways from the tradition. They include economists who work on NEO-ILE issues as well as others whose research is less efficiency-oriented and closer, in various respects, to the older ILE tradition. In this latter group are such scholars as Katharine Abraham, Francine Blau, Clair Brown, William Brown, William Dickens, Richard Freeman, Robert Frank, Harry Katz, Daniel Mitchell, Paul Osterman, Peter Philips, Michael Piore, David Soskice, Myra Strober, and many others. Members of this group need to be more assertive about what it is that makes their work distinctive and differentiates it from both the neoclassical and the NEO-ILE approaches. Other economists, including some whose work falls under the NEO-ILE rubric, are ignorant or contemptuous of institutionalism. This essay is intended to goad them a bit. The discussion begins with an analytic history of institutionalism and then focuses specifically on the ILE approach and its intellectual concerns. Three succeeding sections examine key NEO-ILE concepts—asset specificity, deferred rewards, and opportunism—and subject them to a critical evaluation using ideas derived from the ILE approach. The final section offers some methodological suggestions to guide future work in the NEO-ILE area.

Early Institutionalism

As Hausman (1989) and others show, the view of methodology held by most orthodox economists today is quite similar to that espoused by nineteenth century classical and neoclassical economists like J. S. Mill and J. N. Keynes: A set of assumptions is generated by inductive observation or by introspection; from these assumptions are deduced probabilistic statements (or laws, *ceteris paribus*) that have predictive and explanatory consequences. Empirical analysis then determines whether the consequences are correct and if causal factors have been omitted. This view has had numerous critics over the years, including Friedman (1953). Here, I focus on the criticisms made by the institutional economists.

Institutionalism swept American economics in two waves: the first appeared in the eighteen seventies and eighties, and included the work of Ely, Seligman, and Patten; the second—and more influential—crested during the two decades after 1900, and included the work of Veblen, Mitchell, and Commons. In those days, neoclassical economics was only weakly committed to empirical research, a stance which the institutionalists roundly criticized. Drawing on the inductivism of the German historical school and on the pragmatist credo that the truth of an idea is to be judged by its consequences, the institutionalists called for a stronger factual and empirical orientation in economics. Although institutionalism itself was criticized for excessive description and fact-gathering, at its best it combined the pragmatic emphasis on facts and chance to produce—as in Mitchell's work—a statistical approach to economic research that has its modern counterpart in empirical econometrics as carried out at the NBER (founded by Mitchell) and elsewhere.

The institutionalists were driven by an abiding concern with public policy. They found the neoclassical approach unhelpful in formulating policy and often hostile to the idea that economic and social problems could be ameliorated by the state.[1] Indeed, it was out of their diverse policy concerns— the "labor" question, industrial regulation, municipal ownership, trade protection, public administration—that the institutionalists developed their two main criticisms of orthodox theory: first, that its predictions diverged from empirical reality (they saw the real world as a place where state policies contributed to economic growth; trade unions raised wage levels; unemployment was pervasive; and trade protection facilitated economic development); and second, that these discrepancies arose from a lack of realism in the model's assumptions. Against those assumptions, the institutionalists offered their own: indeterminacy; endogeneity; behavioral realism; and diachronic analysis.

Indeterminacy. Whereas the orthodox model assumed perfect competition and unique equilibria, the institutionalists pointed to pervasive market power and to indeterminacy even under competition. Commons (1924), for example,

---

[1] The American Economic Association was founded in 1885 by Ely (1886) and other early institutionalists, who angered their more orthodox colleagues by including a phrase in the AEA's opening statement that called the state "an agency whose positive assistance is one of the indispensable conditions of human progress." For a more detailed analysis of institutionalism and its origins, see Jacoby (1988).

argued that in the labor market, the employer possessed superior information, resources, and bargaining power as compared to individual workers; the Webbs (1920)—borrowing from Edgeworth—claimed that the labor contract was indeterminate regardless of the degree of competition, leaving its terms to be specified by custom, bargaining, or law.

Endogeneity. In the orthodox view, an individual's wants were taken as given and exogenous to the realm of economic need satisfaction dominated by efficiency forces. The institutionalists held instead that market exchange was mediated by social institutions that determined, and were at the same time determined by, individual wants and behaviors. As Commons (1934) put it, the transaction between two persons, the basic unit of economic analysis, was subject to the working rules of going concerns, but these rules were expressions of collective action and thus subject to change through human volition. Veblen (1919, p. 239) expressed the same idea when he said that economic conduct is "hedged about and directed by [social] relations...of an institutional character," while at the same time, "the growth and mutations of the institutional fabric are an outcome of the conduct of individual members of the group."

Behavioral realism. The orthodox view took from utilitarianism the assumption that *homo economicus* was guided by rational self-interest, whereas the institutionalists derived from pragmatism and other sources their belief that economic theory had to be based on psychological facts rather than on assumptions about economic behavior. From the new empirical disciplines of cognitive and social psychology, they developed their emphasis on habit as a component of rationality. Not only do habits have an historical dimension (they cause past choices to constrain a person's present ones), they also have social and cultural origins and can promote collective action. Commons (1950) saw the latter as a key feature of modern capitalism.

Diachronic analysis. In the orthodox view, economic theory was synchronic: an abstraction from reality that isolated its transhistorical and universal aspects. Following Max Weber, the institutionalists asserted that the abstractions of economic theory were neither timeless nor placeless but instead were an ideal type—an enhancement of features unique to modern Western capitalism.[2] As such, economic theory was "not so much an account

---

[2] Commons (1934) acknowledged his debt to Max Weber, and sociologists again are beginning to consider the relations between economy and society (e.g., see Granovetter, 1985).

of how men do behave as an account of how they would behave if they followed out in practice the logic of the money economy" (Mitchell, 1937, p. 371). The institutionalists realized that nothing was wrong with this approach to theory so long as the distance between abstraction and reality was not great. But their empirical research led them to view this distance as substantial, at least for some parts of orthodox theory, and also as historically variable, because the economy perpetually was "a moving, changing process" (Commons, 1924, p. 376). Hence, they insisted that diachronic analysis—how the economy acquired its features and the conditions that cause those features to vary over time and place—had to be part of economics, alongside synchronic abstraction.

It is an error of long standing to charge that the institutionalists discarded economic abstraction and the deductive method. Possibly the accusation could apply to Veblen and some of the early institutionalists, but it was not true of Commons, Hoxie, Mitchell, and others who followed them. Yet it *is* true that the institutionalists were unable to resolve their dispute with orthodoxy. Commons thought that the way to proceed was to base economic theory on realistic assumptions revealed by empirical research within and outside of the discipline. "The problem now," he explained, "is not to create a different kind of economics—'institutional' economics divorced from preceding schools—but how to give collective action, in all its varieties, its due place throughout economic theory" (Commons, 1934, p. 5). Mitchell had much the same thing in mind when he criticized his friend Veblen for failing to state his ideas in testable terms and said that economic methodology should involve a "passing back and forth between hypothesis and observation, each modifying and enriching the other" (1937, p. 302). But neither man produced even a partially modified version of neoclassicism, although both left a wealth of ideas and data that questioned some of its foundations.

The institutionalist critique had its greatest impact on the field of labor economics, a specialty that emerged in the twenties (McNulty, 1980). Not only were labor markets the site of numerous theoretical anomalies, but they had features that overlapped the concerns of other disciplines to a greater extent than other applied subjects in economics. Both the traders and the commodity traded in labor markets—human effort—were more likely to be affected by psychological and social factors than, say, brokers and bonds (but see Shiller, 1984). Also, labor economics was a field in which practical issues were salient and unavoidable. The "labor" question, broadly defined, was arguably the most pressing problem in American society through the fifties, long after other nations had adapted to trade unionism and the welfare state.

Institutional Labor Economics

There was considerable intellectual continuity between the institutionalists and the institutional labor economists (the ILEs) who succeeded them in the twenties and thirties (e.g., Douglas, Lescohier, Slichter, Wolman) and in the forties and fifties (e.g., Kerr, Dunlop, Lester, Reynolds, Ulman).[3] Like their forebears, the ILEs deprecated the lack of empiricism in orthodox economics and its limited relevance to public affairs. They were deeply concerned with policy problems and actively involved in solving them: the first generation cut its teeth on industrial relations and labor market issues during the First World War; the second generation did much the same thing during the thirties and the Second World War. The ILEs were struck by discrepancies between orthodoxy's predictions and the realities that they observed from their posts in government and through their more systematic empiricism.

The ILEs traced the anomalies they observed—including nonclearing labor markets, wage rigidity, persistent wage differentials, labor immobility, administered (internal) labor markets, and bargaining power—to the same flaws in the orthodox model that the institutionalists had earlier identified. And they championed many of the same alternative assumptions: *endogeneity* (the ILEs thought that market behavior and social relations were mutually determined, as in the ILE emphasis on custom and equity in wage setting); *diachronic analysis* (the ILEs focused on time- and place-specific elements in economic theory and conducted theoretically informed comparative and historical studies, as in the works published under the aegis of Kerr and Dunlop's Inter-University Study of Labor project); and *indeterminacy* (because of the theoretical advances made in the thirties—by Keynes, Robinson, Chamberlin, and others—the second generation of ILEs gave more attention than did their predecessors to imperfect and nonprice competition, yet the effect was the same: an emphasis on indeterminacy in the orthodox model, leaving room for the exercise of discretion, power, and social norms in the labor market).[4]

---

[3] Some have recently asserted a disjuncture between the institutionalists and the ILEs of the forties and fifties, calling the latter "postinstitutionalists" (Segal, 1986) or "neoclassical revisionists" (Kerr, 1988). As I explain below, there *were* differences, but they were not sharp.

[4] The ILEs had relatively less to say about behavioral realism, in part because the academic division of labor began to change during the thirties as new fields like personnel psychology and management split off from labor economics. But these fields became part of the new interdisciplinary umbrella of industrial relations, under which most of the ILEs also chose to gather. From here, the ILEs closely followed developments in those fields and participated in their debates. See note 10.

Methodology. Where the ILEs, especially the second generation, differed from their forebears was in their methodological approach to resolving these anomalies. Rather than espouse (much less attempt) the creation of a new body of theory based on realistic assumptions, the ILEs built a wide range of eclectic, middle-level theories that bridged the abstractions of pure theory and the institutional realities of American labor markets. When received theory failed to predict with a high degree of precision, the ILEs added more realistic elements—diachronic, nonprice, social, political—into their explanations. Critics faulted the ILEs for failing to develop a substitute for neoclassical theory. The middle-level approach was, however, a reasonable and fruitful way to proceed, given the previous generation's failures in this area, and, especially, given the growing realization that neoclassicism's theoretical core was surrounded by impenetrable bands of conditional clauses (see Hutchison, 1938; Latsis, 1976).[5] Nor was this approach unique to labor economics. Industrial organization economics of the forties and fifties, both in the U.S. and the U.K., generated empirical findings that were at variance with neoclassical predictions. Like the ILEs, the industrial organization economists developed a range of eclectic, middle-level, or bridging theories to account for anomalies like rule-of-thumb pricing and the shape of long-run cost curves (e.g., Boulding, 1952; Heflebower, 1952; Walters, 1963).

The ILEs' approach was not invincible, of course. A disinclination toward methodology left them vulnerable to Friedman's (1953) clever attack on realism and descriptive accuracy and to Machlup's (1946) claim that middle-range theories dealt with mere deviations or disturbances from long-run equilibrium. On the heels of those criticisms came other developments that undermined the ILE approach. By the late fifties, the public concerns that had animated the ILEs—remedying labor market inequalities through industrial relations and macro-welfare policies—were less pressing. Moreover, the mathematization of economics cut the ILEs off from the generation of labor economists trained in the sixties and seventies. The ILEs were perceived as dated, and their eclectic, middle-range theories proved difficult to model in formal terms. At the same time, labor economics experienced a neoclassical resurgence with the rise of human capital theory. Increasingly, the thrust was to reconcile labor economics with orthodox theory.

Nevertheless, during the seventies and eighties a new trend emerged in labor economics. Various anomalies from the ILE tradition became the subject of theoretical concern: internal labor markets, wage differentials,

---

[5] In a recent elegiac essay, Clark Kerr (1988, p. 21) faults his generation for failing to produce "an integrated statement" or "consistent theory." Kerr is too hard on himself and his colleagues. True, better modeling could have been done, but the ILEs made the right decision by not attempting a full-blown alternative to neoclassical theory.

wage rigidity, and unionism. Economists again began to study employment institutions, giving rise to the "new efficiency-oriented institutional labor economics" (NEO-ILE). As previously noted, the NEO-ILE is a motley body of research ranging from work that is avowedly institutional to more neoclassical and even Marxian approaches. But throughout the NEO-ILE literature there are theoretical problems which could be rectified by a more conscious application of insights from the ILE tradition. Below, I substantiate this claim by critically examining three central NEO-ILE concepts—asset specificity, deferred rewards, and opportunism.

Internal Labor Markets and Asset Specificity

Asset specificity in various forms plays a key role in the NEO-ILE literature on internal labor markets and related topics. Doeringer and Piore's (1971) now-classic book on internal labor markets was one of the earliest attempts to provide an efficiency-oriented explanation for a phenomenon first identified and discussed by the preceding generation of ILEs. Borrowing from Becker (1964) and focusing on the stability of employment in internal labor markets, Doeringer and Piore gave causal primacy to skill specificity and the informal process by which firm-specific skills are acquired. Skill specificity leads employers to stabilize employment and reduce turnover so that they can recoup their firm-specific investments in employees. At the same time, stability facilitates the informal process of specific-skill acquisition, which occurs on the job through learning-by-doing. Doeringer and Piore also made an historical argument that employment had become increasingly stable due to growing use of mass production technology, whose detailed division of labor necessitated firm-specific skills.

While subsequent research has confirmed an historical shift over the last century in the stability of industrial employment (Carter, 1988), there is little evidence that the shift resulted from a growing reliance on firm-specific techniques or skills. In fact, the evidence suggests that the opposite was true: that technology and job skills became less, rather than more, firm-specific over time. By the early nineteen hundreds, the U.S. was developing a capital goods industry that allowed firms to purchase identical machinery from national vendors instead of having to craft their own, as in the nineteenth century (Jacoby, 1979). As one manager said in 1917, all firms "can buy the same kinds of machinery if they know where to get it; or they can design the same kind. Processes cannot now be kept entirely secret" (Hopkins, 1917, p. 2). Moreover, as contemporary economists were well aware, this standard technology had the advantage of lowering training costs by narrowing job content and de-emphasizing skill specificity (Douglas,

1921).

To escape from this paradox, Williamson (1975) expanded the sources of skill specificity beyond Doeringer and Piore's "technological specificity" to include a host of organizational factors that make incumbents valuable to employers: team accommodations, informal process innovations, and knowledge of codes and procedures.[6] But similar historical problems adhere even to this expanded definition. Take, for example, a firm's codes and procedures. One of the major findings of modern industrial sociology is that work organizations today are more rationalized and bureaucratic than in the past (Bendix, 1956; Jacoby, 1973). As a result, employees (whether in steel mills or universities) find other organizations in the same industry to be more similar—in terms of their codes and procedures—than was true one hundred years ago. Nineteenth-century firms were stamped by the identities of their owners, workplace routines were unstandardized, and workers had to learn the idiosyncrasies of foremen who ran their departments like independent fiefs.

The specificity concept also has empirical problems, chiefly the fact that idiosyncratic elements can be found in most jobs. Restaurant work provides a prime example of an unstructured labor market (one lacking internal labor markets). Yet this work entails process, team, and communications idiosyncracies as unique and elaborate (from restaurant to restaurant) as those found in semi-skilled auto assembly jobs, the *locus classicus* of a structured internal labor market (Whyte, 1948). Surely then, to paraphrase Williamson (1975), one cannot place primary reliance on idiosyncracy to produce structure, for if idiosyncracy is a common employment feature, how is the coexistence of structured and structureless labor markets to be explained?

The preceding claim admittedly lacks detailed documentation, but the same is true of the claims made by adherents of idiosyncracy. Indeed, the major problem with the concept is its vagueness and lack of empirical content. No one has devised a way to measure skill specificity directly. At best, one must make the heroic assumption that the amount of specific skills a worker possesses is proxied by years of on-the-job experience. But that raises even more difficulties than the analogous assumption that years of schooling is a proxy for general human capital. At least in the case of schools, indirect evidence exists (such as test scores) to assess the plausibility of the notion that additional schooling augments general human capital. There is no similar evidence to show that additional job tenure raises one's

---

[6] Asset specificity is central to Williamson's approach. Its absence, he says, would "vitiate much of transaction cost economics" (1985, p. 56).

stock of firm-specific human capital. In fact, the evidence—which shows that tenure is rewarded independently of productivity—runs in the opposite direction (Abraham and Medoff, 1983).

These criticisms do not come directly out of the ILE tradition, but they are consistent with its emphasis on facts, empiricism, and historical specificity. That tradition needs to be reckoned with, rather than dismissed, by those seeking to rationalize internal labor markets in terms of asset specificity. Still, as economists are fond of saying, it takes more than facts to kill a theory; it takes another theory. In this case, at least, other NEO-ILE theories of internalization are available that are more consistent with the facts. However, those theories, too, could benefit from an infusion of the ILE approach, especially its attention to the social and historical contexts in which employment institutions are rooted.

Internal Labor Markets and Deferred Rewards

An efficiency-oriented alternative to idiosyncracy is Goldberg's (1980, 1984) work on internal labor markets. Using an eclectic combination of agency theory (Lazear, 1979), implicit contract theory of the "invisible handshake" variety (Okun, 1981), radical theories of bureaucratic control (Edwards, 1979), and elements from business history (Chandler, 1977), Goldberg argues that, as firm size and throughput rates rose in the late nineteenth century, worker turnover and indiscipline became more costly to employers. At the same time, larger firm size made traditional methods of control (using foremen to monitor and dismiss refractory workers) less feasible and more costly. The search for alternatives led employers to the idea of penalizing premature separations and promoting self-monitoring through the use of deferred compensation (i.e., internal promotion, pensions, and other plans that tie pay to seniority by tilting age-earnings curves, much like posting a bond). Use of these less visible control structures stabilized employment: directly, through reductions in voluntary mobility; and indirectly, through employer-initiated rules restricting unfair, premature dismissal. By imposing rules on themselves that curbed their own opportunism, employers ensured that workers would not discount the value of their deferred compensation and that the latter would retain its incentive effect.

Goldberg's interpretation generates internal labor markets without idiosyncracy. It also has the advantage of being studded with large chunks of historical reality. Nevertheless, at several key points the story does not fit the historical record. These disjunctures point to a more complex interpretation of internal labor markets, one that is less supportive of Goldberg's (and others') view that economic efficiency incentives are sufficient to account for observed institutional outcomes. First, the notion that an increase in average firm size caused internalization is a fallacy of the *post hoc, ergo propter hoc* variety. Undoubtedly there was some relationship in some cases, but, on average, the two events had only a loose and widely varying temporal correlation. Giant manufacturing firms were a common feature of the industrial landscape by 1890, yet in many of them internalization—whether measured by means (pensions, internal promotion lines, employer restraints on dismissal) or by ends (geographic mobility, labor mobility, average tenure) did not occur until four or five decades later (Ross, 1958). One is left wondering why some large employers were so slow to realize the efficiency advantages of internalization and deferred rewards, especially when size-driven changes occurred so rapidly in marketing, production, accounting, and other spheres of management. Moreover, medium-sized firms (those with fewer than 1,000 workers) were often among the first to abolish the traditional system of factory labor administration.

Second, key methods by which internalization supposedly was effected did not become prevalent until the fifties, which is *after* internalization had occurred and the modern pattern had been set for employment stability, tenure, and mobility. Three examples: (i) The proportion of wage-earners eligible to receive severance pay stood at less than 9 per cent in 1946 but rose to 25 per cent by 1964. (ii) Only 2 per cent of wage-earners received pensions in 1929, and by the end of World War II this had risen to only 8 per cent. Again, the big increase came after the war, when the proportion rose to 73 per cent in 1964. (iii) Employer-initiated restraints on dismissal, as measured by the proportion of firms having defined dismissal rules, stood at only 16 per cent in 1940 but rose to 43 per cent in 1964 (Jacoby, 1986; Gordon, Edwards, and Reich, 1982). In other words, deferred rewards and the structures governing them were a consequence, rather than a cause, of internalization. They had less to do with employer control than with employee preferences (deferred rewards are valued by stable employees) and shifts in power and social norms (dismissal rules protect, and severance pay liquidates, vested job rights).

Third, internal labor markets did not spontaneously develop in an ever-growing number of firms. Typically, they were adopted during two periods of crisis for the older system of labor administration—the late nineteen tens and the decade from 1935 to 1945, years during which employee bargaining power was high as a result of labor shortages and/or union threat effects (Jacoby, 1985). This pattern suggests that external pressure was critical in the shift to more structured employment practices, whose putative efficiency incentives many managers remained skeptical of. Some managers were reluctant to stabilize employment out of fear that it would raise labor costs by forcing them to give regular pay increases to incumbent employees. Others held tight to the conviction that intimations of job security eroded discipline and that only close supervision would keep employees in line. The steady increase from 1900 to 1960 in the ratio of foremen to production workers in American manufacturing firms is consistent with this belief (U.S. Bureau of the Census).

Normative efficiency. It would be wrong to suggest that efficiency was irrelevant or that internal labor markets were a random development. Size *did* sometimes influence outcomes, along with other economic variables like product demand stability, inventory accumulation costs, and product diversification (Piore, 1975; Jacoby, 1989). But these variables take us only part of the way. One critical element missing from Goldberg's story is worker preferences, in the form of a "second generation effect." Workers born in the U.S. were more likely than mobile immigrants to value attachments to particular employers and communities. That effect was already felt in the late nineteenth century and then gradually increased over time. It was given major impetus by post-1920 changes in immigration law, which halted much of the reverse-migration to Europe. Workers who might have emigrated before the change in the law now sank roots in the United States. As well, the law caused a drop in immigration, which brought a decline in the proportion of rootless newcomers in the labor force. Consequently, the children of the immigrants who flocked here between 1880 and 1915 made up a growing proportion of the labor force. Presumably, they wanted to remain in the workplaces and communities where their parents had finally settled. Hence, workers' overwhelming concern with job security during the twenties and thirties stemmed from a desire to protect new forms of communal stability from the disruption caused by job loss (Jacoby, 1983).

More was involved in the second generation effect than an inexplicable shift in time-discounting preferences. Immigrants and their children were affected by the norms and attitudes of American society, which emphasized equality, rights, and lack of deference to authority. The industrial workplace, however, sharply contradicted those values, with its visible exercise of the foreman's power and authority; its lack of due process in labor allocation and dismissal; and its rankling status differences between blue- and white-collar workers, with the latter, but not the former, receiving implicit or explicit promises of job security (Jacoby, 1982). The tension between social norms and industrial realities built up and then erupted during the nineteen tens and again (in more organized fashion) during the thirties and forties. Out of these episodes emerged a more stable, impersonal, and rule-bound system of employment.

It is possible to rationalize all of this in efficiency terms, as when Stiglitz (1987, p. 49) argues that "it is in the interests of employers to construct employment relationships that are attractive to workers. In competitive markets firms will be 'forced' to provide such efficient contracts." But because what is attractive to workers is historically and socially specific, Stiglitz's linkage between what he calls the "positive" and "normative" aspects of contracting entails a concept of efficiency that also is historically and socially specific. It can be termed "normative efficiency" and is akin to Leibenstein's (1976) x-efficiency concept. It is different from the kind of efficiency implied or expressed in synchronic NEO-ILE theorizing about labor market institutions, although the two efficiency concepts are best thought of as complements or joint constraints. Thus, in the case at hand, internal labor markets (and employment practices more generally) are a blend of adaptations: to forces that produce allocative or transactional efficiency and to specific historical and cultural forces that produce normative efficiency.[7] Moreover, if Stiglitz's "competitive markets" condition is not met, then there is room for more complexity in the model—including, on the one hand, employer sluggishness in responding to worker preferences; on the other, the use of collective action via unions or government to speed up the response. Without getting into what is usually an abstract and fruitless debate over whether or not power relations shape the organization of work, suffice it to say that most NEO-ILE models either ignore the exercise of unilateral power or doubt that the concept can explain very much (Macneil, 1981; Williamson, 1985). If, however, labor markets are imperfectly competitive, then power—in the form of collective action—has a role to play. It can speed up the process of "efficient" institutional change or cause the adoption of institutional forms that are inefficient. Collective action can be pursued by workers—as in the wholesale replacement during the thirties of millions of individual at-will employment contracts by collective contracts requiring just cause—or by employers, as in the recent political jockeying over dismissal and notice legislation.

Even if labor markets are competitive, externalities across firms can act to deter the provision of a sufficient supply of attractive jobs. These externalities reveal the endogeneity of the employment relationship, taking us into the realm of social costs, social benefits, and social policy, issues not often considered in NEO-ILE models. One example of such an externality was given by Slichter (1919, pp. 426–431), based on his observation of firms

---

[7] The median-voter model of unionism (Freeman and Medoff, 1984) can be classed as a normative efficiency concept.

and labor markets during the nineteen tens. Slichter was concerned that market forces would fail to end the prevalent "drive policy" of close supervision and unstable jobs because the policy was "profitable" and "practical" for employers "dealing with some classes of workers." Yet, he said, what was privately rational had undesirable consequences for "the class interests of [all] employers" as well as for "the general social welfare." The drive policy, explained Slichter, "intensifies class consciousness of labor" and "wears workers out to such an extent that it is equivalent to a decrease in the general supply of labor." To encourage wider pursuit of "a liberal and broadly conceived policy," he urged governments, universities, and employers' associations to take a more active role.

Indeed, around this time state and federal agencies first began to promote "socially responsible" employment practices, many of which fostered internalization. The government took steps such as training hundreds of personnel managers during the First World War, legislating anti-layoff incentives during the mid-thirties, and reforming private dismissal practices during the Second World War. The Wagner Act, too, was partly motivated by the idea that unions would bring industrial stability not only by curtailing strikes but by hastening the demise of drive practices (Casebeer, 1987).

Diachronic specificity. Normative efficiency factors, externalities, and market imperfections add to the specificity of the employment relationship and enmesh it in a web of institutions (unions, legislation, schools) that vary over time and place. Given this specificity, one would expect to find substantial cross-national variation in the structure of internal labor markets and in the labor market outcomes to which they give rise. This is precisely what recent studies have uncovered. For example, as compared to the U.S. or the U.K., Japan and Germany have internal labor markets that are less finely structured and less market- (versus organization-) oriented, while their external labor markets have lower mobility levels (Dore, 1973; Cole, 1979; Osterman, 1988). Others have found that large French and German firms— although neighbors and trading partners—nevertheless exhibit systematic variations in their internal wage structures and mobility patterns. These variations are traceable to differing national educational systems and how the latter are linked to firms (Maurice *et al.*, 1986).

Orthodox economists assert that such variations can safely be abstracted from because they have but "negligible effect" as compared to the more fundamental outcomes produced by long-run forces of competition (Reder, 1989, p. 457). In other words, it is believed that one can neatly disentangle economic/universal from noneconomic/specific factors, and that the former will have causal primacy, at least in the long run. But when it comes to studying labor markets, it would seem safer or, to use an old term, more pragmatic, to hold an agnostic position on these issues and to take each analytical problem as it comes. Otherwise, one runs the risk of making theory a rationalization for, rather than an explanation of, observed phenomena.[8]

To make this point concrete, consider the various theories of wage rigidity that appeared during the seventies as an offshoot of work on internal labor markets. The theories explained wage rigidity as the result of optimizing in the face of risk aversion or turnover costs. These were elegant models, but they were framed solely in functional-synchronic terms without regard to empirical or diachronic factors. The risk-shifting version eventually broke apart on hard factual reefs: the limited incidence and scope of real wage protection (e.g., COLAs) and of income replacement (e.g., SUBs and UI) for American workers on layoff (Oswald, 1987; Brown, 1988). Other research pointed to substantial historical and international variations in wage rigidity, which neither theory could explain as well as models that incorporated specific institutional factors. Thus, with respect to the substantial increase in U.S. wage rigidity since the twenties, Mitchell (1985, p. 36) said, "Perhaps risk aversion and turnover costs increased after the 1920s, but the most significant changes that occurred involved unionization, new public policies, and changing social expectations." As for international variations in wage rigidity (with the U.S. an outlier on this dimension), the best explanation again came from theories that emphasized the institutional structures affecting wage determination: the level, timing, and extent of bargaining; union ideologies and norms; and measures of corporatism, such as implicit social contracts or the political integration of organized labor (Bruno and Sachs, 1985; Flanagan, Soskice, and Ulman, 1983; Gordon, 1982; Helliwell, 1988).

The preceding research on wage rigidity demonstrates that economists working on NEO-ILE topics do not always adhere to an orthodox position. But it is fair to say that an eclectic, interdisciplinary approach—blending abstract economic and specific social and historical factors—remains the exception rather than the rule. Among NEO-ILE economists, the dominant view of other social science perspectives is that they are "rivals" (Williamson,

---

[8] The criticism advanced here is similar to Dow's (1987, p. 26) argument that neoclassical and transactional theories are functional rather than causal explanations of institutional outcomes. Belief in the efficiency of observed structures, says Dow, leads to functionalist explanatory statements of the sort: "governance structure X exists because efficiency requirements dictate X for transactions of type Y... Causal explanations, on the other hand, describe how later structures have emerged out of earlier ones."

1988, p. 183) to economic orthodoxy—substitutes rather than complements—and, judging by citations in NEO-ILE publications, inferior goods to boot.[9]

Opportunism and Shirking

Unlike wage or employment rigidity, opportunism is a topic that most ILEs failed to consider. Nevertheless, the problem of reducing opportunistic behavior in the workplace is interesting and provides a potential link between the NEO-ILE and organizational research in other disciplines. The problem lies at the heart of a variety of NEO-ILE models, including efficiency wage theory (Katz, 1986; Shapiro and Stiglitz, 1984), agency theory (Pratt and Zeckhauser, 1985), and transactions-cost theory. Opportunism is "self-interest seeking with guile. This includes but is scarcely limited to more blatant forms, such as lying, stealing, and cheating" (Williamson, 1985, p. 47). In the workplace, it often takes the form of shirking, which is associated with incomplete or distorted disclosure of information regarding employee effort. To mitigate opportunism in employment requires either hierarchical monitoring and governance procedures or less visible control mechanisms like deferred rewards and supra-market clearing wages that increase the worker's cost of job loss when malfeasance is detected. Some Marxian models of employment rely on similar notions: that as the cost of job loss decreases, opportunism and the need for control both increase (Weisskopf *et al.*, 1983). For some, the similarity is cause for hopes of reconciliation between neoclassical and Marxian economics (e.g., see Putterman, 1986), although Bowles (1985) asserts that the Marxian model differs fundamentally from the NEO-ILE's Hobbesian approach because it specifies opportunism as a feature of capitalist society rather than of human nature.

This is a key difference and Bowles is correct in criticizing the NEO-ILE approach for failing to endogenize the workplace in a social context. But the Marxian model shares with the NEO-ILE approach some dubious features, chiefly an overemphasis on one side of human nature in capitalist workplaces (shirking and conflict) and a tendency to ignore other sides—altruism, morality, trust, cooperation—or to disparage them as false consciousness or disguised self-seeking. Both the NEO-ILE and Marxian models tend to assume certain invariant and fundamental features of human behavior or of capitalism, an approach that pragmatic institutionalists like Mitchell (1969, p. 596) rejected as "a schematic and superficial view of human nature." Thus, with respect to conflict and shirking, a more suitable

---

[9] The result is what Nelson and Winter (1982, p. 405) term "the intellectual autarky of economics."

approach would endogenize workplace relations, while recognizing the rich variety of those relations and not constraining them to a single essence or modality.[10]

Socialization. In detaching the employment relationship from its social and historical moorings, NEO-ILE opportunism models miss the fact that socialization is a prerequisite for, and alternative to, organizational control structures (Parsons, 1949). First, there is primary socialization—in families and schools—which usually supports what employers do inside workplaces and gives meaning to the incentives and penalties found there. Then there is secondary socialization at the workplace itself, which relies on consensual methods of inculcating norms and goals, such as ideologies of authority that must be seen as legitimate if they are to be persuasive. Both types of socialization are required to make workplace controls effective; both also offer alternatives to those controls. For example, studies show that primary schools prepare young people for the disciplinary regimen they will encounter at work. The fit between school and work is not perfect, however. Graduates of professional programs attach high value to professional rewards that are not given by the employer. At the same time, employees imbued with a strong work ethic or a strong sense of corporate loyalty are less likely to require supervision than those who have neither (Andrisani, 1978; Baldamus, 1961; Kohn, 1977; Ouchi, 1980). Hence, raising penalties for shirking is not the only or even the most efficient way to economize on monitoring, just as stiffer sentencing for criminals is not the only or most effective way to deter crime and reduce the number of police.[11]

In modern workplaces that do not rely on corporal force, controls are usually a blend of the utilitarian (economic) and normative (social) types (Etzioni, 1961). Yet NEO-ILE models focus exclusively on utilitarian controls, perhaps because these are relatively less dependent on socialization and can be more easily divorced from a social context. Problems then arise when analysis turns to prescription, as when the NEO-ILE is offered as practical human resource management.

---

[10] Given their disdain for "human relations" and Elton Mayo (cf. Kerr and Fisher, 1957), the ILEs might seem a poor source from which to draw this critique; and, in fact, at times the ILEs were more economistic and conflict-oriented than their forebears. Still, the behavioral realism the ILEs inherited from the institutionalists led them to criticize Mayo on *empirical* grounds and to regularly emphasize moral and social sides of human behavior, as, for example, in analyses of union solidarity, cooperative bargaining, and business leadership.

[11] Hirschman (1985) offers an interesting explanation of why economists deal with undesirable behaviors by proposing to raise their costs rather than relying on norms and sanctions. Leonard's (1987) empirical results question the predictions of efficiency wage models that incorporate shirking.

Compensation provides a case in point. First, the NEO-ILE literature overemphasizes its efficacy and centrality to human resource management. Recent studies show that the impact of financial incentives on productivity is less than that of factors like employee involvement in goal setting (Guzzo and Katzell, 1987). Second, rather than being purely a utilitarian control, as it is portrayed in the NEO-ILE literature, organizational pay setting is enmeshed in normative processes, a point the ILE tradition emphasized (Marsden, 1986). Recent research on equity theory, for example, shows that workers gauge pay differentials according to cultural and organizational norms of fairness (Weick *et al.*, 1976; Carrell and Dittrich, 1978). When wage dispersion exceeds these norms, effort is reduced and turnover increases (Mowday, 1983; Pfeffer and Blake, 1988). Even the pay levels of corporate executives are affected by social factors, such as the reinforcement of hierarchical authority in large firms (Simon, 1957) or the maintenance of equity between CEO and board member salaries (O'Reilly *et al.*, 1988). Although some NEO-ILE pay models incorporate these factors or recognize the existence of normative controls (e.g., Akerlof, 1982), most do not.

That is not unexpected, given that few economists are exposed during their training to social and behavioral sciences other than economics.[12] The standard modeling metaphor learned by graduate students in economics remains that of Robinson Crusoe, alone on his island without a community, a history, or even an employer. The NEO-ILE has given Crusoe a boss but not a great deal more. The imagery in efficiency-wage and principal-agent shirking theories remains that of Crusoe. The metaphor is derived from the classical model of contract, with its mutual suspicion, atomistic individualism, weak ties, and pervasive fear of opportunism. That model is "infused with the spirit of restraint and delimitation; open-ended obligations are alien to its nature; arms-length negotiation is the keynote." The classical or purposive contract stands in sharp contrast to the status contract intended to govern ongoing relationships such as marriages or long-term employment. These contracts are laden with cultural specificity, full of "general and diffuse commitments...[and] bonds and obligations" derived from social relations and cultural norms (Selznick, 1969, pp. 54–55). While Williamson (1979) and some of his followers have grasped the inappropriateness of using purposive contract concepts to describe status relationships, other NEO-ILE theorists have not. And even Williamson remains weak on a key point: that both status and purposive contracts draw on prior social bonds, customs,

---

[12] Colander and Klamer's (1987) survey of graduate students in economics found that only 13 per cent had intellectual interactions with students or scholars in other disciplines; well more than half thought that a thorough knowledge of the economy was unimportant for professional success.

and mores—what Durkheim (1933, p. 206) called the "noncontractual relations of contract"—without which any contract would be impossible to negotiate or to enforce. Abstracting from these elements creates the risk of seriously misunderstanding how markets, including labor markets, work (Hirsch, 1976). Even guile—an important feature of Williamson's concept of opportunism—presupposes the existence and subsequent violation of contractual principles that have their origins in ongoing social relations and social norms (Macneil, 1981).

Trust. Ongoing social relations build trust, another concept whose importance has not been widely recognized in the NEO-ILE literature, except by Williamson (1975) and his followers. Even for Williamson, however, trust is an add-on rather than an integral part of the analysis because his operating assumption—like that of most other NEO-ILE theorists—remains that of pervasive opportunism. Yet, as industrial studies have repeatedly shown, the presumption of innate opportunism is fatal to trust (Gouldner, 1954; March and Simon, 1958). It leads to a proliferation of control structures—supervision, rules, and deferred rewards—intended to inhibit opportunism. These create resentment and distrust among employees, who correctly perceive the controls as expressions of their employer's distrust. Expectations fulfill themselves when worker resentment breeds opportunism and the employer is forced to implement additional controls, now with the conviction that his initial beliefs were justified. Fox (1974) terms this the low trust syndrome: low trust begets low trust in an ever-downward spiral of resentment, opportunism, and control. Imagine an employment system embodying the low trust syndrome; imagine modern Britain, says Fox. Alternatively, imagine vast segments of American industry, filled with complex governance structures intended to attenuate opportunism and distrust but paradoxically producing an opposite result. While there is risk here of being a Pollyanna, NEO-ILE adherents rarely have considered the risks inherent in their own approach.

Concededly, some economists have built trust models which do not assume that opportunism is pervasive but instead treat its occurrence as a probability determined by the cost of its consequences (Klein *et al.*, 1978). For employers and workers, these costs are said to be higher when growth is expected to be rapid than when growth is stable or declining.[13] Thus, in high-growth

---

[13] Under rapid growth, the employer's cost of opportunism is future increased wages for an expanding work force; knowing this, employees are more likely to trust the employer not to take advantage of them. Opportunistic workers stand to lose the income and promotion opportunities associated with high growth; knowing this, employers are more likely to trust them.

firms—like those of Silicon Valley or Japan—opportunism costs are high, and with that comes higher trust, less rigid prices and/or wages, and fewer explicit contracts. This is an interesting approach, although the model tries too hard to rationalize trust in terms of an economic variable—growth rates—without considering the possibility that what contributes to those high growth rates is the prior existence of high levels of trust. As suggested above, it is likely that trust reduces firms' operating costs and raises their growth rates. With trust, employers have less need for control devices and cumbersome governance structures that are costly and can interfere with their ability to adapt quickly to changing market circumstances. Similarly, in the case of suppliers and customers, trust and goodwill can speed up innovation, reduce the cost of restructuring, and obviate costly or cumbersome contractual devices intended to lessen opportunism (Dore, 1987; Perrow, 1986).

An understanding of the economy or of the employment relationship thus requires that we analyze the social relations that underpin them. It is here that economists can learn much from noneconomists about the production of trust (and related conduct like cooperation and altruism) and about the social conditions that promote those behaviors (Etzioni, 1988). Consider the possibility that the NEO-ILE assumption of rampant opportunism is an unwitting time- and place-specific abstraction from modern American society (e.g., see Titmuss, 1970; Landau, 1984). Therein lies the current fascination of American managers with foreign social arrangements and workplace practices. It is more than a little ironic that those managers are presently seeking to promote trust and shrink bureaucratic controls (through decentralization, employee involvement, and union cooperation), while at the same time NEO-ILE theorists are devising models that rationalize in efficiency terms such phenomena as metering, hierarchy, and unilateral management (Alchian and Demsetz, 1972; Jensen and Meckling, 1979; Singh, 1985; Williamson, 1980).

Behavioral realism. The institutionalists' skepticism of *homo economicus* (Veblen's "homogenous globule of desire") has been validated by recent findings in cognitive psychology that question some of economic theory's behavioral precepts. Researchers have shown that expected utility maximization models do not accurately forecast behavior and that economic decisions are often only quasi-rational (Kahneman *et al.*, 1982; Russell and Thaler, 1985). People ignore high consequence events of low probability (e.g., few purchase flood or earthquake insurance) unless they have previously been exposed to them (Kunreuther *et al.*, 1978). These findings raise serious questions about the psychological adequacy of key NEO-ILE concepts such as reputation effects in agency theory or the self-monitoring consequences of efficiency wages. In each case, even if some minority of workers was treated unfairly or caught malingering, an employee who has never been mistreated or caught shirking (the vast majority) will think it unlikely that the employer will treat *her* unfairly (hence an unfair employer's reputation can remain unsullied) or that the employer will detect *her* malfeasance and dismiss her (hence shirking will continue). Thus, even with one's premium-wage job or reputation at stake, there is a threshold level (conceivably quite high) below which those stakes have no deterrent effect.

The new psychology also stresses that search and choice under uncertainty are not entirely rational but instead are guided by heuristic "frames" that are likely to have social and cultural origins. These can explain various behaviors of interest to labor economists, including bargaining, arbitration, tipping, and money illusion. In the case of wages, money illusion is thought to result from social norms regarding the "fairness" of real but not nominal wage cuts (Bazerman, 1985; Kahneman *et al.*, 1986; Dawes and Thaler, 1988). Again, the NEO-ILE's mixed parentage is reflected in the fact that some NEO-ILE researchers have incorporated these findings into their work (e.g., Akerlof, 1980; Kaufman, 1989), although most remain insensible or indifferent to them.

Conclusions: Some Thoughts on Methodology

As the papers in this symposium demonstrate, modern institutional labor economics is complex. It includes those who carry on in the ILE tradition and assert the necessity of middle-range theory and eclectic approaches in labor economics, and others who believe that a neoclassical efficiency (rational actor) approach can and should be extended to cover the field. In some respects the tendencies are similar. Both are in contact with and borrow from neoclassical theory, and both operate at a lower level of generality than neoclassicism's hard core. But they diverge on the issue of whether labor economics' distance from the core should be minimized or maintained. This essay has argued that distance as well as contact between the two is inevitable, necessary, and valuable. Although distance creates theoretical tension, it is something that institutional labor economists, whether NEO or not, should acknowledge and maintain, rather than rationalize or minimize.

In closing, I would like to offer some methodological precepts that can be gleaned from the ILE tradition and from the analysis presented here. These precepts—realism, empiricism, and eclecticism—are not arcane points from the past. They reflect the approach of a sizable group of economists at work today both within and outside of labor economics. Greater consciousness of methodological issues may improve the quality of work presently being done in labor economics and in economics more generally.

Realism. Although Friedman's (1953) dictum on realism of assumptions was the methodological mother's milk of many U.S. economists, philosophers of science now reject his emphasis on prediction. Explanation, they say, matters too. Friedman claimed that a theory's assumptions do not have to be realistic, but realism—what Freeman (1988) calls "informed priors"— enhances a theory's explanatory power. It allows us to know *why* a prediction is valid and to choose among competing theories (Caldwell, 1982; Hausman, 1989). Realism is also necessary in dealing with phenomena that are fixed in time and space, such as the institutional practices that are a focus of the NEO-ILE; and, at a lower level of abstraction, realism is important in analyzing and formulating policy, which includes the managerial actions and decisions that are of concern to the NEO-ILE. At that level, cautioned Knight (1951, p. 83), "account must be taken of many details of situations that fluctuate from case to case and that must be learned from empirical observation at the scene of the action."

Knight's point cannot be overemphasized. For example, when analyzing the labor market factors that determine competitive advantage among advanced industrial nations, details of institutional structure are extremely important. Evidence from comparative studies of firms in the same industry using identical technology shows significant national productivity differences, which are traced to particular and fine-grained institutional features: relations between workers, employers, and unions; linkages between social and industrial structures; and employment customs and practices (Dore, 1973; Lincoln and Kalleberg, 1985; Melman, 1958). Indeed, advanced nations that are successful at international trade are found to have "institutional structures widely different from those prescribed by...textbook models of competition" (Soskice, 1989, p. 2).

Empiricism. Knowing the facts about labor markets and keeping theory close to empirical reality are key parts of the ILE tradition that should be preserved.[14] Facts not only are needed for the verification of theoretical

---

[14] Economics today is more empirical than it was 50 years ago, when reliable economic data were scarce and sparsely used by economists. Yet Wesley Mitchell's jab at the armchair theorizing of his colleagues (which he politely aimed at the classical tradition) still rings true. Classical economics, said Mitchell, "erred sadly in trying to think out a deductive scheme and then talked of verifying *that*. Until a science has gotten to the stage of elaborating the details of an established body of theory, say...filling in a gap in the table of elements—it is rash to suppose one can get an hypothesis which stands much chance of holding good except from a process of verification, modification, fresh observation, and so on" (quoted in Gruchy, 1947, p. 268).

predictions but are elemental substances from which new theories are derived. Often the "stylized facts" that theorists work with are old or faulty. Without fresh infusions of facts the frontiers of scientific discovery remain frozen or mired in sophisticated explanations of the obvious. Too often NEO-ILE (and other) economists rush into print theories based on partial or incorrect factual knowledge; only later do the empiricists come to clean up the mess.[15]

Admittedly, some of those problems stem from the unavailability of facts. We need more data generated from a variety of sources and less reliance on the same limited sets of government or panel data. More data could permit testing of the myriad and contradictory theoretical claims in the NEO-ILE literature (e.g., Are wage structures stable because of efficiency wages, human capital, or noneconomic factors? Do age-earnings profiles tilt due to human capital or to incentive effects?) But as Leontief's (1982) study suggests, it is more convenient and prestigious for economists (including NEO-ILE economists) to "do theory" than to gather and study new facts.[16] The ILE literature bulged with factual material—case studies, surveys, industry studies, and labor market studies—but could have used more theory. Today there is an opposite problem.

Eclecticism. Economists are adept at arguing the irrelevance of other disciplines or of evidence that does not fit optimization models. They can always claim that market competition or learning effects will eliminate any noneconomic intrusion or any short- to medium-term departure from strict rationality. The strength of orthodox theory—and also its weakness—is its ability to rationalize or dismiss anomalous findings and facts.[17] Economists *do* have a point when they argue that other social sciences could benefit by paying more attention to the analytic methods and theoretical precision found in economics. But cross-disciplinary enlightenment flows in both directions. This is particularly true of topics that fall under the NEO-ILE rubric (e.g., work motivation, organizational structure, unionism), which

[15] For example, some able theorists (e.g., Hall and Lillien, 1979; Aoki, 1984) have repeatedly confused the causal relationship between the NLRB's contract bar rule and union contract durations. Since the Second World War, the former has determined the latter, not the reverse (Jacoby, 1987).

[16] Leontief found that two-thirds of the articles published in the American Economic Review between 1977 and 1981 contained no data, a share that makes economics unique among the natural and social sciences (Morgan, 1988).

[17] As demonstrated by a variety of critics (e.g., Nelson and Winter, 1982; Thurow, 1983), these rationalizations depend on a host of subsidiary and questionable assumptions: that markets are competitive and in equilibrium, that strong selection pressures weed out inefficient (including noneconomic) factors, and that long-run equilibrating processes are immune from shocks that would prevent an equilibrium position from being reached.

have received considerable attention from noneconomists. Incorporating perspectives from other disciplines would make NEO-ILE research more powerful by widening its range of evidence. At the same time, it would make NEO-ILE research more attractive and plausible to noneconomists.

Akerlof (1984) compares the unwillingness of neoclassical economists to derive assumptions from other disciplines to French chefs whose unwritten rules forbid the use of certain ingredients like raw fish or catsup. Below, I offer a sampling of ingredients from psychology, history, and sociology that would make for a more well-rounded, tasty, and nutritious intellectual cuisine. Of course, the chef might object that these additives have no place in his or her kitchen, but there is a long tradition in economics (including the ILE approach) that rejects this as excessive parsimony (Hirschman, 1985).

Cognitive and social psychology offer a rich body of empirical research that questions the strict rationality assumptions of the orthodox model. Previous efforts to go beyond that model—with concepts like Simon's (1957) bounded rationality and Leibenstein's (1976) selective rationality—never led economists very far into the domain of psychological research. Recently, however, there has been a welling up of research at the boundaries between the disciplines, although only a bit of it has trickled back into labor economics. Future work remains to be done that would ground rationality assumptions in empirical research on individual decision-making, the purpose of seemingly nonrational factors in utility functions, and the processes by which those functions derive their terms. At the very least, psychologists could teach NEO-ILE economists to make their behavioral assumptions explicit, especially any unconscious or unarticulated views about human nature and work behavior.

As labor economists return to the study of institutions, historical analysis should bulk larger in their research. Unlike markets, institutions and organizations have specific origins and histories; indeed, those origins often determine the course of institutional development (David, 1985). Historical and comparative analyses also reveal what is and is not unique about particular institutions and thus deter the use of inappropriate analytical generalizations. As one economic historian recently asked, how many economists know specifically what is modern or American about "modern American labor markets"? (Wright, 1987). Finally, more attention to historical methods and reasoning can help steer economists away from the kind of teleology that occasionally surfaces in the NEO-ILE, as when history is portrayed as the successive development of more efficient institutional forms.

Sociology has long been avoided by neoclassical economists, in part because holistic concepts like society contradict the normative and methodological individualism that lies at neoclassicism's core. But a variety of sociological concepts nevertheless are implicit in the *ceteris paribus* conditions that link the core to the real world, such as the set of social institutions that permit market exchanges to occur (everything from contract laws to the police to trust). This is what economic sociologists mean when they describe the economy as "embedded" in structures of social relations and social norms (Granovetter, 1985; Lowe, 1935). As shown in this essay, when economists abstract from these social terms or reduce them to maximizing behavior, they create economic man, who, says Sen (1982, p. 99), "is close to being a social moron." Social moronism might be a good approximation to reality in some instances, but it is a misleading oversimplification when applied to labor market behavior. More is involved in taking account of these social terms than simply inserting them into an individual's utility function. This solution can cause analytic problems, especially if preferences are interdependent and require individuals to act against immediate self-interest in the pursuit of social goals (Elster, 1982; Sen, 1985).

It is one thing to advocate for the NEO-ILE a greater reliance on eclectic, middle-level theories grounded in empirical reality. It is an entirely different matter to achieve it. Joining synchronic and diachronic analysis is not easy; nor is it easy to bridge theory and reality, economics and other disciplines, or what R. A. Gordon (1976) called "rigor and relevance." Striking the right intellectual balance depends on the topic at hand, on the uses of our knowledge, on judgment, and on an open mind. In understanding these matters, the ILE tradition—whatever its defects—is an old dog that still has tricks to teach us all.

References

Abowd, John and Steven Manaster. "Option Models of Employment Contracts: A Theoretical and Empirical Framework," Working Paper, Cornell University, 1985.

Abraham, Katharine G. and Henry S. Farber. "Job Duration, Seniority and Earnings," *American Economic Review*, LXXVII (June, 1987), 278–297.

Abraham, Katharine G. and James L. Medoff. "Length of Service and the Operation of Internal Labor Markets," *Proceedings* of the Thirty-Fifth Annual Meeting, Industrial Relations Research Association, New York, 1983, pp. 308–318.

Addison, John T. and Barry T. Hirsch. "Union Effects on Productivity, Profits, and Growth: Has the Long Run Arrived?", *Journal of Labor Economics*, VII (January, 1989), 72–105.

Akerlof, George A. *An Economic Theorist's Book of Tales*. Cambridge: Cambridge University Press, 1984.

——. "Labor Contracts as Partial Gift Exchange," *Quarterly Journal of Economics*, XCVII (November, 1982), 543–569.

——. "A Theory of Social Custom, of Which Unemployment May Be One Consequence," *Quarterly Journal of Economics*, XCIV (June, 1980), 749–775.

—— and H. Miyazaki. "The Implicit Contract Theory of Unemployment Meets the Wage Bill Argument," *Review of Economic Studies*, XLVII (1980), 321–338.

Akerlof, George and Janet Yellen. *Efficiency Wage Models of the Labor Market*. Cambridge: Cambridge University Press, 1986.

Alchian, Arman and Harold Demsetz. "Production, Information Costs, and Economic Organization," *American Economic Review*, LXII (December, 1972), 777–795.

Allen, Steven G. "Declining Unionization in Construction: The Facts and the Reasons," *Industrial and Labor Relations Review*, XLI (April, 1988), 343–359.

——. "Can Union Labor Ever Cost Less?", *Quarterly Journal of Economics*, CII (May, 1987), 347–365.

——. "Unionized Construction Workers Are More Productive," *Quarterly Journal of Economics*, IC (May, 1984), 251–274.

——, Robert L. Clark, and Ann A. McDermed. "Why Do Pensions Reduce Mobility?", Working Paper No. 2509, National Bureau of Economic Research, February 1988.

Amsden, Alice H. "Introduction." In Alice H. Amsden, ed., *The Economics of Women and Work*. Harmondsworth, Middlesex England: Penguin Books, 1980, pp. 11–38.

Andrisani, Paul J. *Work Attitudes and Labor Market Experience*. New York: Praeger, 1978.

Aoki, M. *A Cooperative Game Theory of the Firm*. Oxford: Clarendon, 1984.

Arrow, Kenneth. "Higher Education as a Filter," *Journal of Public Economics*, II (1973), 193–216.

——. "The Economic Implications of Learning by Doing," *Review of Economic Studies*, XXIX (January, 1962), 155–173.

Ashenfelter, Orley and David E. Bloom. "Models of Arbitrator Behavior: Theory and Evidence," *American Economic Review*, LXXIV (March, 1974), 111–124.

Atleson, James B. *Values and Assumptions in American Labor Law*. Amherst, MA: University of Massachusetts Press, 1983.

Azariadis, Costas. "Human Capital and Self-Enforcing Contracts," *Scandinavian Journal of Economics* (1988 Special Issue), 507–528.

——. "Implicit Contracts and Underemployment Equilibria," *Journal of Political Economy*, LXXXIII (December, 1975), 1183–1201.

—— and Joseph E. Stiglitz. "Implicit Contracts and Fixed-Price Equilibria," *Quarterly Journal of Economics*, XCVIII (1983 Supplement), 1–22.

Baily, Martin N. "Wages and Employment under Uncertain Demand," *Review of Economic Studies*, XLI (January, 1974), 37–50.

Baldamus, W. *Efficiency and Effort: An Analysis of Industrial Administration*. London: Tavistock, 1961.

Baldwin, John R. and Paul K. Gorecki. *The Role of Scale in Canada/U.S. Productivity Differences in the Manufacturing Sector, 1970–1979*. Toronto: University of Toronto Press, 1986.

Bazerman, Max H. "Norms of Distributive Justice in Interest Arbitration," *Industrial and Labor Relations Review*, XXXVIII (July, 1985), 558–570.

—— and Henry S. Farber. "Arbitrator Decision Making: When Are Final Offers Important?", *Industrial and Labor Relations Review*, XL (October, 1985), 76–89.

Becker, Gary. "Human Capital, Effort and the Sexual Division of Labor," *Journal of Labor Economics*, III (1985), S33–S58.

——. *Human Capital: A Theoretical Analysis with Special Reference to Education*. New York: Columbia University Press, 1964.

——. "Investment in Human Capital: A Theoretical Analysis," *Journal of Political Economy*, LXX (October, 1962), 9–49.

——. *The Economics of Discrimination*. Chicago, IL: University of Chicago Press, 1957.

—— and George Stigler. "Law Enforcement, Malfeasance and Compensation of Enforcers, " *Journal of Legal Studies*, III (January, 1974), 1–18.

Bendix, Reinhart. *Work and Authority in Industry*. New York: Wiley, 1956.

Black, Fischer. "The Tax Consequences of Long-Run Pension Policy," *Financial Analysts Journal* (July-August, 1980), 3–10.

Blair, D. H. and D. L. Crawford. "Labor Union Objectives and Collective Bargaining," *Quarterly Journal of Economics*, XCIX (August, 1984), 547–566.

Blanchard, Olivier J. and Lawrence H. Summers. "Hysteresis in Unemployment," Working Paper No. 2035, National Bureau of Economic Research, October 1986.

Blau, Francine and Andrea Beller. "Trends in Earnings Differentials by Gender, 1971–1981," *Industrial and Labor Relations Review*, XLI (July, 1988), 513–529.

Blau, Francine and Lawrence Kahn. "Race and Sex Differences in Quit Rates by Young Workers," *Industrial and Labor Relations Review*, XXXIV (July, 1981), 563–577.

Blaug, Mark. "Where Are We Now in the Economics of Education?", *Economics of Education Review*, IV (1985), 17–28.

——. *The Economics of Education: An Annotated Bibliography*. 3rd ed.; Oxford: Pergamon Press, 1976a.

——. "The Empirical Status of Human Capital Theory: A Slightly Jaundiced View," *Journal of Economic Literature*, XIV (1976b), 827–855.

Bloom, David E. "Empirical Models of Arbitrator Behavior Under Conventional Arbitration," *Review of Economics and Statistics*, LXVIII (December, 1986), 578–585.

Bond, Eric W. and Tain-Jy Chen. "The Welfare Effects of Illegal Immigration," *Journal of International Economics*, XXIII (November, 1987), 315–328.

Borsook, I. "Earnings, Ability and International Trade," *Journal of International Economics*, XXII (May, 1987), 281–295.

Boulding, Kenneth E. "Implications for General Economics of More Realistic Theories of the Firm," *American Economic Review*, XLII (May, 1952), 35–44.

Bowles, Samuel. "The Production Process in a Competitive Economy: Walrasian, Neo-Hobbesian, and Marxian Models," *American Economic Review*, LXXV (May, 1985),

16–36.

—— and Herbert Gintis. *Education and Capitalism in the U.S.* New York: Basic Books, 1976.

——. "The Problem with Human Capital Theory--A Marxist Critique," *American Economic Review*, LXV (May, 1975), 74–82.

Brander, James A. "Intra-Industry Trade in Identical Commodities," *Journal of International Economics*, XI (February, 1981), 1–14.

—— and Barbara J. Spencer. "Unionized Oligopoly and International Trade Policy," *Journal of International Economics*, XXIV (May, 1988), 217–235.

——. "Foreign Direct Investment with Unemployment and Endogenous Taxes and Tariffs," *Journal of International Economics*, XXII (May, 1987), 257–279.

——. "Export Subsidies and International Market Share Rivalry," *Journal of International Economics*, XVIII (February, 1985), 83–100.

——. "Tariff Protection and Imperfect Competition." In Henryk Kierzkowski, ed., *Monopolistic Competition and International Trade*. Oxford: Clarendon Press, 1984, pp. 194–206.

Brecher, Richard A. and Ehsan U. Choudhri. "International Migration Versus Foreign Investment in the Presence of Unemployment," *Journal of International Economics*, XXIII (November, 1987), 329–342.

Brown, Charles and James L. Medoff. "Trade Unions in the Production Process," *Journal of Political Economy*, LXXXVI (June, 1978), 355–378.

Brown, Clair. "Income Distribution in an Institutional World." In Garth Mangum and Peter Philips, eds., *The Three Worlds of Labor Economics*. Armonk, NY: Sharpe, 1988, pp. 51–56.

Brown, James N. and Orley Ashenfelter. "Testing the Efficiency of Employment Contracts," *Journal of Political Economy*, XCIV (June, 1986), S40-S87.

Bruno, Michael and Jeffery D. Sachs. *Economics of Worldwide Stagflation*. Cambridge, MA: Harvard University Press, 1985.

Bull, Clive. "The Existence of Self-Enforcing Implicit Contracts," *Quarterly Journal of Economics*, CII (February, 1987), 147–160.

Cain, Glen. "The Economic Analysis of Labor Market Discrimination: A Survey." In Orley Ashenfelter and R. Layard, eds., *Handbook of Labor Economics*. Amsterdam: Elsevier Science Publishers, 1986, pp. 693–785.

——. "The Challenge of Segmented Labor Market Theories to Orthodox Theory: A Survey," *Journal of Economic Literature*, XIV (1976), 1215–1257.

Caldwell, Bruce J. *Beyond Positivism: Economic Methodology in the 20th Century*. London: Allen & Unwin, 1987.

Calvo, Guillermo and Stanislaw Wellisz. "International Factor Mobility and National Advantage," *Journal of International Economics*, XIV (February, 1983), 103–114.

Card, David. "Longitudinal Analysis of Strike Activity," *Journal of Labor Economics*, VI (April, 1988), 147–176.

——. "Efficient Contracts with Costly Adjustment: Short-Run Employment Determination for Airline Mechanics," *American Economic Review*, LXXVI (December, 1986), 1045–1071.

Carmichael, H. Lorne. "Reputations in the Labor Market," *American Economic Review*, LXXIV (May, 1984), 713–725.

——. "The Agent-Agents Problem: Payment by Relative Output," *Journal of Labor Economics*, I (January, 1983), 50–65.

Carnoy, Martin. "Education, Economy and the State." In Michael Apple, ed., *Cultural and Economic Reproduction in Education: Essays on Class, Ideology and the State*. London: Routledge and Kegan Paul, 1981, pp. 79–126.

Carrell, M. R. and J. E. Dittrich. "Equity Theory: The Recent Literature and New Directions," *Academy of Management Review*, III (April, 1978), 202–210.

Carter, Susan B. "The Changing Importance of Lifetime Jobs, 1892–1978," *Industrial Relations*, XXVII (Fall, 1988), 287–300.

Casebeer, Kenneth. "Holder of the Pen: An Interview with Leon Keyserling," *University of Miami Law Review*, XLII (November, 1987), 285–363.

Catanzarite, Lisa M. and Myra H. Strober. "Occupational Attractiveness and Race-Gender Segregation, 1960–80." Paper presented at the Annual Meetings of the American Sociological Association, Atlanta, August 1988.

Chacholiades, Miltiades. *International Trade Theory and Policy*. New York: McGraw-Hill, 1978.

Chandler, Alfred D. *The Visible Hand: The Managerial Revolution in American Business*. Cambridge, MA: Harvard University Press, 1977.

Clark, Kim. "The Impact of Unionization on Productivity: A Case Study," *Industrial and Labor Relations Review*, XXXIII (July, 1980), 451–469.

Closius, Phillip J. and Henry M. Schaffer. "Involuntary Nonservitude: The Current Judicial Enforcement of Employee Covenants Not to Compete--A Proposal for Reform," *Southern California Law Review*, LVII (May, 1984), 531–560.

Cohen, George M. and Michael L. Wachter. "An Internal Labor Market Approach to Labor Law: Does Labor Law Promote Efficient Contracting?", *Proceedings* of the Forty-First Annual Meeting, Industrial Relations Research Association. Madison, WI: 1988, pp. 243–250.

Colander, David and Arjo Klamer. "The Making of an Economist," *Economic Perspectives*, I (Fall, 1987), 95–111.

Cole, Robert E. *Work, Mobility, and Participation: A Comparative Study of American and Japanese Industry*. Berkeley, CA: University of California Press, 1979.

Commons, John R. *The Economics of Collective Action*. New York: Macmillan, 1950.

——. *Institutional Economics: Its Place in Political Economy*. New York: Macmillan, 1934.

——. *The Legal Foundations of Capitalism*. New York: Macmillan, 1924.

Cooper, Russell. *Wage and Employment Patterns in Labor Contracts: Microfoundations and Macroeconomic Implications*. New York: Harwood Academic Publishers, 1987.

Corcoran, Mary, Greg Duncan, and Michael Ponza. "Work Experience, Job Segregation, and Wages." In Barbara Reskin, ed., *Sex Segregation in the Workplace: Trends, Explanations and Remedies*. Washington, DC: National Academy Press, 1984, pp. 171–191.

Cox, Archibald, Derek Curtis Box, and Robert A. Gorman. *Cases and Materials on Labor Law*. 10th ed.; New York: Foundation Press, 1986.

Das, Satya P. "Effects of Foreign Investment in the Presence of Unemployment," *Journal of International Economics*, XI (May, 1981), 249–257.

David, Paul A. "Clio and the Economics of QWERTY," *American Economic Review*, LXXV (May, 1985), 332–337.

Dawes, Robin M. and Richard H. Thaler. "Anomalies: Cooperation," *Journal of Economic Perspectives*, II (Summer, 1988), 187–198.

Deardorff, Alan V. and Robert M. Stern. "Current Issues in Trade Policy: An Overview." In Robert M. Stern, ed., *U.S. Trade Policies in a Changing World Economy*. Cambridge, MA: MIT Press, 1987, pp. 15–72.

Denison, Edward F. *Trends in American Economic Growth, 1929–1982*. Washington, DC: Brookings, 1985.

Dickens, William T. "The Effect of Company Campaigns on Certification Elections: Law and Reality Once Again," *Industrial and Labor Relations Review*, XXXVI (July, 1983), 560–575.

—— and Kevin Lang. "Why It Matters What We Trade: A Case for Active Policy." In Laura d'Andrea Tyson, William T. Dickens, and John Zysman, eds., *The Dynamics of Trade and Employment*. Cambridge, MA: Ballinger, 1988, pp. 87–112.

Dickens, William T. and Jonathan Leonard. "Accounting for the Decline in Union

Membership, 1950–1980," *Industrial and Labor Relations Review*, XXXVIII (April, 1985), 323–334.

Dixit, Avinash. "Optimal Trade and Industrial Policies for the US Automobile Industry." In Robert C. Feenstra, ed., *Empirical Methods for International Trade*. Cambridge, MA: MIT Press, 1988, pp. 141–165.

——. "Strategic Aspects of Trade Policy." In Truman F. Bewley, ed., *Advances in Economic Theory - Fifth World Congress*. Cambridge: Cambridge University Press, 1987, pp. 329–362.

—— and Joseph E. Stiglitz. "Monopolistic Competition and Optimum Product Diversity," *American Economic Review*, LXVII (June, 1977), 297–308.

Doeringer, Peter and Michael Piore. *Internal Labor Markets and Manpower Analysis*. Lexington, MA.: Heath, 1971.

Dore, Ronald P. *Taking Japan Seriously: A Confucian Perspective on Leading Economic Issues*. Stanford, CA: Stanford University Press, 1987.

——. *British Factory/Japanese Factory: The Origins of National Diversity in Industrial Relations*. Berkeley, CA: University of California Press, 1973.

Douglas, Paul H. *American Apprenticeship and Industrial Education*. New York: Columbia University Press, 1921.

Dow, G. K. "The Function of Authority in Transaction Cost Economics," *Journal of Economic Behavior and Organization*, VIII (March, 1987), 13–38.

Duncan, G. J. and F. P. Stafford. "Do Union Members Receive Compensating Differentials?", *American Economic Review*, LXX (June, 1980), 355–371.

Dunlop, John T. "Labor Markets and Wage Determination: Then and Now." In Bruce E. Kaufman, ed., *How Labor Markets Work*. Lexington, MA: Heath, 1988, pp. 47–87.

——. *Industrial Relations Systems*. New York: Holt, 1958.

——. "The Task of Contemporary Wage Theory." In George W. Taylor and Frank C. Pierson, eds., *New Concepts in Wage Determination*. New York: McGraw Hill, 1957, pp. 117–139.

——. *Wage Determination under Trade Unions*. New York: Kelley, 1950.

Durkheim, Emil. *The Division of Labor in Society*. New York: Macmillan, 1933.

Eastman, H. C. and S. Stykolt. *The Tariff and Competition in Canada*. Toronto: Macmillan, 1967.

Economic Council of Canada. *Looking Outward, A New Trade Strategy for Canada*. Ottawa: Information Canada, 1975.

Edwards, Richard C. *Contested Terrain: The Transformation of the Workplace in the 20th Century*. New York: Basic, 1979.

Ehrenberg, Ronald G. and George M. Jakubson. *Advance Notice Provisions in Plant Closing Legislation*. Kalamazoo, MI: Upjohn, 1988.

——. "Advance Notice Provisions in Plant Closing Legislation: Do They Matter?", *Industrial Relations*, XXVIII (Winter, 1989), 60–71.

Ehrenberg, Ronald G. and Robert G. Smith. *Modern Labor Economics*. 3rd ed.; Glenview, IL: Scott, Foresman, 1988.

Ellwood, David T. "Pensions and the Labor Market: A Starting Point (The Mouse Can Roar)." In David A. Wise, ed., *Pensions, Labor, and Individual Choice*. Chicago, IL: University of Chicago Press for NBER, 1985, pp. 19–53.

Elster, Jon. "Sour Grapes: Utilitarianism and the Genesis of Wants." In A. Sen and B. Williams, eds., *Utilitarianism and Beyond*. Cambridge: Cambridge University Press, 1982, pp. 219–238.

Ely, Richard T. "Organization of the American Economic Association," *Publications of the AEA*, I (March, 1886), 1–45.

England, Paula, George Farkas, Barbara Stanek Kilbourne, and Thomas Dou. "Explaining Occupational Sex Segregation and Wages: Findings From a Model with Fixed Effects," *American Sociological Review*, LIII (August, 1988), 544–558.

Ethier, Wilfred J. "Illegal Immigration: The Host-Country Problem," *American Economic Review*, LXXVI (March, 1986), 56–71.

——. "International Trade and Labor Migration," *American Economic Review*, LXXV (September, 1985), 691–707.

Etzioni, Amitai. *The Moral Dimension: Toward A New Economics*. New York: Free Press, 1988.

——. *A Comparative Analysis of Complex Organizations*. New York: Free Press, 1961.

Farber, Henry S. "The Analysis of Union Behavior." In Orley C. Ashenfelter and Richard Layard, eds., *Handbook of Labor Economics*, Vol. II. Amsterdam: North Holland, 1986, pp. 1039–1089.

——. "The Extent of Unionization in the United States." In Thomas A. Kochan, ed., *Challenges and Choices Facing American Labor*. Cambridge, MA: MIT Press, 1985, pp. 15–44.

——. "Splitting the Difference in Interest Arbitration," *Industrial and Labor Relations Review*, XXXV (October, 1981), 70–77.

—— and Harry C. Katz. "Interest Arbitration, Outcomes, and the Incentive to Bargain," *Industrial and Labor Relations Review*, XXXIII (October, 1979), 55–63.

Farber, Henry S. and Daniel H. Saks. "Why Workers Want Unions: The Role of Relative Wages and Job Characteristics," *Journal of Political Economy*, LXXXVII (April, 1980), 349–369.

Feldstein, Martin. "Temporary Layoffs in the Theory of Unemployment," *Journal of Political Economy*, LXXXIV (October, 1976), 937–957.

Feuille, Peter. "Final Offer Arbitration and the Chilling Effect," *Industrial Relations*, XIV (October, 1975), 302–310.

——, Wallace E. Hendricks, and Lawrence M. Kahn. "Wage and Nonwage Outcomes in Collective Bargaining: Determinants and Tradeoffs," *Journal of Labor Research*, II (Spring, 1981), 39–53.

Feuille, Peter and John T. Delaney. "Collective Bargaining, Interest Arbitration, and Police Salaries," *Industrial and Labor Relations Review*, XXXVII (January, 1986), 228–240.

Filer, Randall K. "The Role of Personality and Tastes in Determining Occupational Structure," *Industrial and Labor Relations Review*, XXXIX (April, 1986), 412–424.

Findlay, Ronald and Henryk Kierzkowski. "International Trade and Human Capital: A Simple General Equilibrium Model," *Journal of Political Economy*, XCI (December, 1983), 957–978.

Fischel, Daniel. "Labor Markets and Labor Law Compared with Capital Markets and Capital Law," *University of Chicago Law Review*, IV (1984), 1061–1077.

Flanagan, Robert J. "Compliance and Enforcement Decisions Under the National Labor Relations Act," *Journal of Labor Economics*, VII (July, 1989), 257–280.

——. *Labor Relations and the Litigation Explosion*. Washington, DC: Brookings, 1987.

——. "Implicit Contracts, Explicit Contracts and Wages," *American Economic Review*, LXXIV (May, 1984a), 345–349.

——. "Wage Concessions and Long-Term Union Wage Flexibility," *Brookings Papers on Economic Activity*, 1: 1984b, pp. 183–216.

——, David W. Soskice, and Lloyd Ulman. *Unionism, Economic Stabilization and Incomes Policies: European Experience*. Washington, DC: Brookings, 1983.

Fox, Alan. *Beyond Contract: Work, Power, and Trust Relations*. London: Faber, 1974.

Freedman, Audrey. *The New Look in Wage Policy and Employee Relations*, report no. 865. New York: Conference Board, 1985.

Freeman, Richard B. "Does the New Generation of Labor Economists Know More than the Old Generation?" In B. E. Kaufman, ed., *How Labor Markets Work*. Lexington, MA: Heath, 1988, pp. 205–232.

——. "Unionism and Protective Legislation," *Proceedings* of the Thirty-Ninth Annual Meeting, Industrial Relations Research Association. Madison, WI: 1987, pp. 260–267.

—— and James Medoff. *What Do Unions Do?* New York: Basic Books, 1984.

Friedman, Milton. "The Role of Monetary Policy," *American Economic Review*, LVIII (March, 1968), 1–17.

——. "The Methodology of Positive Economics." In *Essays on Positive Economics*. Chicago, IL: University of Chicago Press, 1953.

——. "Some Comments on the Significance of Labor Unions for Economic Policy." In David McCord Wright, ed., *The Impact of the Union*. New York: Harcourt, Brace, 1951.

Getman, Julius G., Stephen B. Goldberg, and Jeanne B. Herman. *Union Representation Elections: Law and Reality*. New York: Russell Sage Foundation, 1976.

Goldberg, Victor. "A Relational Exchange Perspective on the Employment Relationship." In F. H. Stephen, ed., *Firms, Organization and Labour*. New York: St. Martin's Press, 1984, pp. 127–145.

——. "Bridges Over Contested Terrain: Exploring the Radical Account of the Employment Relationship," *Journal of Economic Behavior and Organization*, I (September, 1980), 249–274.

Goldin, Claudia. "Monitoring Costs and Occupational Segregation by Sex: A Historical Analysis," *Journal of Labor Economics*, IV (July, 1986), 1–27.

Goldthorpe, J. H. *The Affluent Worker: Industrial Attitudes and Behavior*. Cambridge: Cambridge University Press, 1968.

Gordon, David M., Richard E. Edwards, and Michael Reich. *Segmented Work, Divided Workers: The Historical Transformation of Labor in the United States*. Cambridge: Cambridge University Press, 1982.

Gordon, Donald F. "A Neo-Classical Theory of Keynesian Unemployment," *Economic Inquiry*, XII (December, 1974), 431–459.

Gordon, Robert A. "Rigor and Relevance in a Changing Institutional Setting," *American Economic Review*, LXVI (March, 1976), 1–14.

Gordon, Robert J. "Fresh Water, Salt Water, and Other Macroeconomic Elixirs," *Economic Record* (forthcoming).

——. "The Role of Wages in the Inflation Process," *American Economic Review*, LXXVIII (May, 1988), 276–283.

——. "Why U.S. Wage and Employment Behavior Differs from that in Britain and Japan," *Economic Journal*, XCII (March, 1982), 13–44.

Gouldner, Alvin W. *Patterns of Industrial Bureaucracy*. Glencoe, IL: Free Press, 1954.

Gramm, Cynthia, Wallace E. Hendricks, and Lawrence M. Kahn. "Inflation, Uncertainty and Strike Activity," *Industrial Relations*, XXVII (Winter, 1988), 114–129.

Granovetter, Mark. "Economic Action and Social Structure: The Problem of Embeddedness," *American Journal of Sociology*, XCI (November, 1985), 481–510.

Gray, Jo Anna. "On Indexation and Contract Length," *Journal of Political Economy*, LXXXVI (February, 1978), 1–18.

Green, Jerry R. "The Riskiness of Private Pensions." In David A. Wise, ed., *Pensions, Labor and Individual Choice*. Chicago, IL: University of Chicago Press for NBER, 1985, pp. 357–375.

—— and C. M. Kahn. "Wage-Employment Contracts," *Quarterly Journal of Economics*, XCVIII (1983 Supplement), 173–189.

Greenwald, Bruce and Joseph E. Stiglitz. "Keynesian, New Keynesian, and New Classical Economics," Working Paper No. 2160, National Bureau of Economic Research, February 1987.

Gregory, R. G., R. Anstie, A. Daly, and V. Ho. "Women's Pay in Australia, Britain and the United States: The Role of Laws, Regulations and Human Capital." In Robert T. Michael, Heidi I. Hartmann, and Brigid O'Farrell, eds., *Pay Equity: Empirical Inquiries*. Washington, DC: National Academy Press, 1989, pp. 222–242.

Gross, James A. *The Making of the National Labor Relations Board*. Albany, NY: SUNY Press, 1974.

Grossman, Gene M. "International Competition and the Unionized Sector," *Canadian Journal of Economics*, XVII (August, 1984), 541–556.

Grossman, S. J. and O. D. Hart. "Implicit Contracts and Fixed-Price Equilibria," *Quarterly Journal of Economics*, XCVIII (1983 Supplement), 123–156.

Gruchy, Alvin. *Modern Economic Thought: The American Contribution*. Englewood Cliffs, NJ: Prentice-Hall, 1947.

Gustman, Alan L. and Thomas L. Steinmeier. "Pensions, Efficiency Wages, and Job Mobility," Working Paper No. 2426, National Bureau of Economic Research, November 1987.

Guzzo, R. A. and Raymond A. Katzell. "Effects of Economic Incentives on Productivity." In H. R. Nalbantian, ed., *Incentives, Cooperation, and Risk Sharing*. Totowa, NJ: Rowman & Littlefield, 1987, pp. 107–119.

Hall, Robert E. "The Importance of Lifetime Jobs in the U.S.," *American Economic Review*, LXIX (September, 1982), 716–724.

—— and David M. Lilien. "Efficient Wage Bargains under Uncertain Supply and Demand," *American Economic Review*, LXIX (December, 1979), 868–879.

Harris, M. and A. Raviv. "Optimal Incentive Contracts With Imperfect Information," *Journal of Economic Theory*, XX (April, 1979), 231–259.

Harris, Richard. "Applied General Equilibrium Analysis of Small Open Economies with Scale Economies and Imperfect Competition," *American Economic Review*, LXXIV (December, 1984), 1016–1032.

Hart, Oliver, D. "Optimal Labor Contracts under Asymmetric Information: An Introduction," *Review of Economic Studies*, L (January, 1983), 3–35.

—— and Bengt Holmstrom. "The Theory of Contracts." In Truman Bewley, ed., *Advances in Economic Theory*. Cambridge: Cambridge University Press, 1987, pp. 71–155.

Hartmann, Heidi. "Capitalism, Patriarchy and Job Segregation by Sex." In Martha Blaxall and Barbara Reagan, eds., *Women and the Workplace: The Implications of Occupational Segregation*. Chicago, IL: University of Chicago Press, 1976, pp. 137–170.

Hartog, Joop. "Earnings Functions: Beyond Human Capital," *Applied Economics*, XVIII (1987), 1291–1309.

Hashimoto, Masanori. "Firm-Specific Human Capital as a Shared Investment," *American Economic Review*, LXXI (June, 1981), 475–482.

Hausman, Daniel M. "Economic Methodology in a Nutshell," *Journal of Economic Perspectives*, III (Spring, 1989), 115–127.

Hausman, Jerry and Lynn Paquette. "Involuntary Early Retirement and Consumption." In Gary Burtless, ed., *Work, Health and Income among the Elderly*. Washington, DC: Brookings, 1987, pp. 151–175.

Hayes, Beth. "Unions and Strikes with Asymmetric Information," *Journal of Labor Economics*, II (January, 1984), 57–83.

Heflebower, Richard B. "Full Costs, Cost Changes, and Prices." In National Bureau of Economic Research, *Business Concentration and Price Policy*. Princeton, NJ: Princeton University Press, 1955, pp. 361–392.

Helliwell, J.F. "Comparative Macroeconomics of Stagflation," *Journal of Economic Literature*, XXVI (March, 1988), 1–28.

Helpman, Elhanan. "Increasing Returns, Imperfect Markets, and Trade Theory." In Ronald W. Jones and Peter B. Kenen, eds., *Handbook of International Economics*, Vol. I. Amsterdam: Elsevier Science Publishers, 1984, pp. 325–365.

——. "International Trade in the Presence of Product Differentiation, Economies of Scale and Monopolistic Competition: A Chamberlin-Heckscher-Ohlin Approach," *Journal of International Economics*, XI (August, 1981), 305–340.

——. *Trade Policy and Market Structure*. Cambridge, MA: MIT Press, 1989.

—— and Paul R. Krugman. *Market Structure and Foreign Trade*. Cambridge, MA: MIT Press, 1985.

Hendricks, Wallace E. "Labor Market Structure and Union Wage Levels," *Economic Inquiry*, XIII (September, 1975), 401–416.

—— and Lawrence M. Kahn. "The Demand for Labor Market Structure: An Economic Approach," *Journal of Labor Economics*, II (July, 1984), 412–438.

Hicks, J. R. *The Theory of Wages*. 2nd ed.; London: Macmillan, 1964.

Hildebrand, George H. and George F. Delehanty. "Wage Levels and Differentials." In R. A. Gordon and M. S. Gordon, eds., *Prosperity and Unemployment*. New York: Wiley, 1966, pp. 265–301.

Hill, John K. "Comparative Statics in General Equilibrium Models with a Unionized Sector," *Journal of International Economics*, XVI (May, 1984), 345–356.

Hirsch, Barry T. and John T. Addison. *The Economic Analysis of Unions: New Approaches and Evidence*. Boston, MA: Allen & Unwin, 1986.

Hirsch, Fred. *Social Limits to Growth*. Cambridge, MA: Harvard University Press, 1976.

Hirschman, Albert O. "Against Parsimony," *Economics and Philosophy*, I (April, 1985), 7–21.

——. *Exit, Voice and Loyalty*. Cambridge, MA: Harvard University Press, 1970.

Holmstrom, Bengt. "Equilibrium Long-Term Contracts," *Quarterly Journal of Economics*, XCVIII (1983 Supplement), 23–54.

Hopkins, E. M. "Advantages of Centralized Employment," *The Annals*, LXXI (May, 1917), 1–9.

Hurd, Michael D. "Comment on Lazear and Moore." In Zvi Bodie, John B. Shoven, and David A. Wise, eds., *Pensions in the U.S. Economy*. Chicago, IL: University of Chicago Press for NBER, 1988, pp. 188–190.

Hutchens, Robert M. "A Test of Lazear's Theory of Delayed Payment Contracts," *Journal of Labor Economics*, V (October, 1987), S153–S170.

Hutchison, T. W. *The Significance and Basic Postulates of Economic Theory*. London: Macmillan, 1938.

Ichniowski, Casey. "The Effects of Grievance Activity on Productivity," *Industrial and Labor Relations Review*, XL (October, 1986), 75–89.

Ippolito, Richard A. "Why Federal Workers Don't Quit," *Journal of Human Resources*, XXII (Spring, 1987), 281–299.

——. *Pensions, Economics, and Public Policy*. Homewood, IL: Dow Jones-Irwin, 1986.

——. "The Labor Contract and True Economic Pension Liabilities," *American Economic Review*, LXXV (December, 1985): 1031–1043.

—— and Walter W. Kolodrubetz. *Handbook of Pension Statistics*. Chicago, IL: Commerce Clearing House, 1986.

Jackson, Matthew and Edward P. Lazear. "Stock, Options, and Deferred Compensation," Working Paper No. E-88–11, Hoover Institution, February 1988.

Jacoby, Henry. *The Bureaucratization of the World*. Berkeley, CA: University of California Press, 1973.

Jacoby, Sanford M. "Pacific Ties: Industrial Relations and Employment Systems in Japan and the U.S." In H. J. Harris and N. Lichtenstein, eds., *Industrial Democracy in the Twentieth Century*. Cambridge: Cambridge University Press, forthcoming.

——. "The Intellectual Foundations of Industrial Relations." Unpublished working paper, 1988.

——. "The Development of Cost-of-Living Escalators in the U.S.," *Labor History*, XXIX (Fall, 1987), 515–533.

——. "Progressive Discipline in American Industry: Its Origins, Development, and Consequences," *Advances in Industrial and Labor Relations*, III (1986), 213–260.

——. *Employing Bureaucracy: Managers, Unions, and the Transformation of Work in American Industry, 1900–1945*. New York: Columbia University Press, 1985.

——. "Industrial Labor Mobility in Historical Perspective," *Industrial Relations*, XXII (Spring, 1983), 261–282.

——. "The Duration of Indefinite Employment Contracts in the United States and England,"

Comparative Labor Law, V (Winter, 1982), 85–128.

——. "The Origins of Internal Labor Markets in Japan," *Industrial Relations*, XVIII (Spring, 1979), 184–196.

—— and Daniel J. B. Mitchell. "Does Implicit Contracting Explain Explicit Contracting?" In Barbara D. Dennis, ed., *Proceedings* of the Thirty-Fifth Annual Meeting, Industrial Relations Research Association, Madison, WI: 1983, pp. 319–328.

Jensen, Michael C. and W. H. Meckling. "Rights and Production Functions: An Application to Labor-Managed Firms and Codetermination," *Journal of Business*, LII (October, 1979), 469–506.

Jones, Ronald W., Isaias Coelho, and Stephen T. Easton. "The Theory of International Factor Flows: The Basic Model," *Journal of International Economics*, XX (May, 1986), 313–327.

Jovanovic, Boyan. "Job Matching and the Theory of Turnover," *Journal of Political Economy*, LXXXVII (October, 1979), 972–990.

Kahneman, D., J. L. Knetsch, and R. Thaler. "Fairness as a Constraint on Profit Seeking: Entitlements in the Market," *American Economic Review*, LXXVI (September, 1986), 728–741.

——, P. Slovic, and A. Tversky, eds. *Judgement Under Uncertainty: Heuristics and Biases*. Cambridge: Cambridge University Press, 1982.

Kandel, Eugene and Edward P. Lazear. "Peer Pressure and Partnerships," Working Paper in Economics E-89-5, Hoover Institution, January 1989.

Katz, Lawrence F. "Efficiency Wage Theories: A Partial Evaluation." In S. Fischer, ed., *NBER Macroeconomics Annual 1986*. Cambridge, MA: MIT Press, 1986.

—— and Lawrence H. Summers. "Industry Rents: Evidence and Implications," *Brookings Papers on Economic Activity: Microeconomics*, 1: 1989, pp. 209–275.

Kaufman, Bruce E. "Models of Man in Industrial Relations Research," *Industrial and Labor Relations Review*, XLIII (October, 1989), 72–88.

Kennan, John. "The Economics of Strikes." In Orley Ashenfelter and Richard Layard, eds., *Handbook of Labor Economics*, Volume II. New York: North Holland, 1986, pp. 276–310.

Kerr, Clark. "The Neoclassical Revisionists in Labor Economics (1940–1960)--R.I.P." In Bruce E. Kaufman, ed., *How Labor Markets Work*. Lexington, MA: Heath, 1988, pp. 1–40.

—— and Lloyd Fisher. "Plant Sociology: The Elite and the Aborigines." In Mirra Komarovsky, ed., *Common Frontiers of the Social Sciences*. Glencoe, IL: Free Press, 1957.

——. "The Balkanization of Labor Markets." In E. Wight Bakke, ed., *Labor Mobility and Economic Opportunity*. Cambridge, MA: The Technology Press of MIT, 1954, pp. 92–110.

Keynes, J. M. "The Economic Consequences of Mr. Churchill." (1925). Reprinted in *Essays in Persuasion*. New York: Norton, 1963.

——. *The General Theory of Employment, Interest, and Money*. New York: Harcourt, Brace, 1936.

Kiefer, David and Peter Philips. "Doubts Regarding the Human Capital Theory of Racial Inequality," *Industrial Relations*, XXVII (Spring, 1988), 251–261.

Kierzkowski, Henryk. *Monopolistic Competition and International Trade*. Oxford: Clarendon Press, 1984.

Kiker, B. F. and Julia A. Heath. "The Effect of Socioeconomic Background on Earnings: Comparison by Race," *Economics of Education Review*, IV (1985), 45–55.

Klein, Benjamin, R. G. Crawford, and Armen Alchian. "Vertical Integration, Appropriable Rents, and the Competitive Contracting Process," *Journal of Law and Economics*, XXI (October, 1978), 297–326.

Knieser, Thomas J. and Arthur H. Goldsmith. "A Survey of Alternative Models of the

Aggregate U.S. Labor Market," *Journal of Economic Literature*, XXV (September, 1987), 1241–1280.

Knight, Frank H. "Economics and the Ethics of the Wage Problem." In D. McCord Wright, ed., *The Impact of the Union*. New York: Harcourt Brace, 1951, pp. 80–110.

——. *Risk, Uncertainty, and Profit*. Boston, MA: Houghton Mifflin, 1921.

Kochan, Thomas A., Robert B. McKersie, and John Chalykoff. "The Effects of Corporate Strategy and Workplace Innovations on Union Representation," *Industrial and Labor Relations Review*, XXXIX (July, 1986), 487–501.

Kochan, Thomas A., Harry C. Katz, and Robert B. McKersie. *The Transformation of American Industrial Relations*. New York: Basic Books, 1986.

Kohn, Melvin. *Class and Conformity: A Study in Values*. Chicago, IL: University of Chicago Press, 1977.

Kotlikoff, Laurence J. and David A. Wise. "The Incentive Effects of Private Pension Plans." In Zvi Bodie, John B. Shoven, and David A. Wise, eds., *Issues in Pension Economics*. Chicago, IL: University of Chicago Press for NBER, 1987, pp. 283–336.

Krueger, Alan B. "The Evolution of Unjust Dismissal Legislation in the United States," Working Paper, Princeton University, October 1988.

Krugman, Paul R. "Scale Economies, Product Differentiation and the Pattern of Trade," *American Economic Review*, LXX (December, 1980), 950–959.

——. "Import Protection as Export Promotion." In Henryk Kierzkowski, ed., *Monopolistic Competition and International Trade*. Oxford: Clarendon Press, 1984, pp. 180–193.

——. "Increasing Returns, Monopolistic Competition, and International Trade," *Journal of International Economics*, IX (November, 1979), 469–479.

Kuh, E. "A Productivity Theory of Wage Levels—An Alternative to the Phillips Curve," *Review of Economic Studies*, XXXIV (October, 1967), 333–360.

Kunreuther, H. C., R. Ginsberg, L. Miller, P. Sagi, and P. Slovic. *Disaster Insurance Protection: Public Policy Lessons*. New York: Wiley, 1978.

Lancaster, Kelvin. "Intra-Industry Trade under Perfect Monopolistic Competition," *Journal of International Economics*, X (May, 1980), 151–175.

——. *Variety, Equity, and Efficiency*. New York: Columbia University Press, 1979.

Landau, Saul. "Trends in Violence and Aggression: Cross-Cultural Analysis," *International Journal of Comparative Sociology*, XXV (September, 1984), 133–158.

Latsis, Spiro, ed. *Method and Appraisal in Economics*. Cambridge: Cambridge University Press, 1976.

Lawrence, Colin and Robert Z. Lawrence. "Manufacturing Wage Dispersion: An End Game Interpretation," *Brookings Papers on Economic Activity*, 1: 1985, pp. 47–106.

Lazear, Edward P. "Incentive Effects of Pensions." In David Wise, ed., *Pensions, Labor, and Individual Choice*. Chicago, IL: University of Chicago Press for NBER, 1985, pp. 253–282.

——. "Pensions as Severance Pay." In Zvi Bodie and John Shoven, eds., *Financial Aspects of the U.S. Pension System*. Chicago, IL: University of Chicago Press for NBER, 1983a, pp. 57–85.

——. "A Competitive Theory of Monopoly Unionism," *American Economic Review*, LXXIII (September, 1983b), 631–643.

——. "Agency Earnings Profiles, Productivity, and Hours Restrictions," *American Economic Review*, LXXI (September, 1981), 606–620.

——. "Why Is There Mandatory Retirement?", *Journal of Political Economy*, LXXXVII (December, 1979), 1261–1264.

—— and Robert L. Moore. "Pensions and Turnover." In Z. Bodie, J. Shoven, and D. Wise, eds., *Pensions in the U.S. Economy*. Chicago, IL: University of Chicago Press for NBER, 1988, pp. 163–188.

——. "Incentives, Productivity, and Labor Contracts," *Quarterly Journal of Economics*, LXXVII (May, 1984), 275–295.

Lee, Lung-Fei. "Unionism and Wage Rates: A Simultaneous Equations Model With Qualitative and Limited Dependent Variables," *International Economic Review*, XIX (June, 1978), 415–433.

Leibenstein, Harvey. *Beyond Economic Man: A New Foundation for Microeconomics.* Cambridge, MA: Harvard University Press, 1976.

Leonard, Jonathan S. "Carrots and Sticks: Pay, Supervision, and Turnover," *Journal of Labor Economics*, V (October, 1987), S136-S152.

Leontief, Wassily. "The Pure Theory of the Guaranteed Annual Wage Contract," *Journal of Political Economy*, LIV (February, 1946), 76–79.

——. "Academic Economics," *Science*, CCXVII (July, 1982), 104–107.

Lewis, H. Gregg. *Union Relative Wage Effects: A Survey.* Chicago, IL: University of Chicago Press, 1986.

——. *Unionism and Relative Wages in the United States.* Chicago, IL: University of Chicago Press, 1963.

Lilien, David. "The Cyclical Pattern of Temporary Layoffs in United States Manufacturing," *Review of Economics and Statistics*, LXII (February, 1980), 24–31.

Lincoln, James R. and Arne L. Kalleberg. "Work Organization and Workforce Commitment: A Study of Plants and Employees in the U.S. and Japan," *American Sociological Review*, L (December, 1985), 738–760.

Lindbeck, A. and D. J. Snower. "Wage-Setting, Unemployment, and Insider-Outsider Relations," *American Economic Review Proceedings*, LXXVI (May, 1986), 235–239.

——. "Cooperation, Harassment, and Involuntary Unemployment: An Insider-Outsider Approach," *American Economic Review*, LXXVIII (March, 1988), 167–188.

Linneman, Peter D. and Michael L. Wachter. "Rising Union Premiums and the Declining Boundaries Among Noncompeting Groups," *Papers and Proceedings* of the Ninety-Eighth Annual Meeting, American Economic Association. Menasha, WI: 1986, pp. 103–108.

Livernash, E. Robert. "The Internal Wage Structure." In George W. Taylor and Frank C. Pierson, eds., *New Concepts in Wage Determination.* New York: McGraw Hill, 1957, pp. 140–172.

Lowe, Adolph. *Economics and Sociology.* London: Allen & Unwin, 1935.

MacDougall, George D. A. "The Benefits and Costs of Private Investment from Abroad: A Theoretical Approach," *Economic Record*, XXXVI (March, 1960), 13–35.

Machlup, Fritz. "Marginal Analysis and Empirical Research," *American Economic Review*, XXXVII (September, 1946), 519–554. Reprinted in F. Machlup, *Method of Economics and Other Social Sciences.* New York: Academic Press, 1978.

Macneil, Ian R. "Economic Analysis of Contractual Relations," *Northwestern University Law Review*, LXXV (February, 1981), 1018–1063.

Madden, Janice Fanning. "Gender Differences in the Cost of Displacement: An Empirical Test of Discrimination in the Labor Market," *American Economic Review*, LXXVII (May, 1987), 246–251.

Malveaux, Julianne and Phyllis Wallace. "Minority Women in the Workplace." In Karen S. Koziara, Michael H. Moskow, and Lucretia D. Tanner, eds., *Working Women: Past, Present and Future.* Washington, DC: Bureau of National Affairs, 1987, pp. 265–298.

Maranto, Cheryl L. and Robert C. Rodgers. "A Test of the On-the-Job Training Hypothesis," *Journal of Human Resources*, XIX (Summer, 1984), 341–357.

March, James G. and Herbert A. Simon. *Organizations.* New York: Wiley, 1958.

Markusen, James R. "Trade and Gains from Trade with Imperfect Competition," *Journal of International Economics*, XI (November, 1981), 531–551.

Marsden, David. *The End of Economic Man? Custom and Competition in Labor Markets.* New York: St. Martin's Press, 1986.

Marshall, Alfred. *Elements of the Economics of Industry.* London: Macmillan, 1928 ed.

——. *Principles of Economics.* 8th ed.; London: Macmillan, 1927.

Matsuyama, Kiminori. "Export Subsidies as an Outcome of Management-Labor Conspiracy." Discussion paper, Department of Economics, Northwestern University, 1987.

Matthewson, Stanley B. *Restriction of Output among Unorganized Work Groups*. Rev. ed.; Carbondale, IL: Southern Illinois University Press, 1969.

Maurice, M., F. Sellier, and J. Silvestre. *The Social Foundations of Industrial Power: A Comparison of France and Germany*. Cambridge, MA: MIT Press, 1986.

Maxwell, Nan L. "Occupational Differences in the Determination of U.S. Workers' Earnings: Both the Human Capital and the Structured Labor Market Hypotheses are Useful in Analysis," *American Journal of Economics and Sociology*, XLVI (October, 1987), 431–445.

McConnell, Sheena. "Strikes, Wages and Private Information," *American Economic Review*, LXXIX (September, 1989), 810–815.

McDonald, I. M. and R. M. Solow. "Wage Bargaining and Employment," *American Economic Review*, LXXI (December, 1981), 896–908.

McNulty, Paul. *The Origins and Development of Labor Economics*. Cambridge, MA: MIT Press, 1980.

Medoff, James L. and Katharine G. Abraham. "Are Those Paid More Really More Productive: The Case of Experience," *Journal of Human Resources*, XVI (Spring, 1981), 186–216.

——. "Experience, Performance, and Earnings," *Quarterly Journal of Economics*, XCV (December, 1980), 703–736.

Melman, Seymour. *Decision-Making and Productivity*. New York: Wiley, 1958.

Meyer, J. R. "Wage, Price, and National Income." In P. D. Bradley, ed., *The Public Stake in Union Power*. Charlottesville, VA: University of Virginia, 1959, pp. 255–283.

Miller, Merton and Myron Scholes. "Executive Compensation, Taxes and Incentives." In William F. Sharp and Kathryn Cootner, eds., *Financial Economics: Essays in Honor of Paul H. Cootner*. Englewood Cliffs, NJ: Prentice-Hall, 1982, pp. 179–201.

Mincer, Jacob. *Schooling, Experience, and Earnings*. New York: Columbia University Press, 1974.

——. "On-the-Job Training, Costs, Returns, and Implications," *Journal of Political Economy*, LXX (December, 1962), 50–79.

——. "Investment in Human Capital and Personal Income Distribution," *Journal of Political Economy*, LXVI (August, 1958), 281–302.

—— and Boyan Jovanovic. "Labor Mobility and Wages." In Sherwin Rosen, ed., *Studies in Labor Markets*. Chicago, IL: University of Chicago Press, 1981, pp. 21–64.

Mincer, Jacob and Solomon Polachek. "Family Investments in Human Capital: Earnings of Women," *Journal of Political Economy*, LXXXII (March/April, 1974), S76-S108.

Mitchell, Daniel J. B. "Wage Pressures and Labor Shortages: The 1960s and the 1980s," *Brookings Papers on Economic Activity*, 2: 1989, pp. 191–231.

——. "Wage Flexibility In the U.S.: Lessons from the Past," *American Economic Review*, LXXV (May, 1985), 36–40.

——. "Recent Union Contract Concessions," *Brookings Papers on Economic Activity*, 1: 1982, 165–201.

——. *Unions, Wages, and Inflation*. Washington, DC: Brookings, 1980.

——. "Union Wage Policies: The Ross-Dunlop Debate Reopened," *Industrial Relations*, XI (February, 1972), 46–61.

Mitchell, Olivia S. and Gary S. Fields. "The Economics of Retirement Behavior," *Journal of Labor Economics*, II (January, 1984), 84–105.

Mitchell, W. C. *Types of Economic Theory: From Mercantilism to Institutionalism*. New York: Kelley, 1969.

——. *The Backward Art of Spending Money and Other Essays*. New York: McGraw-Hill, 1937.

Morgan, T. "Theory Versus Empiricism in Academic Economics," *Journal of Economic Perspectives*, II (Fall, 1988), 159–164.

Mortenson, Dale T. "Job Search and Labor Market Analysis." In Orley Ashenfelter and

Richard Layard, eds., *Handbook of Labor Economics*, Vol. II. Amsterdam: North Holland, 1985, pp. 849–919.

——. "Specific Capital and Labor Turnover," *Bell Journal of Economics*, IX (Autumn, 1978), 572–586.

Mowday, Richard T. "Equity Theory Predictions of Behavior in Organizations." In R. M. Steers and L. W. Porter, eds., *Motivation and Work Behavior*. 3rd ed.; New York: McGraw-Hill, 1983, pp. 91–113.

Nelson, Richard and Sidney Winter. *An Evolutionary Theory of Economic Change*. Cambridge, MA: Harvard University Press, 1982.

Newmann, George R. and Ellen R. Rissman. "Where Have All the Union Members Gone?", *Journal of Labor Economics*, II (April, 1984), 175–192.

Nordhaus, William D. "Alternative Approaches to the Political Business Cycle," *Brookings Papers on Economic Activity*, 2: 1989, pp. 1–68.

——. "The Worldwide Wage Explosion," *Brookings Papers on Economic Activity*, 2: 1972, pp. 431–464.

O'Reilly, C., B. G. Main, and G. S. Crystal. "CEO Compensation as Tournaments and Social Comparisons: A Tale of Two Theories," *Administrative Science Quarterly*, XXXIII (June, 1988), 257–274.

Oi, Walter. "Labor as a Quasi-Fixed Factor," *Journal of Political Economy*, LXX (December, 1962), 538–555.

Okun, Arthur M. *Prices & Quantities: A Macroeconomic Analysis*. Washington, DC: Brookings, 1981.

——. "The Invisible Handshake and the Inflationary Process," *Challenge*, XXII (January-February, 1980), 5–12.

Osterman, Paul. *Employment Futures*. New York: Oxford University Press, 1988.

——. "White-Collar Internal Labor Markets." In Paul Osterman, ed., *Internal Labor Markets*. Cambridge, MA: MIT Press, 1984, pp. 163–189.

——. "Affirmative Action and Opportunity: A Study of Female Quit Rates," *Review of Economics and Statistics*, LXIV (November, 1982), 604–612.

Oswald, Andrew J. "New Research on the Economics of Trade Unions and Labor Contracts," *Industrial Relations*, XXVI (Winter, 1987), 30–45.

——. "The Economic Theory of Trade Unions: An Introductory Survey," *The Scandinavian Journal of Economics*, LXXXVII (1985), 160–193.

Ouchi, William G. "Markets, Bureaucracies, and Clans," *Administrative Science Quarterly*, XXV (March, 1980), 120–142.

Parsons, Donald O. "The Employment Relationship: Job Attachment, Work Effort, and the Nature of Contracts." In Orley Ashenfelter and Richard Layard, eds., *Handbook of Labor Economics*, Vol. II. Amsterdam: North Holland, 1986, pp. 789–848.

——. "Specific Human Capital: An Application to Quit Rates and Layoff Rates," *Journal of Political Economy*, LXXX (November/December, 1972), 1120–1143.

Parsons, Talcott. *The Structure of Social Action*. New York: Free Press, 1949.

Pencavel, John. "Wages and Employment Under Trade Unionism: Microeconomic Models and Macroeconomic Applications," *The Scandanavian Journal of Economics*, LXXXVII (1985), 197–225.

——. "Wages, Specific Training, and Labor Turnover in U.S. Manufacturing Industries," *International Economic Review*, XIII (February, 1972), 53–64.

Perrow, Charles. "Economic Theories of Organization," *Theory and Society*, XV (1986), 11–45.

Pesando, James E. and Morley Gunderson. "Retirement Incentives Contained in Occupational Pension Plans and Their Implications for the Mandatory Retirement Debate," *Canadian Journal of Economics*, II (May, 1988), 244–264.

Pfeffer, Jeffrey and Allison Davis-Blake. "Salary Dispersion and Turnover Among College Administrators," typescript, 1988.

Phelps, Edmund. "The Statistical Theory of Racism and Sexism," *American Economic Review*, LXII (September, 1972), 659–661.

Phillips, A. W. "The Relation Between Unemployment and the Rate of Change of Money Wage Rates in the United Kingdom, 1861–1957," *Economica*, XXV (November, 1958), 283–299.

Piore, Michael J. "Notes for a Theory of Labor Market Stratification." In Richard Edwards, Michael Reich, and David M. Gordon, eds., *Labor Market Segmentation*. Lexington, MA: Lexington Books, 1975, pp. 125–150.

—— and Charles F. Sabel. *The Second Industrial Divide: Possibilities for Prosperity*. New York: Basic Books, 1984.

Polachek, Solomon William. Personal communication, January 1989.

——. "Sex Differences in College Major," *Industrial and Labor Relations Review*, XXXI (July, 1978), 498–508.

——. "Occupational Segregation and the Gender Wage Gap," *Population Research and Policy Review*, VI (1987), 47–67.

Posner, Richard A. *Economic Analysis of Law*. 3rd ed.; Boston, MA: Little Brown, 1986.

Pratt, J. W. and R. J. Zeckhauser, eds. *Principal and Agents*. Boston, MA: Harvard Business School Press, 1985.

Prescott, Edward C. "Theory Ahead of Business Cycle Measurement," *Federal Reserve Bank of Minneapolis Quarterly Review*, X (Fall, 1986), 9–22.

Putterman, Louis. *The Economic Nature of the Firm*. Cambridge: Cambridge University Press, 1986.

Ramaswami, V. K. "International Factor Movement and the National Advantage," *Economica*, XXXV (August, 1968), 309–310.

Rao, M. J. Manohar and Ramesh C. Datta. "Human Capital and Hierarchy," *Economics of Education Review*, IV (1985), 67–76.

Reder, Melvin W. "Review of B. E. Kaufman (ed.), *How Labor Markets Work*," *Industrial and Labor Relations Review*, XLII (April, 1989), 456–459.

—— and George R. Newmann. "Conflict and Contract: The Case of Strikes," *Journal of Political Economy*, LXXXVIII (October, 1980), 867–886.

Rees, Albert. "The Effects of Unions on Resource Allocation," *Journal of Law and Economics*, VI (October, 1963), 69–78.

——. *The Economics of Trade Unions*. 2nd ed.; Chicago, IL: University of Chicago Press, 1962.

Reich, Michael. "Postwar Racial Income Differences: Trends and Theories." In Garth Mangum and Peter Philips, eds., *Three Worlds of Labor Economics*. Armonk, NY: Sharpe, 1988, pp. 144–167.

——. "Segmented Labour: Time Series Hypothesis and Evidence," *Cambridge Journal of Economics*, VIII (1984), 63–81.

——. *Racial Inequality: A Political-Economic Analysis*. Princeton, NJ: Princeton University Press, 1981.

Renshaw, P. *The General Strike*. London: Methuen, 1975.

Riley, John G. "Testing the Educational Screening Hypothesis," *Journal of Political Economy*, LXXXVII (1979 Supplement), S227-S251.

——. "Competitive Signalling," *Journal of Economic Theory*, X (1975), 175–186.

Riordan, Michael H. and Michael L. Wachter. "What Do Implicit Contracts Do?", *Proceedings of the Thirty-Fifth Annual Meeting, Industrial Relations Research Association*. Madison, WI: 1982, pp. 291–298.

Rogerson, Richard. "Indivisible Labor, Lotteries, and Equilibrium," *Journal of Monetary Economics*, XXI (January, 1988), 3–16.

—— and Randall Wright. "Involuntary Unemployment in Economies with Efficient Risk Sharing," *Journal of Monetary Economics*, XXII (November, 1988), 501–515.

Rosen, Sherwin. "Implicit Contracts: A Survey," *Journal of Economic Literature*, XXIII

(September, 1985), 1144–1175.

Rosenberg, Samuel. *The Dual Labor Market: Its Existence and Consequences.* Unpublished Ph.D. dissertation, University of California at Berkeley, 1979.

Ross, Arthur M. "Do We Have a New Industrial Feudalism?", *American Economic Review,* XLVIII (December, 1958), 903–920.

——. *Trade Union Wage Policy.* Berkeley, CA: University of California Press, 1948.

Ruback, Richard S. and Martin B. Zimmerman. "Unionization and Profitability: Evidence from the Capital Market," *Journal of Political Economy,* XCII (December, 1984), 893–919.

Ruffin, Roy J. "International Factor Movements." In Ronald W. Jones and Peter B. Kenen, eds., *Handbook of International Economics,* Vol. I. Amsterdam: Elsevier Science Publishers, 1984, pp. 255–256.

Russell, T. and Richard Thaler. "The Relevance of Quasi-Rationality in Competitive Markets," *American Economic Review,* LXXV (December, 1975), 1071–1082.

Sachs, Jeffrey. "Real Wages and Unemployment in the OECD Countries," *Brookings Papers on Economic Activity,* 1: 1983, pp. 255–289.

Salop, Steven C. "A Model of the Natural Rate of Unemployment," *American Economic Review,* LXIX (March, 1979), 117–125.

Schultz, Theodore W. "Investment in Human Capital," *American Economic Review,* LI (March, 1961), 1–17.

Schultze, Charles L. "Comment on Industry Rents: Evidence and Implications," *Brookings Papers on Economic Activity: Microeconomics,* 1: 1989, pp. 280–283.

Schwab, Steward. "Is Statistical Discrimination Efficient?", *American Economic Review,* LXXVI (March, 1986), 228–234.

Segal, Martin. "Post-Institionalism in Labor Economics: The Forties and Fifties Revisited," *Industrial and Labor Relations Review,* XXXIX (April, 1986), 388–403.

Selznick, Philip. *Law, Society, and Industrial Justice.* New York: Russell Sage, 1969.

Sen, Amortya. "Goals, Commitment, and Identity," *Journal of Law, Economics, and Organization,* I (Fall, 1985), 341–356.

——. *Choice, Welfare, and Measurement.* Cambridge, MA: MIT Press, 1982.

Shank, Susan E. "Preferred Hours of Work and Corresponding Earnings," *Monthly Labor Review,* CIX (November, 1986), 40–44.

Shapiro, Carl and Joseph E. Stiglitz. "Equilibrium Unemployment as a Worker Discipline Device," *American Economic Review,* LXXIV (June, 1984), 433–444.

Shapiro, Matthew D. and Mark Watson. "Sources of Business Cycle Fluctuations," Working Paper No. 2589, National Bureau of Economic Research, May 1988.

Shefferman, N. W. *The Man in the Middle.* Garden City, NY: Doubleday, 1961.

Shiller, Robert J. "Stock Prices and Social Dynamics," *Broookings Papers on Economic Activity,* 2: 1984, pp. 457–498.

Siebert, Calvin D. and Mahmood A. Zaidi. "The Short-Run Wage-Price Mechanism in U.S. Manufacturing," *Western Economic Journal,* IX (September, 1971), 278–288.

Simon, Herbert A. "Rational Decision Making in Business Organizations," *American Economic Review,* LXIX (September, 1979), 493–513.

——. "The Compensation of Executives," *Sociometry,* XX (March, 1957), 32–35.

Simons, H. D. "Some Reflections on Syndicalism," *Journal of Political Economy* (March, 1944). Reprinted in *Economic Policy for a Free Society.* Chicago, IL: University of Chicago Press, 1948.

Singh, N. "Monitoring and Hierarchies," *Journal of Political Economy,* XCIII (June, 1985), 599–609.

Slichter, Sumner H. *Union Policies and Industrial Management.* Washington, DC: Brookings, 1941.

——. *Modern Economic Society.* New York: Holt, 1931.

——. "The Current Labor Policies of American Industries," *Quarterly Journal of Economics,*

XLIII (May, 1929), 393–435.
——. "Industrial Morale," *Quarterly Journal of Economics*, XXXV (November, 1920), 36–60.
——. *The Turnover of Factory Labor*. New York: Appleton, 1919.
——, J. J. Healy, and E. R. Livernash. *The Impact of Collective Bargaining on Management*. Washington, DC: Brookings, 1960.
Smith, James P. "Race and Human Capital," *American Economic Review*, LXXVI (December, 1984), 685–698.
—— and Finis R. Welch. "Racial Discrimination: A Human Capital Perspective." In Garth Mangum and Peter Philips, eds., *Three Worlds of Labor Economics*. Armonk, NY: Sharpe, 1988, pp. 95–116.
Soskice, David. "Reinterpreting Corporatism and Explaining Unemployment: Coordinated and Non-Coordinated Market Economies." In R. Brunetta and C. della Ringa, eds., *Markets, Institutions, and Cooperation*. London: Macmillan, 1989.
Spence, Michael. "Product Selection, Fixed Costs, and Monopolistic Competition," *Review of Economic Studies*, XLIII (June, 1976), 217–236.
——. *Market Signalling: Informational Transfer in Hiring and Related Screening Processes*. Cambridge, MA: Harvard University Press, 1974.
——. "Job Market Signalling," *Quarterly Journal of Economics*, LXXXVII (1973), 355–375.
Stafford, Frank P. and Greg Duncan. "The Use of Time and Technology by Households in the United States." In Ronald G. Ehrenberg, ed., *Research in Labor Economics*, Vol. 3. Greenwich, CT: JAI Press, 1980, pp. 335–375.
Staiger, Robert W. "Organized Labor and the Scope of International Specialization," *Journal of Political Economy*, XCVI (October, 1988), 1022–1047.
Stevens, Carl M. "Is Compulsory Arbitration Consistent With Bargaining?", *Industrial Relations*, V (February, 1966), 38–52.
Stiglitz, Joseph E. "The Design of Labor Contracts: The Economics of Incentives and Risk Sharing." In H. R. Nalbantian, ed., *Incentives, Cooperation, and Risk Sharing*. Totowa, NJ: Rowman & Littlefield, 1987, pp.47–68.
Stock, James H. and David A. Wise. "Pensions, the Option Value of Work, and Retirement." Working Paper E-88–28, Hoover Institution, 1988.
Strober, Myra H. "The MBA: Same Passport to Success for Women and Men?" In Phyllis Wallace, ed., *Women in the Workplace*. Boston, MA: Auburn House, 1981, pp. 25–44.
—— and Carol Arnold. "The Dynamics of Occupational Segregation Among Banktellers." In Clair Brown and Joseph Pechman, eds., *Gender in the Workplace*. Washington, DC: Brookings, 1987, pp. 107–157.
——. "Toward a General Theory of Occupational Sex Segregation: The Case of Public School Teaching." In Barbara F. Reskin, ed., *Sex Segregation in the Workplace: Trends, Explanations, Remedies*. Washington, DC: National Academy Press, 1984, pp. 144–156.
Tepper, Irwin. "Taxation and Corporate Pension Policy," *Journal of Finance*, XVI (March, 1981), 1–13.
Thurow, Lester C. *Dangerous Currents: The State of Economics*. New York: Random House, 1983.
——. *Generating Inequality*. New York: Basic Books, 1975.
——. "Education and Economic Equality," *The Public Interest*, XXVIII (Summer, 1972), 66–81.
Tirole, Jean. *The Theory of Industrial Organization*. Cambridge, MA: MIT Press, 1989.
Titmuss, R. M. *The Gift Relationship*. London: Allen & Unwin, 1970.
Topel, Robert H. "Comment on Industry Rents: Evidence and Implications," *Brookings Papers on Economic Activity: Microeconomics*, 1: 1989, pp. 283–288.
Townsend, Robert. "Optimal Contracts and Competitive Markets with Costly State Verification," *Journal of Economic Theory*, XXI (October, 1979), 265–293.
Tracy, Joseph. "An Empirical Test of an Asymmetric Information Model of Strikes," *Journal of Labor Economics*, V (April, 1987), 149–173.

——. "An Investigation into the Determinants of U.S. Strike Activity," *American Economic Review*, LXXVI (June, 1986), 423–436.

Tucker, Irvin B., III. "Use of the Decomposition Technique to Test the Educational Screening Hypothesis," *Economics of Education Review*, IV (1985), 321–326.

Ulman, L. "Industrial Relations." In *The New Palgrave: A Dictionary of Economics*. London: Macmillan, 1987, pp. 808–811.

U.S. Bureau of the Census. *Historical Statistics of the U.S.*, pt. 1. Washington, DC: U.S. Government Printing Office, 1975.

Veblen, Thorstein. *The Place of Science in Modern Civilization and Other Essays*. New York: Huebsch, 1919.

Venables, Anthony J. "Trade and Trade Policy with Imperfect Competition: The Case of Identical Products and Free Entry," *Journal of International Economics*, XIX (August, 1985), 1–20.

Verma, Anil. "Relative Flow of Capital to Union and Nonunion Plants Within a Firm," *Industrial Relations*, XXIV (Fall, 1985), 395–405.

Viscusi, W. Kipp. *Employment Hazards: An Investigation of Market Performance*. Cambridge, MA: Harvard University Press, 1979.

Voos, Paula and Larry Mishel. "The Union Impact on Profits: Evidence from Industry Price-Cost Margin Data," *Journal of Labor Economics*, IV (January, 1986), 105–133.

Vroman, Wayne and John Abowd. "Disaggregated Wage Developments," *Brookings Papers on Economic Activity*, 1: 1988, pp. 313–338.

Wachter, Michael L. and George M. Cohen. "The Law and Economics of Collective Bargaining: An Introduction and Application to the Problems of Subcontracting, Partial Closure, and Relocation," *University of Pennsylvania Law Review*, CXXXVI (May, 1988), 1349–1417.

Walters, A. A. "Production and Cost Functions: An Econometric Survey," *Econometrica*, XXXI (January, 1963), 1–66.

Webb, Sidney and Beatrice Webb. *Industrial Democracy*. 3rd ed.; London: Longmans, Green, 1920.

Weick, K. E., M. G. Bougon, and G. Maruyama. "The Equity Context," *Organizational Behavior and Human Performance*, XV (February, 1976), 32–65.

Weisskopf, Thomas, David M. Gordon, and Samuel Bowles. "Hearts and Minds: A Social Model of U.S. Productivity Growth," *Brookings Papers on Economic Activity*, 2: 1983, pp. 381–450.

Weitzman, Martin L. *The Share Economy: Conquering Stagflation*. Cambridge, MA: Harvard University Press, 1984.

——. "Increasing Returns and the Foundations of Unemployment Theory," *Economic Journal*, XCII (December, 1982), 787–804.

Whyte, William F. *Human Relations in the Restaurant Industry*. New York: McGraw-Hill, 1948.

Williamson, Oliver E. "The Economics and Sociology of Organization: Promoting a Dialogue." In G. Farkas and P. England, eds., *Industries, Firms and Jobs: Sociological and Economic Approaches*. New York: Plenum, 1988.

——. *The Economic Institutions of Capitalism: Firms, Markets, Relational Contracting*. New York: Free Press, 1985.

——. "The Organization of Work: A Comparative Institutional Assessment," *Journal of Economic Behavior and Organization*, I (March, 1980), 5–38.

——. "Transaction-Cost Economics: The Governance of Contractual Relations," *Journal of Law and Economics*, XXII (October, 1979), 233–261.

——. *Markets and Hierarchies: Analysis and Antitrust Implications*. New York: Free Press, 1975.

——, Michael L. Wachter, and Jeffrey E. Harris. "Understanding the Employment Relation: The Analysis of Idiosyncratic Exchange," *Bell Journal of Economics*, VI (Spring, 1975),

250–278.

Willis, Robert J. "Wage Determinants: A Survey and Reinterpretation of Human Capital Earnings Functions." In Orley Ashenfelter and Richard Layard, eds., *Handbook of Labor Economics*, Vol. I. Amsterdam: Elsevier Science Publishers, 1986, pp. 525–602.

Wilson, Robert and John Kennan. "Game-Theoretic Models of Bargaining and Interpretation of Strike Data." Unpublished paper, Graduate School of Business, Stanford University, November 1988.

Wolf, Douglas A. and Frank Levy. "Pension Coverage, Pension Vesting, and the Distribution of Job Tenure." In Henry J. Aaron and Gary Burtless, eds., *Retirement and Economic Behavior*. Washington, DC: Brookings, 1984, pp. 53–61.

Wolpin, Kenneth. "Education and Screening," *American Economic Review*, LXVII (December, 1977), 949–958.

Wonnacott, Ronald J. *Canada's Trade Options*. Ottawa: Information Canada, 1975.

—— and Paul Wonnacott. *Free Trade Between the United States and Canada*. Cambridge, MA: Harvard University Press, 1967.

Wright, Gavin. "Labor History and Labor Economics." In A. J. Field, ed., *The Future of Economic History*. Boston, MA: Kluwer Nijhoff, 1987, pp. 313–348.

Wright, Randall. "The Observational Implications of Labor Contracts in a Dynamic General Equilibrium Model," *Journal of Labor Economics*, VI (October, 1988), 530–551.